MW01039314

decolonizing museums

decolonizing museums

REPRESENTING NATIVE AMERICA IN
NATIONAL AND TRIBAL MUSEUMS

AMY LONETREE

First Peoples
New Directions in Indigenous Studies

The University of
North Carolina Press
Chapel Hill

Publication of this book was made possible, in part, by a grant from the Andrew W. Mellon Foundation.

© 2012 The University of North Carolina Press. All rights reserved
Set in Minion and Aller
Manufactured in the United States of America

The paper in this book meets the guidelines for permanence and durability of the Committee on Production Guidelines for Book Longevity of the Council on Library Resources.

The University of North Carolina Press has been a member of the Green Press Initiative since 2003.

Library of Congress Cataloging-in-Publication Data

Lonetree, Amy.
Decolonizing museums : representing native America in
national and tribal museums / Amy Lonetree.
p. cm. — (First peoples : new directions in indigenous studies)
Includes bibliographical references and index.
ISBN 978-0-8078-3714-6 (cloth : alk. paper)
ISBN 978-0-8078-3715-3 (pbk : alk. paper)
1. Indians of North America—Museums. 2. Indians of North America—Public opinion. 3. Ethnological museums and collections—United States. 4. Postcolonialism—United States. 5. Museums—United States—Management. 6. Museum exhibits—Moral and ethical aspects—United States. 7. Racism in museum exhibits—United States. 8. Indians in popular culture. 9. Indigenous peoples in popular culture. 10. Public opinion—United States. 11. United States—Race relations. I. Title.
E76.85.L66 2012
970.004'97—dc23
2012018877

Portions of this work have appeared earlier, in somewhat different form, as "Missed Opportunities: Reflections on the National Museum of the American Indian," in *American Indian Quarterly* 30, no. 3/4 (Summer/Fall 2006): 632–45 (revised form reprinted as "'Acknowledging the Truth of History': Missed Opportunities at the National Museum of the American Indian," in *The National Museum of the American Indian: Critical Conversations*, ed. Amy Lonetree and Amanda J. Cobb [Lincoln: University of Nebraska Press, 2008], 305–27; "Museums as Sites of Decolonization: Truth Telling in National and Tribal Museums," in *Contesting Knowledge: Museums and Indigenous Perspectives*, ed. Susan Sleeper Smith (Lincoln: University of Nebraska Press, 2009), 322–37, reprinted by permission of the University of Nebraska Press, copyright 2009 Board of Regents of the University of Nebraska; "Diba Jimooyung: Telling Our Story," Permanent Exhibition Review, Ziibiwing Center of Anishinabe Culture & Lifeways, *Journal of American History* 95, no. 1 (2008): 158–62, copyright © Organization of American Historians, all rights reserved, excerpted with permission.

cloth   16 15 14 13 12   5 4 3 2 1
paper   16 15 14 13 12   5 4 3 2 1

For Jon

contents

illustrations

preface

This book is about three museums—the Mille Lacs Indian Museum in Minnesota, the Smithsonian's National Museum of the American Indian, and the Ziibiwing Center of Anishinabe Culture & Lifeways in Michigan—and their collaborative partnerships with Indigenous communities. My study of the history of the representation of Native Americans in museum exhibitions explores the significance of these three separate institutions, each of which possesses unique and important collections of American Indian material culture, and how they have developed the exhibitions they present. I have worked at two of these museums and have conducted extensive research at all three. Through these experiences, I have witnessed firsthand the complex and important process of developing community-collaborative exhibitions in the late twentieth and early twenty-first centuries.

One of the most vivid memories of my experience in the museum world—and one that has shaped both my understanding of collaboration and the significance of objects to Indigenous communities—took place in 1995 at the Minnesota Historical Society (MHS). As an exhibit researcher working on *Families*, an exhibition funded by the National Endowment for the Humanities focusing on Minnesota families that opened at MHS in 1995, one of my responsibilities was to locate a Native American family to be featured in the exhibition. One section of the exhibit dealt with the theme of family reunions and their role in maintaining identity. A colleague, Carolyn Anderson, recommended that we consider featuring the Kittos—a Dakota tribal family originally from southern Minnesota. The Kittos' own reunions perhaps best exemplified the importance of family reunions in supporting family identity. For the previous ten years, the Kittos had worked on an extensive genealogical project to trace the history of their family and its involvement in the U.S.-Dakota War of 1862.

That war was one of the most searing and significant events in modern Dakota and Minnesota history. In 1862, after suffering the full onslaught of invasion, colonial oppression, broken treaties, and loss of land and lifeways, the Dakota fought a brief war with the United States in the Minnesota River valley, which left hundreds dead.[1] Following the war, the state of Minnesota pursued swift and violent acts of retribution against the Dakota Nation, including a mass execution of thirty-eight Dakota warriors and a policy of ethnic cleansing that led to the removal of all tribal members from the state. Minnesota governor Alexander Ramsey summarized the scope of the action he planned to take in the aftermath of the war: "The Sioux Indians of Minnesota must be exterminated or driven forever beyond the borders of the State."[2]

The legacy of the events of 1862 still weighs heavily on the hearts and minds of contemporary Dakota people. Reuben Kitto, the family patriarch, began research to trace the history of his ancestor Mazaadidi (Walks on Iron), who was arrested in November 1862 and taken prisoner by the U.S. military for his alleged involvement in the war. Kitto's research later confirmed that Mazaadidi was one of over three hundred Dakota men sentenced to death by hanging by a U.S. military tribunal, but his sentence was later commuted. While Mazaadidi was not one of the thirty-eight Dakota warriors executed on the day after Christmas 1862 in the largest mass execution in U.S. history, he was imprisoned at Camp McClellan in Davenport, Iowa, for several years.

Following a pardon from President Lincoln in 1864 and his subsequent release, Mazaadidi rejoined his wife, Pazahiyayewin (She Shall Radiate in Her Path like the Sun), and their children, who had survived their own harrowing journey out of Minnesota following the war in Dakota Territory. In November 1862, Pazahiyayewin, along with her elderly mother and four children (one of whom was only a few weeks old), was force-marched, along with roughly sixteen hundred Dakota women, children, and old men, over 150 miles from the Lower Sioux reservation to a concentration camp at Fort Snelling.[3] After a horrific winter at the fort under military guard in 1862–63, the surviving Dakota were forcibly removed from the state of Minnesota to a reservation in Dakota Territory in 1863. Mazaadidi and Pazahiyayewin would later settle on the Santee Sioux reservation in Nebraska.[4]

Reuben Kitto's search for his family's history and the knowledge he gained from his research led to a renewed commitment to bringing his family together to honor their cultural heritage and identity. He began sending family members newsletters that described his research, which ultimately led to the family's decision to hold reunions every four years on their ancestral lands. This deeply felt and renewed sense of pride in the family's Dakota identity, shared through the newsletters and at the family reunions, was captured in T-shirts, jackets, hats, and shawls that featured the family's medicine wheel emblem.

The Minnesota Historical Society's exhibition-development team recognized the Kitto family story as a principal illuminator of the importance of family reunions, and they wanted to showcase the family's incredible story. I contacted Reuben Kitto about our interest in featuring the family in the exhibition, and he enthusiastically agreed to meet with museum staff to discuss the possibility. I found out later that his gracious and enthusiastic response had a great deal to do with his friendship with Carolyn Anderson as well as with the kind words that our mutual friend Bonnie Wallace had said on my behalf when Reuben asked her if she knew me following our initial conversations. Bonnie, a much beloved member of the Minneapolis–Saint Paul urban Indian community, knew everyone, and her opinion mattered tremendously to her dear friend Reuben Kitto.

At the time, I remember being surprised by his response. Here was a Native American family with a great story to share who had enthusiastically agreed to work with us almost immediately. I had spent months on the front lines of developing collaborative exhibitions with other Native American communities, and I knew how difficult it was to establish a connection of trust. Without trust, a collaborative partnership is simply not possible. The "love-hate relationship" between Native people and museums is something I was all too familiar with. As both an insider and an outsider to MHS, I had faced numerous challenges in trying to vouch for the museum with Native people. So I was deeply touched when Reuben and the rest of the Mazaadidi and Pazahiyayewin clan were interested in collaborating, and we arranged to meet with members of the family. They had several objects to show us in addition to the ones with the family emblem designed for the reunions.

On the morning of the meeting, I was even more surprised to see over fifty Mazaadidi and Pazahiyayewin family members show up at the museum to meet with the staff and discuss their participation. As the meeting began, they shared with us the contemporary objects they developed for the reunions, but they also brought beautiful family treasures, some of which dated back one hundred years. The treasures were stunning: star quilts given to honor members of the family; a pipe belonging to the women of the clan, who had passed the pipe down through the generations; a Bible translated in Dakota that belonged to a relative who was a missionary on the reservation in the early twentieth century; beautiful beadwork, including a bag made by a master craftswoman in the family; and framed photographs of their relatives.

As the members of the family showed us the objects, they also conveyed a wealth of important information about the pieces—when they were made, who made them, and the materials used—all information that museum curators hope for when documenting objects. In addition, and most important, each of the pieces they presented inspired family members to share personal recollections about the ancestors who originally owned them.

Kunsi (Grandmother) Naomi Cavender shared one story in particular about a beautiful social pipe adorned with feathers and beadwork. She placed it in the center of the table and invited us to feature it in the exhibition. She said it was given to her by her grandmother Louisa Sioux Henry, who smoked the pipe with other women on the reservation in the evenings when they told stories. Kunsi Naomi, visibly moved while remembering the stories she heard as a little girl, said this was an important piece and expressed her desire that people should see it.

We also learned that the pipe symbolized the family's inextricable ties to the history of the Dakota Nation and the U.S.-Dakota War of 1862 and its aftermath. The pipe originally belonged to Louisa's grandmother, who carried Louisa on the horrific forced exile from their Minisota Makoce (Land Where the Waters Reflect the Skies) homelands in 1863. She later gave the pipe to her granddaughter, Louisa, who in turn gifted it to her granddaughter, Naomi. Grandma Naomi would then give it to Reuben Kitto. He restored the pipe with a lovely new stem and feathers and returned it to her. This is the pipe— rich with the meaning of their survivance and the family's deep connections to the Dakota Nation—that the Kittos entrusted to the Minnesota Historical Society for exhibition.

I was deeply honored to be part of the exchange, to be in the presence of beautiful objects, and to be able to listen to the stories that surrounded them. In many respects, this was one of the most important moments in my professional career as an exhibit developer, because it embodied the ideal situation: objects that come with stories shared by those whose families remain deeply connected to the pieces. Conventional museum documentation focuses on the materials used, the time period in which they were made, and the cultural group attributed to the pieces (or provenience). Yet this information does not begin to convey the true significance of the objects. The objects are important because they belong to living Native peoples who maintain deep and ongoing connections to the pieces.

The Mazaadidi and Pazahiyayewin descendants who shared their family treasures and stories with me and my colleagues that summer day in 1995 gave us the opportunity to honor them and their ancestors with an exhibit that celebrated the most important tribal value of all: kinship. By so doing, they also gave the museum an opportunity to present Native American life through a representation that was framed and told by those who were intimately part of that story.

This small exhibit, developed by the Minnesota Historical Society in cooperation with the Mazaadidi and Pazahiyayewin family, drove home to all of us involved with the project one of the most important values to remember in Native representations in museums. Objects in museums are living entities. They embody layers of meaning, and they are deeply connected to the past, present, and future of Indigenous communities. Every engagement with objects in museum cases or in collection rooms should begin with this core recognition. We are not just looking at interesting pieces. In the presence of objects from the past, we are privileged to stand as witnesses to living entities that remain intimately and inextricably tied to their descendant communities.

acknowledgments

Writing this book has been a long and incredible journey for me, and I wish to extend my gratitude to the many people who have helped me. The generosity of friends, family, colleagues, museum professionals, and other scholars has touched me deeply, and I am pleased to have this opportunity to acknowledge them.

This study took root when I was a graduate student at the University of California, Berkeley, and was aided in its early stages by Ronald Takaki, a kind and enthusiastic mentor who demonstrated by his illustrious career what it means to be an activist scholar. Ron was a brilliant writer, terrific mentor, and inspiring teacher, and I am honored to have worked with him. Alex Saragoza and Waldo Martin also deserve recognition for their support and for guiding me through the early stages of this work. A special thank-you goes to Professor Steven Crum, who shared his vast knowledge of Indigenous history with me during my years as a graduate student and beyond. Steve is a talented and rigorous historian and remains one of my greatest role models. I am truly blessed to have worked with such outstanding scholars and fine people. Thanks are also due to the many people in the Berkeley community who made my time there both memorable and enjoyable—Carmen Foghorn, Stella Moore, Rhacel Parrenas, Ebba Segerberg, Rowena Robles, Nancy Kim, Dee Bielenberg, Charlotte Cote, Annette Reed-Crum, Luis de la Garza, Iyko Day, Gerald Vizenor, Lily Castillo-Speed, and John Berry. I have learned from all of them.

I am grateful to those at the three museum sites that I have studied who helped make this project a reality. Their generosity and support of this research meant the world to me and made this book possible. At the Minnesota Historical Society, Kate Roberts, Nina Archabal, Rachel Tooker, and Shana Crosson shared their memories of the Mille Lacs Indian Museum project with me. Travis Zimmerman, current site manager at the Mille Lacs Indian Museum, generously gave of his time to inform me of future directions for the site. A special thanks is due to Jack Rumpel for copying the images of the exhibits for inclusion in the book. I began my museum career at the Minnesota Historical Society in the early 1990s, and I consider those years to be some of the most important in my intellectual and career trajectory. Along with the individuals mentioned above, I would also like to thank Marx Swanholm, Merry van den Honert, Celeste Brosenne, Brad Thiel, Sarah Libertus, Rick Polenek, Heather Esser Koop, Marcia Anderson, Brian Horrigan, Carolyn Anderson, Ellen Miller, Barbara Franco, Paul Martin, and Kendra Dillard, who helped shape my understanding of new museum theory and the best methods for putting it into practice.

Both former and current members of the staff at the Smithsonian's National Museum of the American Indian—George Horse Capture, Emil Her Many Horses, Truman Lowe, Gerald McMaster, Harvey Markowitz, Susan Secakuku, James Volkert, Ann McMullen, and Bruce Bernstein—generously gave of their time and provided me with invaluable information on the exhibition-development process at the museum. I owe a special thanks to the late Lou Stancari, who graciously processed my request for photos to include in this research.

I had the good fortune of attending a conference at the Ziibiwing Center of Anishinabe Culture & Lifeways in 2006, which helped launch an amazing research experience that dramatically altered the course of this project. From the moment I set foot in the center, I knew it was a special place, and I am honored to tell part of its story here. I thank the Saginaw Chippewa Indian Tribe of Michigan, its tribal council, and the Ziibiwing Center and its board of directors for this experience. Bonnie Ekdahl, William Johnson, Judy Pamp, Paul Johnson, and Amanda Agosto generously shared their insights on the development of the Ziibiwing Center, and I am grateful for all they shared. Jennifer Jones and Anita Heard graciously processed my request for photographs for inclusion in the volume. The center's current director, Shannon Martin, has been incredibly generous with her time and support for this project, and I am consistently in awe of her dedication and energy. That Shannon is now a dear friend is a great blessing. I offer my sincere admiration and thanks for the amazing work that all of these people do at this important site of Saginaw Chippewa history and memory. *Miigwetch!*

I have received generous financial support over the years from many sources. Thank you to the Ho-Chunk Nation of Wisconsin, to the American Indian Graduate Center, and to the Smithsonian Institution's Office of Fellowships and Grants for their support, as well as to the University of California, Berkeley, for a Chancellor's Postdoctoral Fellowship for Academic Diversity, to San Francisco State University for a Faculty Affirmative Action Award, to the University of California, Santa Cruz, for faculty research awards, to UCLA's Institute of American Cultures for a Visiting Scholar Award in the American Indian Studies Center, and Arielle Read and Dante

Noto at the University of California Humanities Research Institute on the uc Irvine campus for the use of an apartment and office during my residency in Southern California in 2010. A lion's share of the writing happened while on fellowship at UCLA, and I would like to acknowledge the members of the American Indian Studies Center who made my time there productive and enjoyable: Rebecca Hernandez Rosser, Angela Riley, Mishuana Goeman, David Delgado Shorter, Ken Wade, Pamela Grieman, and Christine Dunn.

To the wonderful community of scholars who have supported me and whom I am fortunate to have as friends—Waziyatawin, Myla Vicenti Carpio, Lisa Dyea, Dian Million, Robin DeLugan, Beatriz Tapia, Alexandro Gradilla, Julie Davis, Nancy Marie Mithlo, Amanda Cobb Greetham, Alexis Bunten, Patricia Schechter, Anita Gonzalez, Jennifer Denetdale, Karen Leong, James Riding In, Patricia Pierce Erikson, Joanne Barker, Andrew Jolivette, Melissa Nelson, and Clayton Dumont—I express my heartfelt appreciation. Waziyatawin, Myla, and Lisa, were with me from the very beginning of this journey, and I could not have made it without their love and laughter. A special thanks goes to my writing partner and Anishinabe sister, Sonya Atalay. Sonya came into my life in 2002, and what an honor it has been to write our first books together. She has been with me every step of the way during the writing process, consistently providing encouragement, editorial suggestions, and unwavering support. She is a brilliant archaeologist whose commitment to producing ethical and rigorous scholarship in service to Native people is a source of inspiration. My mother always told me that the best things in life are things that money cannot buy, and Sonya's friendship and love is truly one of those gifts. *Miigwetch* to my dear friend and source of strength!

I arrived at the University of California, Santa Cruz, in 2007, and I am grateful to my wonderful colleagues and friends there who have supported me on this journey: Dana Frank, Beth Haas, Felicity Schaeffer-Grabiel, James Clifford, Diane Gifford-Gonzalez, Lucian Gomell, Christine Hong, and Dean William Ladusaw. My colleagues in American studies—Catherine Ramirez, Kimberly Lau, Eric Porter, and Renya Ramirez—are generous scholars and I treasure our time together. Renya is my Ho-Chunk sister and I value her love and friendship. I could not ask for a more supportive and dynamic academic home.

I would also like to acknowledge the participants in the Scholarly Writing Retreat organized by the always gracious Mitch Reyes over many summers at Lewis and Clark College. I have attended the retreat for the last four years and completed various stages of this book there. The opportunity to gather with other committed scholarly writers helped jump-start this book in 2008, and I credit the supportive and stimulating environment for bringing me to the finish line. Thank you to Mitch Reyes for sharing his expertise on the writing process and his beautiful campus with all of us. A special thanks goes to fellow veteran retreater Kristin Moss for her support and helpful editorial suggestions. I look forward to sharing the final product at our next gathering.

I am grateful to Mark Simpson-Vos, my editor at the University of North Carolina Press, for asking important questions that helped shape the direction of this work. I also thank Zachary Read (assistant editor), Ron Maner (managing editor), and Katie Haywood (copyeditor) for their editorial help, and the production and marketing teams for their work on behalf of the book. I benefited tremendously from two anonymous reviewers engaged by the University of North Carolina Press who offered excellent editorial suggestions that helped improve the manuscript.

A special note of thanks goes to Denise Breton, who took time away from her day job as editor of Living Justice Press to share her editing talents with me. She is a gifted writer in her own right and a copyeditor extraordinaire, and I am indebted to her for helping me strengthen my voice. She is a loving and dear friend, and I am fortunate to have her in my life. Thanks are also due to Dyani Reynolds-White Hawk for the use of her lovely painting *Seeing*, which graces the cover.

To my Ho-Chunk family, the Lonetrees, I offer my gratitude for encouraging me to dream big and for providing me with the love and good humor to help me get there. My *cuwi* Kathy Lonetree-Whiterabbit was one of my biggest supporters, and her love for our family and tribal nation is truly inspiring. I owe a debt of gratitude to my Whitman relatives, whose work ethic set the standard for me. They are true role models. I am grateful for the love and support of my brother and sisters, nieces and nephews, and all our good times together and crazy card games that consistently remind me there is more to life than work. My mother, Loretta Lonetree, was my source of strength during this process, and I am grateful for the many sacrifices she made to help me achieve my goals, and for her love and guidance. I wish to acknowledge my late father, Rawleigh Lonetree, who is with me always in spirit and whose quiet strength and dignity remain my shining example. He instilled in me a fierce pride in my Ho-Chunk identity and a great loyalty to family, and I hope this work brings honor to his memory.

My final note of thanks goes to my partner, Jon Daehnke, whose love and unwavering support help keep me on course. At times I thought I would abandon this project and move onto something else, but Jon had enough faith for both of us. He shared his excellent editorial skills and immense knowledge of Indigenous history and heritage studies with me, and the book is far better for it. For his strength, love, inspiration, and all the times he made me laugh—I dedicate this book to him.

It is a blessing to have such wonderful people in my life. I have learned from all of them, and I say *pinagigi* for helping me bring this project to fruition.

Throughout the book, I use the term "Indigenous" or "Native" when focusing on Indigenous peoples in the United States, and in some instances when I am making a broader connection to communities from throughout the hemisphere or from Australia and New Zealand. I also use the term "American Indian" or "Native American" when referring specifically to tribal peoples in the United States. As often as possible, I have included tribally specific names of the communities and people that I am discussing. For example, a primary focus of the book is on two Anishinabe (also known as the Ojibwe or Chippewa) tribal museums, and I use the names that the respective communities use when identifying themselves. The Saginaw Chippewa Indian Tribe of Michigan uses the term "Chippewa" in its official government title; but "Anishinabe" (a term meaning original people) is used consistently throughout the tribe's museum, and I use this term, along with the plural "Anishinabek" or "Anishinabeg," when referencing the community and museum. In the case of the Mille Lacs Band of Ojibwe, the official government name includes "Ojibwe," which I use throughout chapter 2, but I also use "Anishinabe" in places as well. There are various spellings for "Anishinabe" or "Anishinaabe" and "Ojibwe" or "Ojibwa" and I have used the spelling that those to whom I am referring prefer. All direct quotes include the name as spelled in the original source.

decolonizing museums

one

INTRODUCTION

Native Americans and Museums

Museums can be very painful sites for Native peoples, as they are intimately tied to the colonization process. The study of the relationship between Indigenous peoples and museums—the tragic stories of the past as well as examples of successful Native activism and leadership within the museum profession today—has preoccupied my professional life both inside and outside the academy. Museums have changed significantly from the days when they were considered "ivory towers of exclusivity."[1] Today, Indigenous people are actively involved in making museums more open and community-relevant sites.

We certainly see this new development reflected in exhibitions, which are the most prominent, public face of a museum.[2] Native Americans have witnessed a shift from curator-controlled presentations of the American Indian past to a more inclusive or collaborative process, with Native people often actively involved in determining exhibition content. It is now commonplace and expected that museum professionals will seek the input of contemporary communities when developing exhibitions focusing on American Indian content.[3] This new relationship of "shared authority" between Native people and museum curators has changed the way Indigenous history and culture are represented and has redefined our relationship with museums. The efforts today by tribal communities to be involved in developing exhibitions point to the recognition that controlling the representation of their cultures is linked to the larger movements of self-determination and cultural sovereignty.

In this book, I seek to understand the role museums play within contemporary Indigenous communities as part of the self-determination and cultural sovereignty movement. It is a comparative study of the representation of Native Americans in museum exhibitions at the Mille Lacs Indian Museum in Minnesota (a collaborative project with the Minnesota Historical Society and the Mille Lacs Band of Ojibwe), the Smithsonian's National Museum of the American Indian (NMAI), and the Ziibiwing Center of Anishinabe Culture & Lifeways in Michigan. Through an analysis of the dynamic and complex process of determining exhibition content at these institutions, I explore the changing representations of Indigenous history and memory in a diverse group of museums that hold significant Native American collections. This study of both national and tribal museums examines the complexities of this new relationship between Native Americans and museums as reflected in the exhibitions produced at all three sites—both the positive outcomes as well as the challenges that remain.

SETTING THE STAGE: DEVELOPMENTS IN MUSEUM PRACTICES

The three museums featured in this book embody important ideological shifts in contemporary museum practices. As a museum practitioner and a scholar of Native American history and museum studies, I witnessed first-hand how curators, staff, and communities negotiated the new terrain of collaborative and tribal museums. I worked for two of the museums highlighted in the book, as I will describe in detail in later chapters, and I conducted extensive research (interviewing, archival research, and participant observation) at all three sites. The questions framing the study include the following: How have representations of Native American history and culture changed over time, and what role did Indigenous activism and new museum theory play in the process? How effective are these new representations in challenging the public's understanding of the Native American past and present? Are the new exhibits successful in their educational efforts? What does a decolonizing museum practice involve, and are these museums sites for decolonization?

In order to address these questions, I have relied on archival materials relating to the development of the exhibitions, interviews with key staff members involved in the development process, and a close visual analysis of the texts, objects, and images in the exhibitions themselves. I follow the lead of Patricia Pierce Erikson, who, in her scholarship on the Makah Cultural and Research Center, claims that she is doing more than just engaging in travel writing. By employing ethnographic methodology, her critical analysis offers a far more nuanced and complicated understanding of the Makah museum. As she argues, "One needs to know the history of the surrounding community, the collections, the staff, and the mission statement in order to understand how the museum sees itself and is seen by others."[4]

When I first embarked on this comparative study of the changing representation of Native American history and culture in both national and tribal museums, few scholarly monographs existed on the subject. Then, in 2002, Erikson's important study on the Makah was published,[5] a book with superb insight and rich analysis. The text explores a range of highly relevant and interconnected issues: the genealogy and development of the Makah Cultural and Research Center (one of the first large-scale tribal museums in the nation), Makah history and memory as embodied in the exhibitions, the Makah communities' relationship with anthropologists, and ethical research practices in Indigenous communities. Drawing upon the theoretical concept of "contact zones" advanced by Mary Louise Pratt and applied to museums by James Clifford, Erikson argues that "Native American museums/cultural centers are hybrid embodiments of Native and non-Native perspectives. As a synthesis of cultural forms, they reveal a process of collaboration between diverse peoples amid conditions of unequal empowerment. Native American museums/cultural centers are both translators and translations, agents of social change and products of accommodation."[6] I have found Erikson's work invaluable in shaping my understanding of the complex subjectivity of tribal museums and in recognizing their role in changing mainstream museum practices.

In the years since, a few more published works have been added to the monographs that focus on specific Indigenous museums. John J. Bodinger de Uriarte has produced a book on the Mashantucket Pequot Museum, and Gwyneira Isaac's study of the Zuni Museum was published in 2007.[7] These two books have made significant contributions to our understanding of the complex subjectivity presented at tribal museums, which have been growing in numbers since the late twentieth century. In addition to these monographs, several articles explore the process of collaboration between mainstream museums and Indigenous people and the influence of new museum theory and practice in the late twentieth century.[8]

These texts have added considerable insight to the field and shed much light on changing museum practices. However, these works focus mostly on case studies. This book is unique in that it includes but also goes beyond the case-study format. As I tell the stories of one tribal museum and two collaborative partnerships between mainstream institutions and Native American communities, I examine the museums and their genesis as part of a broader historical development. The cases reveal the changing relations not only between Indigenous people and museums in the late twentieth and early twenty-first centuries but also within the museum world and in society.

In the context of changing museum practices, I focus on three key developments that pertain to Native Americans. First, collaborative partnerships between Native Americans and mainstream museums have increased over the last thirty years. A few collaborative projects did exist before this period; however, most scholars would agree that we have witnessed a significant rise in the number of collaborations during this time as well as significant changes in how these collaborations have been negotiated. Second, the number of tribal museums has grown since the self-determination era of the 1970s. Third, Native cultural centers and museums that are exclusively tribally owned have emerged, too, and these tribally determined spaces are having a significant impact both on their communities and on museum practices. They are changing the fundamental stance of Native representations through museums as well as the accountability that these centers have to their communities. This book explores three case studies that shed light on these trends.

DECOLONIZING MUSEUMS IN THE SERVICE OF
TRUTH TELLING AND HEALING

While I have been working on this project over the last several years, I have thought critically about how museum sites can assist in tribal nation building, empowerment, and healing. Concurrently, museum studies scholars have been exploring the possibilities for expanding the role of museums in what scholar Ruth Phillips has referred to as the "second museum age."[9] This emerging vision makes museums more open and community-relevant sites, and a new museum theory and practice is developing alongside this work.

One can see signs of this shift in many places: the emergence of tribally owned and operated museums across the United States; the transition of many mainstream museums from a "temple" to a "forum"; the collaborative partnerships between museums and so-called source communities and interested publics; a more responsive museum practice that seeks to "share authority," influenced by postmodernism and broader human rights issues; the increase of scholarship that engages how museums can serve as social service agencies; and the establishment of the International Coalition of Sites of Conscience project.[10] All of these developments are significant and have dramatically changed the museum landscape.

For Native peoples, the question around museums has been, How can we begin to decolonize a very Western institution that has been so intimately linked to the colonization process? A decolonizing museum practice must involve assisting our communities in addressing the legacies of historical unresolved grief. Doing this necessarily cuts through the veil of silence around colonialism and its consequences for Native families and communities. Tribal museums serve many functions, of course, and they have done a decent job of challenging the many stereotypical representations of Native history produced in the past. They have served as sites of "knowledge-making [and] remembering"[11] for our communities, and they have educated the general public on the many silences that exist regarding the Indigenous experience.

But one of the most important goals, I believe, is to assist communities in their efforts to address the legacies of historical unresolved grief by speaking the hard truths of colonialism and thereby creating spaces for healing and understanding. I draw upon the theory advanced by Lakota scholar and social worker Maria Yellow Horse Brave Heart, who, along with her colleagues Lemyra DeBruyn and others, is involved in the Takini Network, a nonprofit organization. These leading Native scholars in the field of historical unresolved grief and trauma have not only defined these concepts but also offered workshops to assist Indigenous communities in the healing process. Brave Heart defines historical trauma as a "cumulative emotional and psychological wounding over the lifespan and across generations, emanating from massive group trauma experiences."[12] Historical unresolved grief is "the impaired or delayed mourning" that occurs as a result of the many traumas that Indigenous people have suffered, including genocidal warfare and forced removals, the deliberate spread of disease, assimilation programs such as the boarding schools and the termination and relocation programs of the 1950s, land loss, desecration of sacred sites, racism, and ongoing crushing poverty.[13] This psychological pain leads to the "historical trauma response," which gives rise to the many social problems that continue to plague Indian Country.

Given that the Native American holocaust, which spanned centuries, remains unaddressed in both Native and non-Native communities, truth telling is perhaps the most important aspect of a decolonizing museum practice of the twenty-first century, however painful it may be. The process assists in healing and promotes community well-being, empowerment, and nation building. It opens the door to transformation on all sides of harm. As Brave Heart and DeBruyn write: "The connectedness of the past to present to future remains a circle of lessons and insights that can give us both the consciousness and the conscience to heal ourselves. Understanding the inter-relationship with our past and how it shapes our present world will also give us the courage to initiate healing."[14]

This decolonizing project involves more than moving museums away from being elitist temples of esoteric learning and even more than moving muse-ums toward providing forums for community engagement. A decolonizing museum practice must be in the service of speaking the hard truths of colo-nialism. The purpose is to generate the critical awareness that is necessary to heal from historical unresolved grief on all the levels and in all the ways that it continues to harm Native people today. As Ojibwe scholar Lisa Poupart writes, "Culturally and individually we must recognize our past and present traumas and grieve our losses on a new path of healing."[15] Tribal museums bear the responsibility to assist in telling the difficult stories—honestly and rigorously—in our twenty-first-century museums, so that future generations can know the past and find the means to heal.

During the review process for this book, one of the reviewers raised the issue, which I have observed as well, that some communities do not want to address the legacies of colonialism in their exhibits. They suggest that these topics have been covered and that they want to emphasize Indigenous sur-vival instead. This statement falls in line with other critiques I have heard over the years against speaking the hard truths of Native history in exhibi-tions. We have all heard these critiques: we do not want to offend visitors (many of whom are non-Natives); we do not want to "hang out our dirty laundry" by discussing painful aspects of either our history or our contem-porary social problems; we do not want to "subscribe to the language of vic-timization"; people have heard these stories already; and museums are not social service agencies.[16] I respect those who voice these concerns, but I do not agree with them.

It is time for us as communities to acknowledge the painful aspects of our history along with our stories of survivance, so that we can move toward healing, well-being, and true self-determination. Some may argue that dis-cussing this history keeps Indigenous people mired in the horror of victim-ization and hence entrenched in the victimhood narrative. In my experience, this statement could not be further from the truth. Emphasizing Indigenous survivance is critical, of course. It concerns me, however, when we fail to pro-vide the context that makes our survival one of the greatest untold stories. Americans—and most of the world—seem somehow stubbornly unaware of what Indigenous peoples on this continent have actually faced. Telling the full story of the Native American holocaust proves a testament not to Native victimhood but to Native skill, adaptability, courage, tenacity, and countless other qualities that made our survival a reality against all odds. Our survival is more than remarkable. It is proof of the power of our cultures, traditions, and peoples, proven in the face of the ultimate test.

We know these challenges, and our children need to know them to fully appreciate their forebears and how we came to where we are today—our survival and our strengths. The history of genocide is, after all, a documented and obvious reality. What always surprises me, then, is how unwilling many of our communities have become to present a hard-hitting analysis of colonialism in our exhibitions within museums.

Dakota scholar Waziyatawin explains how important it is to understand Indigenous survival within its colonial context and what is at stake if we fail to do so. She writes: "An analysis of colonialism allows us to make sense of our current condition, strategically develop more effective means of resistance, recover the pre-colonial traditions that strengthen us as Indigenous Peoples, and connect with the struggles of colonized peoples throughout the world to transform the world. When colonialism is removed from the analysis, we have little alternative other than to simply blame ourselves for the current social ills. This blaming the victim strategy only increases violence against our own people."[17]

This call for museums to address colonialism and to address the legacies of historical unresolved grief fits squarely within a broader intellectual project in the Indigenous studies field, namely, to work from a decolonizing paradigm. To trace the genealogy of the decolonization literature and its impact on the field of Indigenous history over the last several decades, I draw upon the excellent work of Seminole historian Susan Miller. In her article "Native America Writes Back: The Origin of the Indigenous Paradigm in Historiography," she asserts that a cadre of Native American historians are working to change the field. They are advancing a new "Indigenous paradigm" within their writing that includes four central concepts: Indigenousness, sovereignty, colonization, and decolonization.[18] This new turn in historical scholarship draws heavily upon the work of Maori scholar Linda Tuhiwai Smith and her seminal volume, *Decolonizing Methodologies: Research and Indigenous Peoples*, published in 1999.[19]

Whereas previous generations of historians have tended to shy away from using the term "colonialism" when they write about Native Americans within the United States, naming colonialism and its ongoing effects is a central project of Indigenous historians who are part of the decolonization paradigm, and I have witnessed this transformation firsthand within the field.

The writings of these Indigenous studies scholars over the last decade have greatly changed the discourse as they no longer shy away from using colonialism as an analytical framework. This group of historians moves beyond speaking euphemistically about the colonial relationship between the United States and tribes, instead asserting in clear terms that the relationship has been, and remains, colonial.[20]

Miller acknowledges that American historians no longer claim that the contest over control of North America had to do with Indigenous people impeding "Progress," nor do they persist in offering the simplistic "conflict of cultures" argument. However, many American historians still "characterize U.S. violations of the nation-to-nation relationship with tribes as 'tragic' or . . . 'ironic'; and historians often take shelter in passive voice, which permits one to say that 'a wrong was done' without naming the culprit."[21] Scholars writing from the Indigenous paradigm employ more powerful and precise terms to describe what happened, including "genocide" and "atrocity," and they do not shy away from naming the perpetrators of the violence in our history.

Those following the Indigenous paradigm adhere to a research methodology that includes producing scholarship that serves Native communities; following Indigenous communities' protocols when conducting research; rigorously interrogating existing scholarship and calling out the "anti-Indigenous concept and language" embedded in existing literature; incorporating Indigenous languages, such as place-names, names of people, and proper nouns; and, finally, privileging Indigenous sources and perspectives over non-Indigenous ones.[22] Miller clearly and forcefully states that the United States has not come to terms with or fully reckoned with its colonial past and writings from this paradigm are challenging these silences.

One of the strengths of Miller's extensive historiographical essay is the attention she gives to the central tenet of decolonizing scholarship, namely, service to Indigenous communities as the primary goal. Service should be the goal of our museums as well. They should assist communities in understanding colonization as the origin of historical and ongoing harms. This understanding is key to creating the critical consciousness among Native people that is necessary to do the important work of decolonizing. Decolonization is not a "futile effort to return to the past," Miller and others argue, but a process that allows Native people to move toward healing from the devastating effects of colonization. As Cree scholar Winona Wheeler states:

> Decolonization entails developing a critical consciousness about the cause(s) of our oppression, the distortion of history, our own collabo-

ration, and the degree to which we have internalized colonialist ideas and practices. Decolonization requires auto-criticism, self-reflection, and a rejection of victimage. Decolonization is about empowerment—a belief that situations can be transformed, a belief and trust in our own peoples' values and abilities and a willingness to make change. It is about transforming negative reactionary energy into the more positive rebuilding energy needed in our communities.[23]

One of the central components of the movement is to revive tribal languages and cultural ceremonies that were previously persecuted by the government, revive institutions and technologies, and continue participation in activities and cultural practices that never lapsed.[24]

For those writing and representing the Indigenous experience, employing colonialism as an overarching interpretative framework does not automatically give Native people victimhood status. Historian Jeffrey Shepherd contends that "colonization and persistence can exist in the same geographical and interpretative space."[25] I would argue that, if we aim to create moving exhibitions that honor the history, memory, and collective experience of our relatives for future generations, we must work toward the goal of decolonization in museums.

What a great irony that places inextricably linked to the colonization process are also the sites where the difficult aspects of our history can and must be most clearly and forcefully told. Only by doing so can we address the legacies of historical unresolved grief. But before exploring further how museums can employ decolonizing methodologies, we must first take a look at their history. Museums have played a major role in dispossessing and misrepresenting Native Americans, and this has been a critical part of the identity of Euro-American museums.

NATIVE AMERICANS ON DISPLAY:
EARLY COLLECTING AND EXHIBITIONS

The history of museum representation of Native peoples begins with the development of anthropology as an academic field. While earlier forms of exhibition existed, such as the cabinets of curiosities, this is when we witness large-scale exhibitions seen by a broader public and in a diversity of places. In the late nineteenth and early twentieth centuries, many anthropologists made their careers on systematically collecting American Indian material culture. These collecting practices clearly influenced the types of exhibitions that curators developed, which in turn influenced the public's understanding of Native culture through the way that museums presented the objects. A majority of these objects were collected during the period when Indians were supposed to vanish from the American landscape—"the Dark Ages of Native history," as scholars of the period have referred to it.[26] This fact alone speaks volumes about the types of presentations that tribes oppose and are moving away from in their current exhibition practices. As art historian Janet Berlo writes, "For the past 100 years these bits and pieces, facts and objects, have been arranged and rearranged in a changing mosaic in which we have constructed an image that we claim represents Native American art and culture."[27] She goes on to argue that these exhibitions convey as much about the collectors themselves as the cultures they propose to represent.

The great collections in America were assembled during this period and were housed in several important museums. The key institutions established at this time include the Smithsonian in 1846, the Peabody Museum of Archaeology and Ethnology at Harvard in 1866, New York's American Museum of Natural History in 1869, and Chicago's Field Museum of Natural History in 1893.[28] These museums aggressively pursued the collecting of Native American ethnographic and archaeological material. During this period, the Smithsonian's collection grew dramatically "from 550 items in 1860 to more than 13,000 in 1873."[29]

The time period in which many important museums in the United States were formed and collecting began coincides with what many view as the nadir of Native existence on this continent. As a result of European colonization of the Americas, tribal nations across the Western Hemisphere experienced great population declines. By the turn of the twentieth century, it is estimated that only 250,000 Indians were alive in the United States. The number is staggering when you consider that the estimated precontact population was 5 million within U.S. borders. The dramatic demographic decline resulted from disease and the genocidal policies enforced throughout the Americas. Scholars have referred to it as the American Indian holocaust.[30] Native people were believed to be "vanishing," and anthropologists at the turn of the twentieth century thought they were in a race against time. They saw themselves as engaged in "salvage anthropology" to collect the so-called last vestiges of a dying race.

Paradoxically, at the same time that these collectors were in search of the "most authentic" or oldest type of tribal artifacts for their collections, Native communities were experiencing extreme pressures to assimilate into American society—to give up the very ways of life that produced these objects and that the objects reflect. The U.S. government enacted a series of assimilation policies during this period. For example, from a desire to disrupt tribal communal ownership of land and to transform Indians into landowners, the United States passed the Dawes Act in 1887, forcing a model of individual land ownership on Native peoples by dividing Indian lands into separate allotments. Each Indian family received 160 acres, and leftover lands were then sold to the highest bidder. Tragically, tribal communities lost a significant portion of their reservations through this policy. Before the passage of the Dawes Act, 138 million acres of land were held in trust—land that tribes were guaranteed under federal treaties. By 1934, however, only 52 million acres of land remained in tribal hands.[31]

At the same time, government-funded boarding schools subjected American Indian children to an educational program aimed at destroying Indigenous culture and kinship relationships. Children suffered enormously at these schools, which were designed to assimilate them and prepare them for positions at the lower rungs of American society. Federal officials were also "determined to eradicate Native religious practice and impose Christianity on Indian people."[32] Violating the American principle of freedom of religion, government agents arrested Native people who participated in their traditional religious ceremonies.

Not surprisingly, social scientists and historians view the late nineteenth century and early twentieth as a time of great loss. During this time, Native peoples faced enormous upheavals and suffering, and this is precisely when most of the collecting took place. Native Americans were told that there was no place for them as tribal people in contemporary society, yet the material culture identifying their tribal uniqueness was highly valued. In his book *Captured Heritage*, historian Douglas Cole traces the history of collecting on the Northwest Coast and describes the staggering quantity of materials collected by, in many instances, questionable means: "By the time it ended there was more Kwakiutl material in Milwaukee than in Mamalillikulla; more Salish pieces in Cambridge than in Comox. The city of Washington contained more Northwest Coast material than the state of Washington, and New York City probably housed more British Columbia material than British Columbia herself."[33]

Disease played a critical role in this wholesale collecting. Not only did its devastating impact lead to the notion of Indians as a vanishing race, but disease also played a role in dispossessing tribal peoples of their material culture by disrupting traditional ownership patterns. In her work on the Makah Nation entitled *Drawing Back Culture*, Ann Tweedie examines the disruptions that separated objects from tribal members within this particular Northwest Coast tribal nation. Disease decimated the community, and by 1860, the Makah lost half of their population to smallpox. Like other Northwest Coast societies, the Makah had highly developed patterns of personal ownership of both tangible and intangible heritage, and the population loss disrupted these ownership patterns within the community. One of the tribal members explains:

> A lot of people died of smallpox. And they'd find these objects [that had been put away] and they'd say "Well. Jees." You know. "Nobody owns these. Let's go sell them." And some families . . . entire clans died from the smallpox epidemic so a lot of these objects got to other places and they really had no ownership. It was really hard to tell when you lost all those linkages to the past.[34]

It is important to point out that not all objects left Native hands under duress during this period. Native art pieces developed for the tourist industry are an example of objects that tribal communities either sold or voluntarily parted with. Across the country, creating tourist art on reservations became a method for Indigenous people to carve out ways of making a living during extremely difficult economic times. For instance, women from my tribe made baskets for sale in Wisconsin Dells, Wisconsin, and tribal people throughout the United States made a living selling their artwork. However, even when objects were sold voluntarily, we must remember the deeper historical context.[35] Extreme poverty and ongoing colonial oppression permeated tribal life at the time, as it does for many Native people today. These brutal realities should never go unacknowledged, especially since questions over the ownership of cultural objects have not ended. The ongoing struggles over repatriation are a case in point.

COLLECTING HUMAN REMAINS

Museums were also interested in collecting human remains during this period. There has always been a fascination with collecting remains and funerary objects.[36] Scholars can date this practice to the Pilgrims in 1620, and even to one of the Founding Fathers of the United States, Thomas Jefferson.

Collecting Native American skeletal remains dramatically increased in the early nineteenth century, because scholars began using human remains to explain physical and cultural differences between peoples. Scholars such as Samuel G. Morton—often recognized as the father of physical anthropology

—actively collected human remains for their studies. The collecting of human crania in particular increased, as "scholars attempted to relate intelligence, personality, and character to skull and brain size."[37] Morton believed that a person's intelligence directly correlated to the size of his or her brain, and he and others conducted "experiments" measuring several hundred skulls belonging to members of different races. The measurements of cranial capacity and skull shape were really a way to racialize ethnic groups and "to validate theories of white supremacy."[38] Morton quickly discovered that there were few skulls available for study, and he provided economic incentives to soldiers, settlers, and government agents to enter Native American graves in order to collect the remains. The high numbers of Native American deaths due to disease and other forces of colonization made the collectors' task easier.[39]

The desire for Native American skulls and bodies for scientific research continued throughout the nineteenth century. In 1867, George A. Otis, curator of the Army Medical Museum (AMM), urged field doctors to send Native American human remains to the AMM. Otis later entered into an agreement with the Smithsonian: the AMM would receive osteological remains and would send the burial and cultural items associated with the deceased to the Smithsonian. In 1868, U.S. Army Surgeon General Joseph Barnes also issued a request to medical officers and field surgeons to collect human remains for scientific research. Because of these orders, roughly forty-five hundred Native American crania ended up in the collections of the AMM, many of which were transferred to the Smithsonian Institution in the 1890s.[40] Numerous other remains of Native Americans ended up in European collections.

Anthropologists certainly played a role in the early collecting of Native American human remains. Franz Boas, who made his reputation in part by gathering the oral traditions of the Native American cultures of the Northwest Coast, also collected Native people's physical bodies. While conducting ethnographic work with the Kwakwaka'wakw, Boas robbed graves after dark, noting that "it is most unpleasant work to steal bones from a grave, but what is the use, someone has to do it."[41] During his early research on the Northwest Coast, Boas collected roughly one hundred complete skeletons and two hundred skulls belonging to Kwakwaka'wakw and Coast Salish peoples. Boas mostly sold these human remains to the Field Museum in Chicago, but he also sold some later remains to parties in Berlin, Germany.[42] Numerous other celebrated figures of anthropology, such as Aleš Hrdlička and George Dorsey, voraciously collected Native American human remains during this time.

The passage of the Antiquities Act of 1906 had ramifications for the relationship between anthropology and Native Americans—both living and dead. The Antiquities Act was supposed to protect the cultural resources of the United States by creating a permitting process for archaeological excavation and by establishing punishments for looting. But in practice, it further reified the authority that anthropologists held over Native American material culture, including human remains. The act failed to directly consider the interests that Native Americans might have in their own material culture, and it legislated the appropriation of that culture by anthropologists. In effect, the act turned Native American human remains into archaeological resources and made them the property of the federal government.[43] As Clayton Dumont notes, "The legislation made no distinction between graves that were thousands of years old and the interment of one's mother at a tribal cemetery a week or even day prior."[44] By the time the Native American Graves Protection and Repatriation Act passed in 1990, scholars estimate that museums, federal agencies, and private collectors held anywhere between 300,000 to 2.5 million Native American bodies and untold millions of cultural objects.[45]

EARLY MUSEUM DISPLAYS

The exhibitions developed in the late nineteenth century and well into the twentieth clearly reflect the mind-set of the period. The notion of Indians as a vanishing or dying race was prevalent in most of the exhibitions that were developed well into the twentieth century. Exhibitions also tended to reinforce the view of static, unchanging cultures. Certainly, the diorama—a popular display technique used in natural history museums—tended to do this by depicting Indians as frozen in time and by displaying them near dinosaurs and other extinct animals. Additionally, objects were presented and defined by Western scientific categories—anthropological categories of manufacture and use—and not by Indigenous categories of culture, worldview, and meaning. Native societies were often defined by functional technology: we are only what we made. Exhibitions also obscured the great historical, cultural, and linguistic diversity of tribal nations by dividing Native people into cultural groups, giving a sense that all tribes are the same or at least the same in one particular region. At a time when Indians were believed to be on the road to extinction, exhibit techniques showed no desire on the part of curators to make connections with living Indians or to address an object's cultural relevance.

In his book *Cannibal Tours and Glass Boxes*, the late Michael Ames, former director of the University of British Columbia's Museum of Anthropology, describes the manner in which ethnographic collections were displayed. He outlines four styles that evolved over the years. The first type, cabinets of curiosities, preceded the development of professional anthropology collections in North America. The style developed in Europe beginning in the sixteenth century. The cabinets were private collections assembled by rich merchants and world travelers who desired to own natural history pieces along with "artificial curiosities," objects made by people from distant, exotic places.[46] Objects in the cabinets were crammed together and overflowing. The intent was to "select objects that would stimulate admiration and wonder and reflect upon the daring exploits, special knowledge, or privileged status of the collector."[47] Placing Native American cultural objects with flora and fauna was a common display technique used in the cabinets. It is important to note that the cabinets of curiosities formed the basis of many museum collections in Europe, including the Musée de l'Homme in France and the British Museum.[48]

The second type of exhibition practice, according to Ames, was the "natural history approach" used in early anthropology museums. This approach is linked to the development of the field of anthropology, and it ushered in the professionalization of museum staff. The displays presented material culture as "specimens" and Native people as "parts of nature like the flora and fauna, and therefore their arts and crafts were to be classified and presented according to similarity of form, evolutionary stage of development, or geographical origin."[49] These evolution-oriented and typology-organized display strategies are still practiced today in museums throughout the world, most notably at the Pitt Rivers Museum at Oxford University.

Ames refers to the third type of display technique as "contextualism," which he associates with modern anthropology. This mode of presentation was heavily influenced by the work of anthropologist Franz Boas, who sought to display objects in "fabricated settings that simulated the original cultural contexts from which they came."[50] Through this contextualized interpretative strategy, Boas believed that objects could be viewed "from the Native point of view," and he employed this approach at the American Museum of Natural History in New York City, where he began his museum career. The exhibits or dioramas placed objects in a simulated environment of a particular culture or time period.[51] Several important institutions still featured exhibits reflective of this interpretative strategy into the late twentieth century, including the Smithsonian's Museum of Natural History on the National Mall in Washington, D.C., and the Field Museum in Chicago.

Ames characterizes the fourth type of exhibition presentation as the "formalist perspective." This exhibit technique differed from the contextualist style developed by Boas, because it favored an emphasis on form in presenting particular objects, rather than on the context from which they came. Formalist presentations sought to identify the material culture of so-called primitive societies and portrayed the pieces as fine art.

Both formalists and contextualists were critical of each other's approach. Formalists have argued that the contextualist approach "is no less an arbitrary arrangement than the old curiosity cabinet, because the simulated context of the exhibition represents the mental reconstruction of the anthropologist further elaborated by the technical artistry of the exhibit designer."[52] The contextualists, on the other hand, reject the presentation of art objects that are not placed within their proper anthropological context. Ames argues that as long as the contextualists remain in anthropology or natural history museums and the formalists remain in art museums, tensions between the two could stay at a minimum.

The four approaches that Ames outlines are all outsider approaches to interpreting Indigenous people and cultures—and all are incomplete. He recognized the importance of a fifth approach, the "insider's point of view," which includes the perspectives of Native peoples themselves in the presentation of their material culture. According to Ames, what is key is "how the insider and outsider perspectives might interact and build upon one another in the process of truth-seeking and understanding."[53] During his tenure as director of the University of British Columbia's Museum of Anthropology (1974–97, 2002–4), Ames initiated collaborative exhibition projects with First Nations communities. This site is now viewed by many as the international leader in moving the museum world forward with efforts to share curatorial authority and collaborate with Indigenous communities in all aspects of museum practice. Today collaboration is becoming more the norm than the exception, and institutions across the country seek to work closely with "source communities" on exhibitions focusing on their history and culture.

NATIVE ACTIVISM AND ACADEMIC EPIPHANIES:
THE MOVE TO COLLABORATION

The move to collaboration in all facets of the museum world, including exhibitions, is gaining ground and is now considered a "best practice" within the field by many. As Robin Boast states, "Dialogue and collaboration [are] the name of the game these days and there are few museums with anthropological, or even archaeological, collections that would consider an exhibition that did not include some form of consultation."[54] What led to this new commitment to collaboration within the museum world?

Many scholars have emphasized the roles that both postmodernism and the international discourse on human rights have played in this new direction in museums. They have argued that postmodernism has led to self-reflection among anthropologists and museum curators on "the ways in which earlier, objectifying traditions of material culture display have supported colonial and neo-colonial power relations";[55] and the "evolving discourse of human rights has, in the years since its broad codification in the 1948 UN Universal Declaration of Human Rights, been vigorously argued to extend to cultural property and the protection of traditional indigenous knowledge."[56]

Fair enough. However, it is equally important to keep in mind that American Indian activism, which includes a wide range of activism, played no small role in this shift. In both the United States and Canada, Native activism was on the forefront of asserting Indigenous participation in developing exhibitions and in deciding what should be done with collections. Scholars have argued that the Native American challenge to museums began in the 1960s and was linked to the larger American Indian self-determination movement. Anthropologist Patricia Pierce Erikson argues that this movement inspired a range of Indigenous activism on issues involving museums. Native activists have worked to change museum practices by (1) protesting stereotypical displays of Native American history and culture at mainstream institutions; (2) protesting the collecting, display, and holding of American Indian human remains; (3) seeking to change museums from the inside by having Native people enter into the profession; (4) challenging the authority of Western museums to represent Native American communities without including the Native perspective; and (5) pressuring for the repatriation of Native American cultural objects, human remains, funerary objects, and objects of cultural patrimony.[57]

A change in Canadian exhibition practices also began during this period. In the 1970s, the Cranmer potlatch collection was returned to the Kwakwaka'wakw—a well-publicized event—and two tribal museums were established in the community. These positive steps reflected a change in the relationship between museums and Native people. Additionally, the Canadian Museums Association and the Assembly of First Nations Task Force on Museums, which was established in 1988, published a report, *Turning the Page: Forging New Partnerships between Museums and First Peoples*, following the

1988 successful boycott of the exhibition *The Spirit Sings: Artistic Traditions of Canada's First Peoples* by First Nations communities. The report recognized that Native groups "own or have moral claim to their heritage and therefore should participate equally in its preservation and presentation."[58] The report went on to recommend that First Peoples should be equal partners with museums in all presentations of their history and culture.

Another watershed moment for Native rights happened with the 1990 passing of the Native American Graves Protection and Repatriation Act (NAGPRA) after nearly two decades of Native activism and struggle. Its passage represents a significant achievement for American Indian people, and it has been critical in heightening Native involvement in the museum world. In a nutshell, the law requires "federal agencies (excluding the Smithsonian Institution) and museums . . . to return human remains and associated funerary objects upon request of a lineal descendant, Indian tribe, or Native Hawaiian organization."[59] NAGPRA is important human rights legislation. It was designed first and foremost to address the historical inequities created by a legacy of past collecting practices, the continual disregard for Native religious beliefs and burial practices, and a clear contradiction between how the graves of white Americans and the graves of Native Americans were treated. As Walter Echo-Hawk, the Pawnee attorney involved in the fight to get this legislation passed, aptly put it: "If you desecrate a white grave, you wind up sitting in prison. But desecrate an Indian grave, and you get a Ph.D."[60] NAGPRA attempts to address these inequities by giving Native American communities greater control over the remains of their ancestors and the cultural objects held at museums. In the context of my analysis of the Ziibiwing Center of Anishinabe Culture & Lifeways (chapter 4), I will address the ongoing efforts by tribal communities to decolonize NAGPRA.

Another major development that has changed the relationship between museums and Native peoples is the tribal museum movement. In an important act of self-determination, Native communities are controlling the representation of their cultures through these tribal institutions as well as challenging the representations of Native peoples at mainstream museums. Once again, Indigenous activism has been critical to changing the relationship between tribal nations and museums, and this needs to be acknowledged. Native involvement in the museum world did not happen because of academic epiphanies by non-Native academics or curators, but as result of prolonged and committed activism.

It is, of course, beyond the scope of this work to provide an in-depth history of tribal museums and how they have developed in the United States and

Canada. However, some background on their development might be useful to help readers understand the broader context for the two tribal museum case studies featured here, the Mille Lacs Indian Museum in Minnesota and the Ziibiwing Center of Anishinabe Culture & Lifeways in Michigan. (The former is considered a "hybrid tribal museum" and the latter is entirely Native controlled.) Both museums developed in tandem with broader movements within the United States and Canada, and in both cases, the impetus was to challenge how mainstream, Western institutions have consistently misrepresented Native history and culture.

While a few tribal museums emerged in the first part of the twentieth century, such as the Osage Tribal Museum in 1938, most scholars acknowledge that the first significant wave of tribal museum development occurred in the 1960s and 1970s as part of a broader movement of economic development. During this period, tribal communities began establishing museums to promote tourism, cultural preservation, and economic growth.[61] Some sought funding through a granting program with the Economic Development Administration (EDA). The EDA offered funding for federally recognized tribes to establish businesses for employment and to create other revenue-generating opportunities, and some tribes took the offer and opened museums, and in the years that followed, some museums prospered, while others failed.[62] In his report *Tribal Museums in America*, George Abrams comments on the uneven success rates of these early facilities: "While the earlier EDA projects provided money for bricks and mortar, oftentimes there was little consideration of how the museum or the tribe was to fund annual budgets, staff, acquiring and maintaining collections, upkeep of the building, etc. It was to become apparent for those who were involved in the actual implementation of tribal museums that buildings are not museums, and museums are not buildings—a view commonly held by the profession at large."[63]

Over the last several decades, tribal museums and cultural centers have continued to be built throughout Indian Country, and they open on a regular basis. The exact number of tribal museums fluctuates, depending on the criteria used to determine eligibility, with most placing the number of tribal museums in North America around two hundred. A recent Smithsonian survey considers tribal museums to be "museums that retain Native authority through direct tribal ownership or majority presence, or that are located on tribally controlled lands, or that have a Native director or board members."[64] If we use a strict definition of exclusive Native control through Native governance, the number drops to between 120 and 175 tribal museums in North America.[65]

Generalizing about the types of exhibitions featured in tribal museums is difficult. As I often tell my students, we need to remember that each museum is as unique as the community it proposes to represent. Many tribal cultural centers and museums are very small places with only a few staff people and small exhibitions. In the last twenty years, however, several tribes have built large multimillion-dollar facilities, and their exhibitions exemplify the finest in contemporary exhibit development. Several sites that I have visited include the Museum at Warm Springs (Warm Springs, Oregon), the Tamástslikt Cultural Institute (Pendleton, Oregon), the Makah Cultural and Research Center (Neah Bay, Washington), and the Mashantucket Pequot Museum and Research Center (Mashantucket, Connecticut). These tribal museums have state-of-the-art exhibits that equal or surpass current exhibits at mainstream museums in terms of design and construction. While the exhibit content is unique, the overall feel of these spaces is contemporary, sophisticated, and beautiful.

Obviously, I do not have the space to describe in detail the content of these and other tribal museums. However, I would like to comment on an overall pattern that I, along with other scholars, have observed in museum content at many of the tribal museums and cultural centers in the United States. In their exhibitions, tribal museums often emphasize Native American survival and cultural continuance: the obvious, yet powerful reminder that "we are still here." JoAllyn Archambault summarizes this emphasis and the overarching exhibit philosophy behind it when she writes, "What binds it all together is a persuasive insistence on the importance of the present and the future, both of which are founded on ties to the past."[66]

Many of our tribal museums have indeed done an excellent job of conveying the ongoing presence of Native communities. They have also shown a desire to challenge the existing stereotypes of Native American history and culture that are prevalent in our society. However, I come back to the need to name colonialism and its impact on our history and our communities today. To date, with the exception of the Ziibiwing Center of Anishinabe Culture & Lifeways in Michigan, most of the tribal museums that I have visited do not provide visitors with a rigorous, critical discussion of colonialism and its ongoing effects.

In her survey of tribal museums in the Southwest conducted under the auspices of a National Endowment for the Humanities "Extending the Reach" grant, Apache scholar Rebecca Hernandez also observed a reluctance to discuss challenging or difficult topics within the exhibitions. She found that many tribal museums follow exhibition didactic practices that are comparable to those of mainstream institutions, particularly in a shared desire to avoid an extensive analysis of colonialism and its ongoing effects. She acknowledges the important educational role that tribal museums and cultural centers play and their many accomplishments in that capacity. However, she also noticed a tendency to "avoid discussion or delineation of controversial events, difficult historical facts and current political dilemmas" in the sites that she visited.[67] One could argue further that the many collaborative projects pursued by Native people and mainstream museums manifest a similar tendency to avoid tough and challenging topics.

THE EMERGENCE OF COLLABORATIONS AND FRAMEWORKS
FOR UNDERSTANDING THEM

While several recent studies provide rich descriptive information on the process of developing collaborative exhibitions, the first scholar to offer a theoretical framework for this process is art historian and museum studies scholar Ruth Phillips. In her introduction to "Community Collaboration in Exhibitions: Toward a Dialogic Paradigm" in *Museums and Source Communities*, edited by Laura Peers and Alison Brown, Phillips asserts that there is "a spectrum of models . . . bracketed by two distinct types."[68] She is careful to acknowledge that there is no prototypical model or single collaborative process. Each project is firmly rooted in the institutional history of the particular museum and is dependent on the relationships that develop between individuals in the museums and on the community advisory boards. Still, even though each project is unique, Phillips proposes two models that most collaborative projects fall into: the multivocal model and the community-based model.

According to Phillips, the multivocal exhibit model allows for multiple perspectives in the exhibitions. The voices of curators, scholars, and Indigenous people are all present in the interpretative space and offer their own interpretations on the significance of the pieces and themes presented from their respective disciplinary and personal backgrounds. An example of this model was *Creation's Journey: Masterworks of Native American Identity and Belief*, which opened in 1994 at the NMAI's George Gustav Heye Center in New York. I will discuss this exhibit and its genesis more fully in chapter 3.

Phillips characterizes the second of the two models as a community-based approach: "The role of the professional museum curator or staff member is defined as that of a facilitator who puts his or her disciplinary and museological expertise at the service of community members so that their messages can be disseminated as clearly and as effectively as possible."[69] The community is given final authority in all decisions related to the exhibition, from the themes and objects that will be featured to the design of the actual exhibition. The tribal perspective has primacy in interpretation in this model, and exhibition text is typically in the first person. The Minnesota Historical Society employed this approach for the Mille Lacs Indian Museum, which opened in 1996, and the NMAI used it for their Washington, D.C., site, which opened in September 2004.

One of the most significant features of these two new types of exhibitions, especially the community-based model, is the desire to move away from object-based presentations that focus on the functions and uses of objects according to ethnographic categories. Instead, the exhibits make stronger connections to the relationships that pieces have to contemporary communities. As scholar Trudy Nicks has acknowledged, "Museums now accept that many contemporary indigenous groups see objects as living entities. . . . [and] the significance of objects is no longer restricted to past contexts of manufacture, use, and collecting, but now takes into account the demonstrated meanings they may have for indigenous communities in the present and for the future."[70]

In these new interpretative strategies, the curators are less willing simply to showcase great objects. Instead, they allow concepts to lead the exhibition planning—concepts that have been developed in consultation with community advisory boards. Objects are still central to the exhibition, but they are selected to illustrate certain themes: the importance of family, elders, and Indigenous communities' relationship to the land; contemporary survival; sovereignty; education; and language, to name a few. Displaying objects in ways that convey both their historic and their contemporary resonances is central in these presentations.

With Phillips's framework and with the new interpretative methods that are the direct result of collaborations in developing museum exhibits, I want to discuss some of the ups and downs that I see in the museum practices that have followed. Scholars and communities recognize that the collaborative process is a welcome shift in power dynamics within museums. But ongoing issues remain. We must not allow these narratives of collaboration to become too tidy or celebratory, or we could become complacent. We now have many examples of both tribally controlled museums and collaborative partnerships that have evolved since the latter part of the twentieth century. In this book, I focus on three museums that I have studied over an extended period of time. But I also want to acknowledge other places where collaborative exhibitions as well as tribal museums have developed.

At the University of Arizona, for example, faculty and graduate students, including Shelby Tisdale, assisted in developing the Cocopah Museum and Cultural Center, which opened in the mid-1990s on the Cocopah reservation in Arizona. In her doctoral dissertation, Tisdale describes the process of bringing this project to fruition. Individuals from the University of Arizona spent years working with members of the community to develop a center that would meet the community's stated goal of cultural preservation and education in a changing world. Community members also brought hopes for economic development—hopes that mirror the goals and objectives of other tribal museum projects and collaborative ventures. Most significantly, the museum's identity or subjectivity is not static or fixed. Tribal members continue to engage in conversations about how this particular new form of cultural preservation can assist them in addressing issues of critical importance. The result is a museum that is fluid and in flux, changing in response to changes in the community it serves.[71]

Other institutions have also played a role in shifting museums from being strictly curator-controlled sites to more inclusive and collaborative spaces. The Denver Art Museum, the Denver Museum of Natural History, the Arizona State Museum, the Museum of Indian Arts and Culture (and its affiliated Laboratory of Anthropology) in Santa Fe, New Mexico, all come to mind as having contributed significantly to changes in museum practices. Bruce Bernstein, for example, first developed community-collaborative types of exhibits in Santa Fe at the Museum of Indian Arts and Culture/Laboratory of Anthropology. He later served as the assistant director for cultural resources at the Smithsonian's National Museum of the American Indian, where he provided vision for the NMAI's ambitious program of community-curated exhibition development. When he came on board with the NMAI in 1997, his commitment to community collaboration played a decisive role in determining the course that the NMAI would follow in developing its exhibits. I will discuss this collaborative project—its strengths and weaknesses, as I see them—more fully in chapter 3. Clearly, collaboration in exhibition development has greatly influenced contemporary museum practice as it relates to Native Americans, and the literature is replete with examples of positive new directions. However, I caution against moving too quickly to celebratory narratives of a "mission accomplished" variety that sometimes permeate the literature.

Cambridge University archaeologist Robin Boast recently wrote an article for *Museum Anthropology* in which he interrogates both the move to collaboration and the recent literature in the field that offers a generally positive picture of the collaborative process. Boast rigorously questions the current state of museum practices and our understanding of "museums as contact zones"—a widely accepted theoretical framing of the collaborative process. I quote from his point in its entirety, as I find his to be the most forceful statement yet on the need not to move so quickly to celebratory narratives. Doing so obscures the glaring power imbalances that remain and thereby reduces the real potential to dramatically shift museum policies and practices.

> The key problem, as I see it, lies deeper—deep in the assumptions and practices that constitute the museum in the past and today. . . . The new museum, the museum as contact zone, is and continues to be used instrumentally as a means of masking far more fundamental asymmetries, appropriations, and biases. The museum, as a site of accumulation, as a gatekeeper of authority and expert accounts, as the ultimate caretaker of the object . . . as its documenter and even as the educator, has to be completely redrafted. Where the new museology saw the museum being transformed from a site of determined edification to one of educational engagement, museums of the 21st century must confront this deeper neocolonial legacy. This is not only possible but, I would argue, could renovate the museum into an institution that supported the enrichment, rather than authorization, of collections. To do this, however, requires museums to learn to let go of their resources, even at times of the objects, for the benefit and use of communities and agendas far beyond its knowledge and control.[72]

As Boast says, moving too soon to celebratory narratives runs the risk of obscuring "far more fundamental asymmetries, appropriations, and biases." Tidy stories of successful collaboration may mask persistent neocolonial relations within the museum world. We must be mindful of these dynamics, because they still hold sway. We have ample evidence of this type of masking from Native people's experiences with repatriation and museum noncompliance with the Native American Graves Protection and Repatriation Act. Twenty years and counting after the passage of the law, Native Americans continue to struggle with many mainstream museums over the return of Native remains and cultural items. The scientific community seems preoccupied with emphasizing successful collaborations with Indigenous communities in many other areas, but this enthusiasm is disingenuous when it masks ongoing issues around academic, scientific, and museum noncompliance with the law. I will discuss these serious concerns in greater depth in chapter 4.[73]

In the chapters that follow, I will focus, then, on three different museums that have engaged the challenging work of collaborative exhibition development over the last few decades. The work is significant given its attention to the complex and ever-changing relationship between Indigenous people and museums, which many describe as a love-hate relationship. My main concern is to explore how museums can serve as sites of decolonization. I argue that they do this through honoring Indigenous knowledge and worldviews, challenging the stereotypical representations of Native people produced in the past, serving as sites of "knowledge making and remembering" for their own communities and the general public, and discussing the hard truths of colonization in exhibitions in an effort to promote healing and understanding.

Unlike previous studies that focus on the relation between Native Americans and museums, this book is comparative and draws upon data collected from my ten-year, multisite museum project. My analysis rests not just on one museum but on three different sites of Indigenous self-representation. I recount the complex and dynamic story of how these projects have come to fruition.

While one of the sites featured in this book, the National Museum of the American Indian, has received attention in the scholarly literature, the other two museums, the Mille Lacs Indian Museum and the Ziibiwing Center of Anishinabe Culture & Lifeways, have not. While they are both Anishinabe museums, each museum's development is unique and exemplifies a significant temporal argument on the changing relationship between Indigenous people and museums. Both illustrate how new museum theory has been put into practice. The Mille Lacs Indian Museum, a "hybrid tribal museum" located in Minnesota, is an important collaborative partnership between the Minnesota Historical Society and the Mille Lacs Band of Ojibwe. The collaborative process followed at this site between a state historical society and an Ojibwe community helped pave the way for the type of large-scale collaborative project pursued by planners of the Smithsonian's National Museum of the American Indian with Native communities across the hemisphere.

In the case of the Ziibiwing Center, I am the first museum studies scholar who has conducted extensive research there. This fact is significant given that the Ziibiwing Center is perhaps the most innovative tribal museum in the country. The museum advances a decolonizing agenda by framing the entire exhibition within the context of the Anishinabe oral tradition, and it also presents the hard truths of colonization in its exhibitions to address the legacies of historical unresolved grief. The present tribal involvement in exhibit development demonstrates the links between self-representation and larger movements of Native American self-determination and cultural sovereignty.

IN ADDITION TO this introductory chapter, the book includes four chapters. Chapter 2 focuses on the development of the Mille Lacs Indian Museum, an Ojibwe museum in Minnesota that has undergone significant changes in representation throughout its history since it opened in 1960. Closed for several years during major renovation and revision, the museum reopened in 1996 as a tribal museum. My examination of this museum addresses how one Native community constructed a collective public memory and history by developing a tribal museum—in this case, a "hybrid" tribal museum. In doing so, they took the lead in shaping the public's perception of their past. This is a significant site of Indigenous self-representation, and the site translates new museum theory into practice. I was fortunate to witness the process firsthand as an exhibit researcher in 1994–95.

My next chapter focuses on the Smithsonian's National Museum of the American Indian and explores the complexities of the new collaborative relationship between Native communities and museums on the national stage. I examine the NMAI's significance to the changing historical relationship between Indigenous people and museums. I also question the assessment of several scholars that the NMAI is a decolonizing museum. While the NMAI advances an important collaborative methodology in its exhibitions, I argue that its historical exhibitions fail to present a clear and coherent understanding of colonialism and its ongoing effects. My critiques focus mostly on the institution's presentation of Native American history in the *Our Peoples* gallery. I argue, first, that the presentation conflates an Indigenous understanding of history with a postmodernist presentation of history, and, second, that it fails to tell the hard truths of colonization and the genocidal acts committed against Indigenous people. Given these silences, I contend that the museum fails to serve as a site of truth telling and remembering. Instead, it remains very much an institution of the nation-state. Thus, I caution against referring to this site as a "tribal museum writ large" or, even more problematically, as a "decolonizing museum," which several scholars have done.

Building on this discussion of how museums can serve as sites of decolonization through truth telling in exhibition spaces, I conclude my case studies with an examination of an Anishinabe tribal museum in Michigan, the

Ziibiwing Center. This community-based museum on the Saginaw Chippewa reservation embodies, I believe, important decolonizing practices. In chapter 4, I explore how the Ziibiwing Center represents the hard truths of colonialism and genocide in its exhibitions. As one of the newest tribally owned and operated museums in the nation, the Ziibiwing Center both borrows from and builds upon the last thirty years of tribal museum development. The center reflects some of the most current and innovative exhibition strategies, including thematic rather than object-based exhibits, an effective use of multimedia, more storytelling and use of the first-person voice, and, most significantly, emphasis on Anishinabe survival within a colonial context.

Because of these critical components, I argue that the museum reflects a decolonizing agenda. How the Saginaw Chippewa represent their story as a people reflects more closely an Indigenous understanding of history and honors the oral tradition. Moreover, the people's courage and ability to speak the hard truths of colonization in their exhibitions has given the museum a vitality and community connectedness that energize their ongoing programming. Notwithstanding the inevitable bumps that arise, this museum is working closely with the community, and the Ziibiwing Center offers a compelling case study of what a vibrant tribal museum can achieve. I end the book with a concluding chapter that focuses on how to transform museums into "places that matter" for Native Americans. Key to this endeavor will be our readiness to extend our understanding of museums to embrace their potential to become "sites of conscience" and decolonization.

Finally, I hope this volume will add another angle to the important conversations about the changing relations between Indigenous people and museums. My research is deeply rooted in my own identity as a Ho-Chunk scholar and museum professional. For most Native people, what is inside tribal museums or any museum that contains Native representations is not a matter of detached, academic interest—something about which we debate as part of our professional careers. We can do this, but the meaning of this work goes much deeper for us. The museum content involves life, ancestors, culture, our continued existence, and future generations.

Mindful of this, I hope that what comes through in my analysis of these institutions is the heartfelt emotion that these sites evoke for many Native people. In my attempt to honor the storytelling traditions of our communities, I have decided to include in the text many first-person testimonies by both Native and non-Native actors. These first-person accounts are rich in description, and they convey what I believe are interesting, thought-provoking commentaries. Moreover, while this work is theoretically informed and methodologically sound, I never want to lose sight of my Native sensibilities and forget to tell a story. For Native people, the story that follows is about our cultural survival and self-determination. There are many ways to tell this story. Here, I will tell it through the ever-changing, complex, contested, and dynamic process of representing Native peoples in both national and tribal museums in the late twentieth and early twenty-first centuries. For all the theory that infuses this work, I hope that readers will also engage this work as a good story—one that continues beyond these pages.

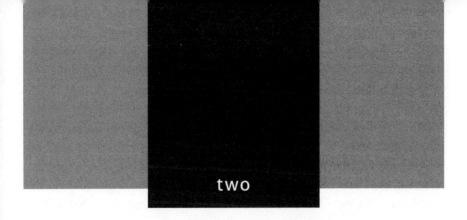

two

COLLABORATION MATTERS

The Minnesota Historical Society, the Mille Lacs Band of
Ojibwe, and the Creation of a "Hybrid Tribal Museum"

BEGINNINGS

In a letter dated 14 March 1997, W. Richard West, Southern Cheyenne and founding director of the Smithsonian's National Museum of the American Indian (NMAI), wrote in support of the Minnesota Historical Society (MHS) receiving an award from the American Association for State and Local History. MHS had recently opened the Mille Lacs Indian Museum at one of its historic sites and had collaborated with the Mille Lacs Band of Ojibwe on all phases of the museum's development. West emphasized the importance of this collaboration as being critical to his work at the NMAI. He stated, "The project's system of community liaisons, quite literally, was in my mind, as I, in the early years of this institution, established a series of direct consultations with Native communities that preceded all planning for facilities and public programs here."[1]

That the collaborative exhibition-development process pursued by the Minnesota Historical Society with the Mille Lacs Band of Ojibwe helped Richard West chart the course for his work at the Smithsonian's National Museum of the American Indian speaks volumes. It shows not only the quality of the representations that developed but also the significance of the Mille Lacs Indian Museum to the changing relationship between Indigenous people and museums. How did this collaboration between a state historical society and an Indigenous nation come to fruition and garner the recognition that West's letter reveals? During the initial planning stages for the new museum, some believed that the Mille Lacs Indian Museum would have local and perhaps regional implications. But others recognized early on that this project could also have national importance.

The Minnesota Historical Society's attempt to collaborate with the Mille Lacs Band of Ojibwe to develop a museum with a new subjectivity as a "hybrid tribal museum" is the focus of this chapter.[2] What happened in Minnesota in the 1980s and 1990s may have happened elsewhere in the museum world, but it is a story worth recognizing as an embodiment of new museum theory put into practice that culminates in new representations of Native American history and culture reflecting the finest in collaborative exhibition development in the late twentieth century.

In this chapter, I explore the development of the Mille Lacs Indian Museum, which is located in Onamia, Minnesota. The museum has undergone significant changes in representation throughout its more than fifty-year history. In 1996 it reopened as a hybrid tribal museum. That is, its current form developed through a collaborative partnership between MHS and the Mille Lacs Band of Ojibwe. My examination of this museum's development occurs within the larger theme of how Native communities have constructed a collective public memory and history through the medium of tribal museums—or, in this case, a "hybrid" tribal museum. In doing so, Native communities have attempted to take control of the public's perception of their past. The Mille Lacs Indian Museum is a significant site of Indigenous self-representation and reflects an enactment of new museum theory into practice that I witnessed firsthand as an exhibit researcher in 1994 during the redesign process.

This shift in museum development raises a number of significant themes, which I explore. To start, I trace the genealogy of the site from its beginnings as a trading post to its years as an MHS museum to its new subjectivity as a hybrid tribal museum. Next, I track how a new exhibition interpretative strategy that privileges the voices and perspectives of the Mille Lacs Band of Ojibwe emerged at this museum. Finally, I explore the complexities of collaborative exhibition development between a mainstream museum and an Indigenous community. The complexities that arise from a collaboration of this nature persist in the ongoing life of the museum and the kind of programs that the museum offers.

The identity of the Mille Lacs Indian Museum is somewhat contested. Its status is unique, as MHS director Nina Archabal described: "While this museum is not a tribal museum in strict parlance—it is not owned by the Band, the building is not owned by the Band, the collection is not owned by the

Band, the Band is not responsible for its operation or its debt or any aspect of it—they are however very much the owners, the spiritual owners of what finally came out of the Mille Lacs Museum."[3] On one hand, it is a state museum, as Archabal mentioned, and it is part of the historic sites network of the Minnesota Historical Society. On the other hand, it is located on tribal lands and provides primacy in interpretation to the Mille Lacs Band. Given this complex subjectivity, I argue that, while the Mille Lacs Indian Museum represents an important collaborative exhibition and museum project by privileging the voice and perspective of the Mille Lacs Band of Ojibwe, it has not yet fully achieved a decolonizing museum practice. The Minnesota Historical Society maintains financial and administrative control. Moreover, the complicated history and genealogy of the site remain an absent-present at the museum, as current programming at the site does not carry forward or complement a decolonizing museum practice.

Still, Richard West recognized what the Mille Lacs Indian Museum does represent: a place that did the work of collaboration in exhibition development "immensely well"—and at a time when few other museums were following a similar course. Close to twenty years later it is now commonplace to share curatorial authority and engage in collaborative exhibition planning that privileges Indigenous voices and perspectives. At Mille Lacs the new museum theory heavily influenced its methodology and became embodied in the exhibitions that opened in 1996.

METHODOLOGICAL STRATEGIES

My engagement with the Mille Lacs Indian Museum began in 1994–95 while I was on staff at the Minnesota Historical Society. I have followed the museum's development and reception ever since. Because I was present at the creation of the Mille Lacs Indian Museum as a participant observer, I had an invaluable opportunity to engage with the Ojibwe community advisory board as well as with members of the Minnesota Historical Society Exhibits Department as they decided which narratives and stories would be privileged in the exhibitions. While serving as an exhibit researcher from June to December 1994, I assisted in the overall conceptual development of the permanent galleries.

As part of my work on the project, I attended monthly advisory board meetings with Mille Lacs Band members and MHS staff. I also attended community gatherings—powwows, feasts, the tribal chair's State of the Band Address, and celebrations for the grand openings of new tribal facilities.

This was an especially active period for tribal infrastructure development. Throughout the early to mid-1990s, new community-owned facilities were opening on a regular basis. These new facilities were built with the proceeds from the Band's tribal gaming operations at Grand Casino Mille Lacs and Grand Casino Hinckley, both of which opened following passage of the Indian Gaming Regulatory Act of 1988.

My job responsibilities also involved researching the Band's history and culture at libraries and archives in Minnesota and beyond. I conducted oral history interviews with elders and artists from the community; some of these interviews were later used in the exhibitions. And I researched collections related to the Band, including objects, archival records, and photographs that were held at MHS. My main goal was to find archival materials that would enhance the content ideas that the community advisory board was putting forth for the exhibitions. The new Mille Lacs Indian Museum opened in 1996.

I returned to MHS in May 2001 to gather documentation for the exhibitions that were launched at the new facility. I collected the final exhibition text, object lists, curators' records, records from the Historic Sites Department, images, grant proposals, media and public relations materials, and audience research evaluations that had been completed in 1996. I also conducted interviews with key members of the project team who had been involved in museum development. When I returned to the Mille Lacs site itself, I interviewed tribal members who were employed as interpreters about their views of the museum.

The opportunity to return to the museum after years away from the project allowed me to reflect on my experiences as an exhibit researcher in 1994. I viewed firsthand the narratives and objects that were included in the final product. Many of the content ideas were enhanced, and certainly some story lines had changed from the early years of content discussions. Surprisingly, though, many of the key themes that were discussed in the early days comprised the core presentation. These themes had simply been enhanced by documentary evidence, including objects and oral histories obtained from tribal members.

Since that time, I have followed the museum's reception and ongoing life, and I have returned to the site whenever my schedule allowed. In June 2010, I spent time at Mille Lacs interviewing its current site manager, Travis Zimmerman, on the state of the museum fourteen years after its opening. He discussed both the successes and challenges of the museum as he saw them. The museum has suffered several cutbacks over the years as part of the state budget crisis in Minnesota over the last decade. In spite of this, there seems to be new energy at the site, and Travis and his staff are making plans to extend programming and to revise the exhibitions.

In the examination that follows, I engage the museum's past, present, and future with a critical eye. What is the museum's status then and now as an embodiment of an important collaborative process between a mainstream museum and a tribal nation? Even after numerous engagements with its exhibitions over the past sixteen years, I find that one of the most striking aspects of the Mille Lacs Indian Museum is the power of its stories. This hybrid tribal museum located on a rural reservation in northern Minnesota has become an important site of tribal history and memory, which its exhibits vividly capture. The Band's stories of cultural continuance are powerfully rendered and convey their pride as a tribal nation. Former site manager and Mille Lacs Band member Joycelyn Shingobe Wedll claimed: "We wanted to focus on our strengths as a community. We wanted to show how we were able to live through the injustices and still be strong in our culture, our language, our community—how we hung onto the very things outside people wanted to destroy. Our spirit was never broken."[4]

THE MILLE LACS BAND OF OJIBWE: THEIR HISTORICAL BACKGROUND AND THE SIGNIFICANCE OF THE MUSEUM

The Mille Lacs Band of Ojibwe are an Algonquian-speaking people who originated on the east coast of North America and migrated to the Great Lakes region. The reasons for the migration are many, including both internal and external forces. Ojibwe scholar Anton Treuer states, "In part because of tribal warfare and in part because of the prophecies, the Ojibwe slowly began moving westward around fifteen hundred years ago."[5] The oral tradition of the Ojibwe people mentions specific prophecies that encouraged their migration to "the land where food grows on the water." This brought them into present-day Michigan, Minnesota, and Wisconsin. At the time of contact with the French in the seventeenth century, the Ojibwe were "already well established at Sault St. Marie [Michigan] and the surrounding area and no longer had ties to their old village sites on the Atlantic Coast."[6]

In the seventeenth century, the Ojibwe first entered the Mille Lacs region, the ancestral homeland of the Dakota people, and by the mid-eighteenth century, they had expelled the Dakota from the area.[7] During the nineteenth century, the Ojibwe in Minnesota were forced to sign several treaties with the U.S. government that resulted in major land cessions, and an 1855 treaty established the Mille Lacs reservation, along with six other reservations for the Ojibwe, in northern Minnesota.[8]

In the nineteenth century and well into the twentieth, the U.S. government placed increasing pressure on the Mille Lacs people to give up their lands at Mille Lacs and settle on the White Earth reservation farther north. The Mille Lacs Band successfully resisted these efforts, and a defining characteristic of its identity today is its status as "nonremovable." The Mille Lacs Band of Ojibwe currently has more than four thousand enrolled members, the majority of whom reside in one of three districts that comprise their north-central Minnesota reservation.[9]

The Mille Lacs Band story, though unique in many respects, resonates with the experiences of tribal nations across the United States as well as with broader themes in Native American history. Alongside their stories of resistance are stories of invasion, violence, disease, warfare, forced surrender of vast amounts of lands through treaties signed with the U.S. government, destruction of tribal economies, and forced assimilation programs. Both sets of stories form a significant part of the Band's heritage. Indeed, the innovative ways that the Mille Lacs people have responded to the last 200-plus years of colonization are more than just stories of survival. These narratives reflect Native survivance, a concept advanced by Gerald Vizenor, a White Earth Ojibwe writer and literary scholar. He defines "survivance" as

> a sentiment heard in creation stories and the humorous contradictions of tricksters and read in the tragic wisdom of literature; these common sentiments of survivance are more than survival reactions in the face of violence and dominance. Tragic wisdom is the source of Native reason, the common sense gained from the adverse experiences of discovery, colonialism, and cultural domination. Tragic wisdom is a pronative voice of liberation and survivance, a condition in native stories . . . that denies victimization.[10]

One of the defining characteristics of the Mille Lacs community is the ability of its members to preserve their language and culture in the face of ongoing colonization. Scholars and Ojibwe leaders alike have long acknowledged that this community has "fared better than most of their neighbors" in maintaining their culture.[11] As Anton Treuer explains, the Mille Lacs people have been able to preserve their Big Drum culture and their traditional religious ceremonies "in the face of consistent efforts to remove them from their homeland, including the burning of their homes in 1901 and the withholding of allotments until 1926 for all who did not relocate to White Earth."[12] He acknowledges the power of the drums and the strong leadership on the reservation as critical to the people's ability to retain this cultural knowledge for all Ojibwe communities: "The people of Mille Lacs have maintained regional Big Drum culture for all Ojibwe people through the strength of their teaching and the strength of their learning."[13] One could argue that the exhibitions at the new Mille Lacs Indian Museum have the potential to become part of this ongoing tradition at Mille Lacs of cultural preservation, education, and continuance.

The exhibition-planning process for the Mille Lacs Indian Museum emerged in the early 1990s, when the community was experiencing rapid cultural, economic, and political change due to its successful tribal gaming enterprises. Mille Lacs leaders believed that it was critical to contextualize these changes within a historical framework. Their priority was raising the historical consciousness of Band members to help them understand not only their past but also the myriad changes in their contemporary lives.[14] The overarching narrative structure of the exhibition was to emphasize Mille Lacs Ojibwe survivance. As I will discuss later, its final form in place today does not provide an extensive context on colonialism and its ongoing effects. Yet the exhibition does place the Mille Lacs voice at the center of the narrative. It presents a rich, ongoing history, but it does so in a manner that avoids challenging or difficult topics, specifically, the impact of colonialism.

THE MILLE LACS INDIAN MUSEUM: THE HISTORY OF THE SITE

The genealogy of the Mille Lacs site as a trading post and later as a museum begins in 1919, when Harry and Jeanette Ayer moved to the Mille Lacs area, where they spent forty years operating a trading post on the reservation.[15] During their tenure at Mille Lacs, they also developed several other businesses, including a fishing-resort complex and a boat-building company. Many of their businesses employed Mille Lacs Band members. Ever the opportunists, the Ayers capitalized on the emerging tourist industry following completion of Minnesota Scenic Highway 169, and they developed a highly profitable business selling Native arts and crafts to tourists. They later opened a museum on the site to showcase their collection of artifacts, most of which were collected from the Mille Lacs Ojibwe people during the early to middle part of the twentieth century.

While the Ayers were successful in their various ventures, their story parallels those of other white traders across the country. The exploitative practices of white traders on reservations during this period made the traders far wealthier than those whose goods they marketed. As Roger and Priscilla Buffalohead argue in their important tribal history, *Against the Tide of American History: The Story of the Mille Lacs Anishinabe,* "[Harry] Ayer's talent for turning the special knowledge of the Chippewa [or Ojibwe] into business enterprises profited himself far more than it did the people."[16] In 1959, the Ayers donated their 1,400-artifact collection, museum, and property to the Minnesota Historical Society. Many in the community believe that the Ayers acquired the land under dubious and unethical circumstances. In 1960, the Minnesota Historical Society renamed the site the State Indian Museum and held a dedication ceremony on the reservation.[17]

Under the Minnesota Historical Society's ownership, the museum remained a popular tourist destination, and Mille Lacs Band members continued their association with the site. They were employed as tour guides, sales clerks, and craft demonstrators. Beginning in the late 1970s, they were also employed as site managers. During this period, the museum buildings began deteriorating, risking the safety of the exhibits and objects. In response, MHS began planning a new museum. This ended up being a seventeen-year process, which culminated in the opening of the new building on the site in 1996.

In the early years of MHS control, the museum was not tribally controlled or even tribally partnered. Although some tribal members worked as guides, craft demonstrators, and sales clerks, they did not have much input in developing the exhibitions. The lack of Ojibwe curatorial input was evident in the exhibits. Kate Roberts, the MHS curator and the Mille Lacs Indian Museum co-curator, recalled:

> What had been up there prior to this museum was the standard interpretation of Native American culture. It started very early, with a large precontact section and went through and talked about seasonal living—we all know the topics that were typically covered in those Native histories. It in no way brought the stories up to the present. And that was the number one goal of the community advisory board [for the new museum]—to make sure that people know we are still here, we are still alive, and we are not still living as they portrayed it.[18]

The exhibitions in the old site did indeed reflect their time. They tended to use outdated ethnographic subject headings, and objects were placed on pedestals and mounted in glass cases. All of the interpretative text was presented in a distant, third-person, curatorial voice, and the Mille Lacs Ojibwe's perspective on their history was notably absent. The few quotes from community members that the curators included described historical events from their perspective, but contemporary images did not accompany the quotes. Incorporating both would have conveyed the continuance of the Mille Lacs Ojibwe culture.

Additionally, culturally sensitive topics, such as spirituality, that are now typically excluded from museum presentations were featured in the old museum. For example, a display describing the Midewiwin Society, the original spiritual practices of the Anishinabe, included disrespectful and erroneous information. It also featured culturally sensitive ceremonial objects. Following the advice of Roger Buffalohead, a Ponca Indian historian hired by MHS to revise the exhibits in the early 1980s, the Midewiwin materials were removed from display. He argued that the Midewiwin was still a "viable religion" and that the current display was "written from the perspective of the dominant culture and in certain places [was] either demeaning of the system of religious beliefs or provided interpretations that [were] mis-leading."[19]

During the exhibition-planning process for the new museum (1993–96), the community advisory board—comprised predominantly of elders— recommended that all things associated with the Midewiwin religion, including objects, music, clothing, and symbols, not be displayed.[20] The exhibition-development team at MHS honored this request. Discussions of spiritual and ceremonial life were not included in any of the new exhibits, nor were sacred objects. At the time of the museum opening, tribal member Darren Moose stated the reason for this decision: "It's a private part of us. It's all we have left."[21]

In the years following Buffalohead's revisions, a majority of the interpretation in the old museum, though influenced by changing ethnohistorical scholarship, still focused mostly on the Band's pre-twentieth-century experience. The older museum also provided significant coverage of Dakota history and Dakota-Ojibwe relations, including the warfare that ensued between the two nations in the eighteenth century. These topics would eventually receive scant attention at the new site. The community advisory board wanted this to be a Mille Lacs tribal museum, not a pantribal Minnesota Indian museum or an Ojibwe national museum.

CHANGING RELATIONSHIPS, CHANGING AUTHORITY: THE SEVENTEEN-YEAR STRUGGLE TO BUILD THE NEW MUSEUM

The lack of the Band's involvement from 1960 to 1979 resulted in a museum that was clearly not a site of tribal history and memory. But after an extensive self-study by the Minnesota Historical Society that began in 1979, a shift occurred. Mille Lacs Band members increasingly participated in planning for the new museum. These consultations led to the museum eventually evolving into a site that represents the Mille Lacs Indian community through the exhibitions in the new museum that opened in 1996, while the Minnesota Historical Society maintained financial and administrative control over the site.

The evolution of this site as a hybrid tribal museum came after years of consultation, research, and collaboration between the two parties. In 1979, under the direction of the newly appointed deputy director, Nina Archabal, the site was evaluated through a self-study funded by the National Endowment for the Humanities (NEH). The consultants hired to review the Mille Lacs site were all leading museum professionals and scholars with extensive experience working with Native American communities in various capacities. They included George H. J. Abrams, director of the Seneca-Iroquois National Museum; Nancy O. Lurie, curator of anthropology at the Milwaukee Public Museum; and Thomas Vennum Jr., ethnomusicologist in the folklife program at the Smithsonian Institution.[22]

All of the consultants recognized the historical significance of the site and stressed the importance of developing the new museum to showcase its collection. As Thomas Vennum claimed, "By accident and bequeathal, the MHS now finds itself the guardian of one of the richest tribal treasures in the country—the Ayer collection."[23] Vennum stressed the symbolic importance of the site to Ojibwe people, in that it marked "the permanent establishment of the Ojibwa in Minnesota." It also served as a place where their ceremonial life continued. Furthermore, he described Batiste Sam and Maude Kegg, the two Mille Lacs Ojibwe women who were conducting the lion's share of the interpretation at that time, as "national treasures" because of their "vast knowledge of the culture."[24]

Given the historical significance of the site to the larger Ojibwe communities in the Great Lakes region and Canada, Vennum recommended establishing a national Ojibwe museum. This idea would resurface in 1984 after another NEH-funded study.[25] However, the idea would later be abandoned as the Mille Lacs community advisory board emphasized that the new museum should be a Mille Lacs Ojibwe museum, not an Ojibwe national museum. This focus is what finally made it to the exhibition floor as the Mille Lacs Indian Museum in 1996.[26]

The consultants also stressed the importance of establishing a community advisory board comprised of Mille Lacs tribal members to advise MHS on the development of the museum. Noting the previous lack of involvement of the tribal people as a serious concern, they encouraged MHS to develop such a board to ensure that this facility would indeed represent the history of the community it proposed to represent. Vennum reported that during his visit to the museum in 1979 as part of the self-study, the site manager at the time, Mille Lacs Band member Floyd Ballinger, told him that the Mille Lacs community did not visit the museum. Vennum viewed this as a major concern and cautioned MHS staff about proceeding with plans that did not involve the Mille Lacs Band:

> This to me should be a strong warning to the MHS—if the community cannot identify with the present site, will it feel anything but resentment about more of the same conceived along the standard, "bigger and better," White formula? According to the plans I have seen, the total facility will be the most imposing structure on the reservation, housing the historic treasures of the Mille Lacs people which, for reasons of history, fell into White hands which continue to guard them and make decisions about their disposal. Unless the Mille Lacs site is somehow made more meaningful to the community, under these circumstances, I can foresee a potential for trouble.[27]

The recommendation to begin discussions with the Mille Lacs Band on the planning of the new site corresponded with then deputy director Nina Archabal's commitment to include them in the process. In an interview with Archabal, she recalled her concern over the lack of involvement of the Mille Lacs Band in the early stages of the process in 1979:

> When I arrived here and became deputy director, I learned two things: that [Mille Lacs was] no ordinary place with no ordinary people with no ordinary collection; and I learned that the Society had a plan to replace the building. I remember very well a meeting at the Hill House early on with a number of staff members. . . . I remember hearing a presentation about the Society's plan to replace the Mille Lacs Indian Museum building, and I asked what I thought was a reasonable question . . . : "What involvement did the Mille Lacs Indian community have in the decision about replacing this building and about the kind of work we would be doing?" And the answer was, "None—we don't really have a relationship with the Mille Lacs community," even though at that time we were employing Mille Lacs people to help with the interpretation and to welcome our guests at the museum. That was deeply disturbing

for me to hear. That was . . . not based on any kind of knowledge of the field, prevailing standards; it was based on common sense. And I said this project cannot go forward without involvement from the Mille Lacs people.[28]

During the interview, Archabal discussed the challenges of building trust with the community. The site had embodied a history of exploitation and exclusion for the Mille Lacs Band, as their relationship with Harry and Jeanette Ayer had been complex, to say the least. Band members recounted the history of the relationship to Roger Buffalohead, which he wrote about in *Against the Tide of American History*, and later to George Horse Capture in 1984, and the story is fraught with colonial entanglements. While working on the project in 1994, I heard some Band members mention the land title issue (I will give more attention to this story later in the chapter) and the questionable ethics of the Ayers, but these issues did not come up regularly in conversations.

By 1994, in some ways one could argue that the struggles over how to interpret the Ayers' story at the revised museum had been resolved. The new museum would emphasize the Mille Lacs Band story, while the "Trading Post" exhibit nearby would discuss the Ayers' presence on the reservation. However, the absence of the history of the Ayers' relationship with the Band is very much an absent-present at the Mille Lacs Indian Museum. What is missing are the Band's views of the Ayers' presence. Their experiences with the Ayers are part of the deep history of the site as well, and what has been left unexpressed may yet be overshadowing Band members' relations with the museum today.

Certainly, the legacy of that relationship was evident in the early days of the new museum, when MHS was trying to move forward with the revised project. Nina Archabal recounted an awkward first meeting with then tribal chair Arthur Gahbow. The meeting was indicative of the lack of trust between MHS and the Mille Lacs Band that existed at the time. She recalled:

I remember my first meeting with Art Gahbow, who was then head of the Mille Lacs Band. This would have been in 1978 or 1979, and I would say, to be perfectly frank, that his attitude was not particularly welcoming. As I came to know him, Art Gahbow was a great jokester and a great prankster. I didn't understand that initially, and I remember going in to see him. It was late in the afternoon, and I was with then director Russ Fridley. Art was eating popcorn, and he didn't offer us any popcorn, which I thought was a little odd, and as I think about it now, I think about it as quite un-Indian not to share his food. He sat there . . . with his back to us. And when we talked to him about the society having some ideas about building a new building there, he told us that the Band controlled a strip of land between the highway and the museum site, and his plan was to put a turnstile up there and to collect tolls to keep people out of the museum. So, I figured this was hardly a good way to begin, but we began. . . .

That was a hard beginning, but from then on, with hard work and persistence and, I would say, with a good heart on the part of this institution, we moved forward, and we learned a whole lot. I remember having an open house at the museum building early on to begin that process of involving local people. And we were giving away food—literally giving away food. We had nice platters of food that we had purchased from some caterer and spread them out and invited people. And, to my very great shock, no one came. And I think that was a measure of just how distrustful people were. I have to believe that, at that point, with the community having over 80 percent unemployment, free food under any situation other than the most strained social relations would have been something that would have drawn people out, and it didn't. That was very disturbing to me and another sign of just how deep-seated the distrust really was.[29]

Building trust with the Mille Lacs Band members became a major goal for those working on the project, and plans were initiated to involve Band members in the development process. The recommendations by the consultants, combined with strong leadership and support at MHS led by Nina Archabal, led to the formation of a museum advisory board at Mille Lacs in the early 1980s. The individuals involved with planning the museum changed over time. However, the following Mille Lacs Band members, many of whom were also part of the Mille Lacs Reservation Curriculum Committee, played a significant role in the early development of the project: Floyd Ballinger, Francis Boswell, Maude Kegg, Batiste Sam, Georgiana Day, and Joycelyn [Shingobe] Wedll. Non-Band member Don Wedll, employed by the Band as the commissioner for natural resources, played a key role on the committee as well.[30] The consultation process between Band members and MHS included both formal and informal meetings. For MHS staff, it involved spending time on the reservation, getting to know people, and finding out from them what they wanted for the museum—their ideas. As Nina Archabal recalled:

We began a process in which I myself was involved in making repeated visits to the community to get to know people. That was certainly the major objective: to gain some understanding and some relationship with them, and also to get some idea from them, to involve them in the process of thinking about what the museum could be, what its content ought to be, what purposes they might have for it. We began to hold a series of meetings. . . . I would guess there were close to twenty of what I would call group gatherings of various kinds. . . . We would begin by having lunch with the elders. There was an elder nutrition center on the reservation, and we would go to the nutrition center instead of inviting people to the museum. I remember very well the meals and what we ate, but I remember particularly learning the protocols. The elders always ate before we ate, and they ate at a separate table, and then we would be served the food and we would eat as well. Then we would go and sit together and talk about their ideas, their feelings, their connections, their hopes and dreams for a museum, but [we would] also get a sense of who they were and get to know a little about this community and what really went on. We would then stay on in the afternoon. And we invited schoolchildren to come, and we gave away pizza and Coca-Cola, and that did draw young people, because we were interested in learning what the young people wanted and how they saw their own community. I remember those as being very lively gatherings. . . . Then, in the evening after dinner, we would also bring the adults together and oftentimes the children came with the adults. . . . I would say that, over time, these efforts not only were related to the museum but my own personal recollections of them are as much social gatherings and friend-making occasions . . . getting to know them by sitting around, literally just kind of hanging out together. Those meetings, I think, were incredibly important.[31]

Archabal's description of the process of collaboration mirrors what others have experienced with collaborative processes elsewhere over the last decade. The collaborative exhibition-development process becomes a time of relationship building and getting to know one another—establishing good relations. Reflecting on the development of Glenbow Museum's permanent gallery *Nitsitapiisinni: Our Way of Life*, which opened in Calgary, Alberta, in 2001, Curator Gerald Conaty emphasized the importance of working with a community where contacts have already been made. He stated that the museum's decision to focus on Blackfoot history and culture for its revised First Nations gallery stemmed from wanting to build on already-established relationships, which take years to build: "By then, we had a strong relationship [with the Blackfoot], and if you're going to do something collaboratively, you have to have that relationship, and it takes years to develop. And I knew who to talk to. That's also key. . . . We had that relationship."[32]

Another interesting point about the process at Mille Lacs is that Nina Archabal took the Mille Lacs Indian Museum project outside of the usual purview of the MHS Historic Sites Department and placed it under her control in the deputy director's office. From the beginning—and most likely heavily influenced by the consultants in the self-study—the Minnesota Historical Society recognized the potential that the revised Mille Lacs Indian Museum could embody as a critical new direction in museum practice. The Mille Lacs Indian Museum could place the institution on the proverbial map of more community-based museum practices. It could also provide an opportunity for MHS to do the right thing, and the Minnesota Historical Society could garner national recognition as a museum pursuing cutting-edge collaborative work with Native peoples.

During the initial stages of planning the museum, tribal members, including Tribal Chair Gahbow, believed that the museum could be an important economic development enterprise for the reservation. The plans for the new site corresponded with other economic development initiatives the Band was considering at that point. MHS and tribal leaders saw its potential as a "primary magnet for related commercial development [that would] . . . include a lodge, restaurant, service station, and convenience store."[33] Certainly, this mirrors the development of other tribal museums during the period, which were being established to "exploit the tourist industry and growing public interest in Indian cultures."[34]

Additionally, tribal leaders envisioned these museums as helping to address the high unemployment rates plaguing Indian Country. The museums could create jobs close to home, so Native people could remain in their communities. In *Concept Plan for the New Mille Lacs Indian Museum and Cultural Center*, published in 1985, the planning committee clearly viewed the project as an opportunity to capitalize on the public's interest in American Indian history and culture. The document claimed that visitors could be "a source of income to the community businesses surrounding the museum and an important market for community-made arts and crafts sold at the museum shop."[35]

The Band believed that the museum could offer important educational possibilities as well. Tribal leaders hoped the museum could serve dual educational purposes—both for their own community and for the public. Tribal youth could learn Ojibwe artistic traditions and they could also learn about their history and culture through exhibitions and programming. Non-Indian visitors could learn about the complex history of Native American people, and the site could also dispel commonly held stereotypes predominant in American society.

The plans for the new museum as an economic development enterprise changed with the successful gaming operations that were established on the Mille Lacs reservation in the late 1980s. The revenues from these businesses provided the community with funds to build schools, clinics, government facilities, and day care centers, making it unnecessary for the museum to fulfill the role as a community center and commercial enterprise. As a result, MHS and the Mille Lacs Band scaled back their plans for the site and focused their efforts on developing a facility that would serve exclusively as a museum.

Following years of consultation with the Mille Lacs Band, two self-studies, and the development of a building plan, MHS successfully secured a $4 million appropriation from the state of Minnesota to build the new museum in 1988. This award—as well as other grants, including over $1 million from the Economic Development Administration and $500,000 from the National Endowment for the Humanities for exhibition development—provided the necessary funding to complete the project.[36]

After securing the crucial $4 million state appropriation in 1987, planning for the museum stalled for several years due to a complicated land title issue. The negotiations and eventual resolution of the problem represent a critical juncture in the history of the museum. In 1993, after years of negotiations, MHS and the Mille Lacs Band eventually reached a decision. In fifty years, the Mille Lacs Band would have the exclusive rights to acquire the land and the museum from the Minnesota Historical Society.

Here is what happened. The problem over the land title issue arose during the consultation process with the elders at Mille Lacs. It became evident that MHS did not hold clear title to the land on which the museum was located, and this created a major problem for MHS. It could not invest the $4 million appropriation from the state of Minnesota without "substantial certainty of land tenure or ownership."[37] During community meetings, elders and others kept raising the issue that the land that Harry Ayer transferred to MHS in 1959 had a clouded title. At the time of the transfer, both the Minnesota Chippewa tribe and the Mille Lacs Band opposed the transfer, but the Bureau of Indian Affairs approved it nonetheless. Ayer also transferred to MHS roughly one hundred acres of prime lakefront property that he acquired during his tenure on the reservation.[38]

George Horse Capture, a Native American museum professional hired as a consultant for the project in 1984, made note of the land title controversy in his report to MHS. He described the seriousness of the land question and the Band's position to MHS and claimed that "the people believe that the land acquisition of Mr. Ayer may not have been legal, and certainly not moral." He went on to recommend that the society return the lands to the tribe to "start the new museum project on an ideal footing by assisting the band in the best way possible."[39]

Eventually, in 1993, after years of consultation with the Band and the Minnesota Historical Society, a land transfer agreement was finalized. The Mille Lacs Band signed a quitclaim deed, which allowed MHS to use the 3.7-acre tract of land it needed to build the new museum. In exchange, MHS agreed to "give the [Mille Lacs] Band the exclusive right to reacquire the same land and any improvements on it at no cost upon the expiration of the fifty-year period from the date of the initial transfer."[40] MHS also agreed to transfer back to the Band the additional 101 acres of prime lakefront property that it had acquired from Harry Ayer in 1959.

The agreement to allow the Mille Lacs Band to acquire the land and the museum within fifty years served as a turning point for the project. Plans for the new museum and for the exhibitions to be featured in the new site were clearly influenced by the idea that the Band would be the site's eventual owner.

With the land question settled, planning for the new museum accelerated. Architect Thomas Hodne was hired to design a new building. And MHS began consulting with Band members to determine which narratives, objects, and images would be featured in the museum exhibitions. The advisory board, comprised of Mille Lacs Band members Batiste Sam, Sandi Blake, Brenda Boyd, Kenny Weyaus, Eve Kuschel, and Betty Kegg, met with MHS Exhibits Department staff on a monthly basis to discuss exhibition planning. While exhibition story lines were being developed, staff members were also trying to secure funding from the National Endowment for the Humanities, and they were eventually awarded an NEH grant in 1994.

During the three-year exhibition-development process, two broad goals influenced the development plans for the Mille Lacs Indian Museum. The larger Minnesota Historical Society American Indian Advisory Board defined these two goals. First, the board wanted to convey that "Indian people and their stories are not just part of the ancient past but are part of the present as well."[41] The Mille Lacs team hoped to meet this goal by offering exhibits that covered contemporary life extensively. A majority of the floor space in the new museum would take the Mille Lacs story to the present day, so their representations would not lock the people in a historic past.

Second, the advisory board wanted the exhibitions to challenge deeply entrenched stereotypes of American Indian life.[42] They believed that the exhibitions could dispel stereotypes by giving primacy to the Mille Lacs Band perspectives on historical events. The exhibition team relied heavily on quotes from interviews conducted with Band members to reinforce the point that Indian people have their own versions of history. On the subjects selected for representation, their voices would predominate throughout.

These goals seem commonplace today, as most tribal museums and mainstream museums that collaborate with Indigenous communities emphasize contemporary survival as the overarching theme in their galleries. However, during this period, the advisory board's move reflected a significant shift in the representation of Native Americans in museums. The emergence of this narrative strategy is critical, as James Clifford argues: "For indigenous people, long marginalized or made to disappear, physically and ideologically, to say 'We exist' in performances and publications is a powerful political act."[43]

A NEW INTERPRETATIVE STRATEGY: MOVING AWAY
FROM OBJECT-BASED PRESENTATIONS

During the monthly consultations between the Band members and MHS, both groups realized that the Ayer Collection could not serve as the basis for the exhibits, though it is certainly an outstanding collection. What drove the content decisions for the new museum were not objects but concepts. The advisory board put forward ideas that focused on contemporary life. From day one, as Kate Roberts, co-curator, recalled, the Band's sovereign status was central to the new museum. From this basis, Band members identified contemporary issues to be covered, including education, treaty rights, powwows, economic development projects, language-retention programs, and casinos. In an interview with Roberts, I asked her about the decision not to develop an object-based exhibition based on the Ayer Collection. She replied:

> You know, that almost happened by default. Initially, I thought it would be the showcase, because I had been told what a fabulous collection it is—and it is. But it is also extremely limited in time span and in type of material. I mean, if we were doing a fabulous exhibit on Ojibwe crafts, that collection would be wonderful, but we weren't. . . . Much of the Ayer Collection didn't end up in the exhibit, and we ended up having

to acquire a lot of contemporary objects and a lot of things outside of the Ayer Collection that we felt were necessary to make our points. . . . It ended up not being an object-driven exhibit, which kind of surprised me. Going in, I would have thought—given that we had the collection already—that those objects would drive the exhibit. But as it turned out, the topics that we ended up covering are not necessarily topics tied to objects. You think of topics like sovereignty—that's a concept; it's not object based.[44]

The decision to focus on contemporary themes that are not object based created particular challenges for the exhibit development team. Developing concept-based displays was much more complex and nuanced, as Roberts explained:

I mentioned the fact that there weren't objects to support some of these topics, but also just the nature of the topics themselves. This idea of sovereignty which was so key to the committee's understanding of who they were and what they wanted to get across to people. I think that came up in our very first conversation—"We are a sovereign people." I didn't know what that meant and didn't have any idea of what that meant. And then, when I found out what it meant, I thought, "That is not an exhibit; that's a book. How do you make that into an exhibit?" So, that was probably my biggest challenge: taking conceptual matter, taking what the Band prides itself on—its independence, its sovereign status—taking that spirit and somehow trying to make it into an exhibit. And that was difficult.[45]

The concepts and themes that eventually made it to the exhibition floor at the new Mille Lacs Indian Museum clearly reflect the directives of the advisory board to focus on the Band's survival and on contemporary issues central to its members' lives today. I would argue that it is necessary for exhibit developers, if they hope to convey the continuance of Native cultural traditions, to abandon the idea of allowing objects to lead content (especially since a majority of the objects in museum collections are historic pieces) and instead allow for concepts to drive decisions about exhibition content. Not only do all of the exhibitions at the new museum thoughtfully convey the people's historic struggles to remain at Mille Lacs, but they also honor tribal survivance.

A notable absence in many of the exhibitions, however, is a direct analysis of colonialism and its ongoing effects. The exhibits clearly emphasize topics that are less controversial and are presented in ways that are not confrontational. The narrative first and foremost privileges the voices and perspectives of Mille Lacs Band members, and their voices are prominent throughout. The curatorial team was clearly aware of the larger scholarly literature in Native American history of the 1980s and 1990s, new museum theory and practice, and Mille Lacs Band tribal history and culture. The exhibitions reflect a rigorous approach based on these sources. They also present a stunning synthesis of these multiple lines of evidence and thought, offering a powerful statement of Indigenous self-representation.

While the museum's identity as a hybrid tribal museum is present, what makes it to the exhibition floor in many respects looks and feels similar to other tribal museums developed during this period. I observe, for example, similarities to the Museum at Warm Springs on the Confederated Tribes of the Warm Springs Reservation in Oregon. Members of the MHS staff visited that museum, along with several other tribal museums in the Pacific Northwest, during the development process in 1994. Kate Roberts later mentioned that the Museum at Warm Springs provided great inspiration and was their "closest ally or model." Even though the Mille Lacs Indian Museum's subjectivity as an MHS historic site is ever present, the exhibit team pursued their methodology with a tribal museum model in mind. Reflecting on this methodology and the hybrid nature of the museum, Roberts stated:

> The other challenge, I think, was being part of MHS. . . . Was it or was it not a tribal museum? Well, it became clear to me the more I went up there that I needed to view it in my own mind as a tribal museum if I was going to have any sort of satisfaction or if I was going to be able to work with [Band members]. I had to see it as my facilitating their telling their story. I'm not convinced that everyone at MHS ever felt that way. . . . So, that was a challenge, I think, from the start until the finish. [It] was being part of this large institution, but also very much needing to act independently and sort of walking that fine line between being the person who was facilitating the tribe's wishes and needing to come back and answer to the folks here who were concerned about what we were going to say to legislators or what we were going to say to funders.[46]

"LEARN ABOUT OUR PAST": THE STORY OF THE MILLE LACS BAND OF OJIBWE—EXHIBIT WALK-THROUGH

In the preceding sections, I have outlined the historical background of the Mille Lacs Band, traced the genealogy of the Mille Lacs Indian Museum first as a trading post and later as an MHS-controlled museum, analyzed the seventeen-year process to redesign the museum, and examined the development of the new exhibition interpretative strategy used at Mille Lacs. Now I will discuss the exhibitions that opened at the new Mille Lacs Indian Museum in 1996 by providing a walk-through of the galleries.

The new Mille Lacs Indian Museum contains rich textual material, beautiful images, and cultural objects that convey a powerful story. One of the major strengths of the museum is the curators' awareness of the audience and their ability to convey important messages persuasively to the visitor. In their overall design and interpretative strategy, the Mille Lacs Indian Museum exhibitions include text panels that are conversational and engaging. They use storytelling in the first-person voice. And the exhibits incorporate photographs, interactives, and innovative media—all of which are emblematic of the broader exhibition program that the Minnesota Historical Society followed in the 1990s.

While the content of the exhibition is obviously different from that of other MHS exhibits, the overall tone, design, and feel of the gallery space reflect the Minnesota Historical Society's exhibition techniques during this period. Visitors are not overwhelmed when they enter the museum, and ideas are presented in a "visitor friendly" manner. Interesting lead-in questions and statements, beautiful designs, and striking images are prominently displayed. The design goes a long way toward supporting the curatorial directives for this exhibit, and it presents the Mille Lacs Band's history and culture in a manner that visitors can engage. Perhaps most significantly, the curators do not attempt to provide a multivocal exhibition narrative: the Mille Lacs Ojibwe interpretative voice is privileged throughout. The words of art historians, historians, traders, collectors, and curators are submerged, and the community's voice is most prominent.

The exhibition-development team, along with the tribal members who served on the committee, did extensive research on the Band. They closely examined existing literature and scholarship on the community, and they conducted oral history interviews with tribal members. The depth and breadth of the information included in the museum are impressive and reflect the long and rigorous collaborative exhibition-development process. Most significantly, the Mille Lacs people themselves speak in an authoritative first-person voice throughout the exhibit. As one of the curators explained: "The voices of the Mille Lacs Band are heard throughout the exhibit: reminiscences taken from oral histories and interviews on life at Mille Lacs today are incorporated in print form. In addition, interactive media stations present Band members describing their work, demonstrating their music, and speaking their language."[47]

The Ojibwe language is used, along with English, throughout the galleries "as a reminder to all visitors that it is a living language used and taught in many communities."[48] The use of first-person testimony provides a more personal feel to the exhibit. It clearly reflects an aboriginal curatorial prerogative that Michael Ames has defined as "more holistic or inclusive" than non-Native curatorial perspectives.[49]

By describing the contemporary and historical experiences of the Mille Lacs Band, the new museum movingly conveys the take-home message that "the Mille Lacs Band of Ojibwe has retained its culture, traditions, and its home for over two centuries, often against great odds."[50] As visitors walk through this 7,000-square-foot exhibition space, they encounter the meaning behind this message through the displays.

The museum's introductory section grounds the exhibit experience on core Ojibwe tribal values, conveyed through the teachings of Mille Lacs elders. Included are five cases focusing on families, elders, spirituality, identity, and language. On one side of the panel is an English version of the text; on the other side, the Ojibwe version. The following text panel introduces visitors to the museum. It is presented in the first-person plural—not a distant third-person curatorial voice—and exemplifies the structure of all the museum's text panels. It states:

Our Strength and Our Hope

"Our strength comes from the traditions we learn from our elders.
Our hope comes from our young, who possess the power of a million
new ideas." Wewinabi (Arthur Gahbow), 1988

Mille Lacs became our home over two hundred years ago. We worked
hard to make a place for ourselves here, and we've worked hard to
keep it.

Take a look around our community. Our history is alive. The events of
the past are evident in the way we live, work, and govern ourselves. Our
lives are shaped by the traditions and ideals of those who have gone
before us.

Gagwe gikendadaa gaapi izhiwebak.
Inaabidaa nii gaan ke yaa
Learn about our past. Look to our future.[51]

Life-size images of both contemporary and historic Mille Lacs Band members visually bring home the point that today's tribal members are part of continuing traditions and an ongoing cultural life.

The introductory section of the museum also includes a time line of Mille Lacs Band history. This section is certainly more reminiscent of earlier museum presentations that conveyed historical events in a linear format. During the planning process in 1994, members of the Minnesota Historical Society's exhibition team were reluctant to present the story in this manner, recognizing how ineffective these methods have been in presenting American Indian history or historical events in general. Nonetheless, the team deferred to the wishes of the Mille Lacs Band members and their desire to have their history all lined up and to have some dates on things.[52] The curators, however, strategically avoided a book-text-on-a-wall presentation. Instead, they presented images of individual leaders and Band members along with maps and engaging texts.

Even though a majority of the panels in the museum are in the first person, the historic time-line section of the museum uses a more distant, third-person, curatorial-voice narration. Here, the items present historical information: accounts of tribal delegations to Washington, D.C., in the nineteenth century; treaty texts from the nineteenth century; an image of Ojibwe chief Migizi in Washington; early reservation school photos; and an article on the hardships of reservation life in the 1940s from the *Minneapolis Morning Tribune*, with a headline reading, "Onamia Indians Starving, Nun Says."[53]

The next section that visitors encounter is "Our Living Culture," which explores Ojibwe music, dance, and language. The opening text panel for this section speaks to the centrality of their culture in their lives and encourages tribal members: "Listen carefully. Watch closely. Ask about what you don't understand. The more we know about our culture, the stronger it will become."[54] The text panel is clearly directed to tribal members. It acknowledges that they have experienced cultural loss over the last two centuries, and it encourages members who are in the process of learning their culture to continue asking and learning. The panel's level of intimacy engages one of the museum's intended audiences: the Band members themselves. The advisory board aimed to offer this site as a place for tribal members to come in and learn more about their own culture, and this goal is clearly expressed in the space.

"Our Living Culture" opens with a moccasin game exhibit comprised of objects from older games and images of Mille Lacs people still playing the game today. Blending historic and contemporary objects and images is a technique commonly used by museum curators to convey cultural continuance, and the strategy persists throughout the museum. Included in this section is a film of a moccasin game shot by Monroe Killy in the 1940s outside the trading post. The film includes the songs that accompany the game, which makes this section even more compelling. But although Killy made the film, the exhibit keeps the focus on the Band members. Monroe Killy's name is listed in photo captions, but his story and his experiences with the Mille Lacs Band are not told here. In this museum, the collectors, photographers, traders, historians, anthropologists, and government officials who interacted with the Mille Lacs Band are not given prominence in interpretation. Their voices are secondary to those of the Band members themselves.

The centerpiece of this exhibit section is the powwow dance circle, complete with life-size mannequins in dance attire. This section borrows a great deal from the Milwaukee Public Museum's popular powwow display, which was part of a larger exhibition, *A Tribute to Survival*. This exhibition, which opened in 1993, focused on the urban Indian community in Milwaukee.[55] In "Our Living Culture," each mannequin is in a different dance pose, and each style of Native dance is represented in the circle: women's traditional dance, women's fancy shawl, and women's jingle dress (a style originating with the Ojibwe people); and men's traditional dance, men's fancy dance, and men's grass dance. The photography and film footage featured in this section were taken at the Mille Lacs Band's annual powwow in July 1994.

Along the outer circle of the powwow area is an exhibit on Ojibwe music. The musical instruments of the Mille Lacs Band on display include drums and flutes—both traditional and contemporary. The section includes videos and listening stations, which are designed to help visitors understand the uniqueness of the music.

A sign that reads, "Why are these bags called bandolier bags?" greets visitors as they enter the section of the exhibition showcasing the Ayer Collection. This is the only section in the new museum that focuses specifically on Harry and Jeanette Ayer and their relationship to the Mille Lacs Band during their years on the reservation. (A display in the "Trading Post" exhibit near the museum focuses on the Ayers and will be discussed later.) This section was designed to be a changing exhibition of objects from the Ayer Collection. The first display that opened in 1996 featured bandolier bags, a highly regarded Ojibwe art form. The older bandolier bags collected by Harry Ayer in the first half of the twentieth century are featured alongside those made by artists from the Mille Lacs community in the 1980s and 1990s. Placing the historic and the contemporary together once again reinforces the message that the Mille Lacs community is a living culture with ongoing cultural traditions. Bandolier bags made by master artists Batiste Sam and Maude Kegg—both of whom worked at the museum site and served as advisors to the project—are included in this section.

Across from the Ayer Collection is a section focusing on military veterans. This section generated a great deal of controversy during the MHS's exhibit vetting meetings. Veterans are held in high esteem in tribes throughout the country, and from the very beginning, members of the Mille Lacs community advocated for a section focusing on veterans in their community. As exhibit researcher Shana Crosson explained: "We kept hearing from day one that this was crucial—to have something in the [exhibit featuring] veterans. . . . It absolutely had to be in there."[56] During the development stage for the exhibitions, MHS leaders voiced their concerns over the use of this somewhat dated—and, in their minds, unsophisticated—presentation. As Nina Archabal explained:

I looked at that and my first reaction to that was this is what a very naive historical organization might do. Sophisticated historical organizations like this one do not do major sections on veterans. It just didn't feel right. And again, I was told this is important, and we need to let this happen. It needs to go forward. And it was very interesting. I will sort of fast-forward for a moment. Rick West, who is a very good friend and the head of the National Museum of the American Indian, came to the opening of the museum. After we had all the celebrations and the dinner and the speeches were over and most of the people had gone, he and I walked around the museum together just to have a look. And we got to the section on the veterans. He stopped, and he said to me, "Of all the honors my father ever had, he was most proud of being a veteran." And I thought to myself, "Thank God!" I once again departed with my—what I would call—sort of my Western way, and said, "Okay, being a veteran is important; we will do a section on veterans." What a lesson that was that night! Of all the things he could have said about the museum, what he said was, "My father was most proud of being a veteran."[57]

Curators Kate Roberts and Joycelyn Shingobe Wedll were, in fact, eventually successful in arguing for including this story, even though they faced opposition from Nina Archabal and Deputy Director Ian Stewart. Archabal and Stewart's decision to acquiesce to the wishes of the Mille Lacs Band demonstrates the changing identity of this site and the desire to have it be an interpretative space that privileges the Band's voice. Just as the land settlement represented a watershed moment in the development of the new building, so, too, the decision to have a space focusing on veterans—in spite of the attitude at MHS that "sophisticated historical organizations like this one do not do major sections on veterans"—demonstrates the interpretative shift that occurred during the planning process. This would be the Mille Lacs Band's story, and their perspectives would be privileged throughout.

Within the "Veterans" section, a wall displays the names of the Mille Lacs Band members who served in the U.S. military throughout the twentieth century. One case highlights the experiences of veteran Darren Moose, who served in the U.S. Army during the Persian Gulf War. Moose loaned several of his personal possessions for the exhibit, including an army uniform, badges, a knife, currency from the faraway lands where he was stationed, photographs, and a bayonet and shield. Again, the theme of cultural continuity is vividly captured in this section. Honoring veterans is a core Ojibwe value, and this section names and recognizes the individuals, both past and present, who served their community.

Through a tall archway, one enters the section of the museum that focuses on sovereignty, called "Nation within a Nation." It addresses a central issue related to contemporary Mille Lacs Indian identity: the Band's sovereign status. This remains one of my all-time favorite exhibitions in a tribal museum, as it embodies the significance of Indigenous curation and exhibition methods. While several tribal museums touch upon this topic in their galleries today, "Nation within a Nation" represents one of the first exhibits devoted to tribal sovereignty ever developed, whether in a tribal or a mainstream museum. The section's main objective is to extensively describe the unique relationship that the Mille Lacs Band of Ojibwe has with the U.S. government and the people's rights as members of a sovereign nation.

As visitors enter this section, a powerful introductory panel presents the concept of tribal sovereignty. I believe this is one of the finest text panels that I have encountered at a tribal museum that both introduces the meaning of tribal sovereignty as a political term and evokes the feeling of what it means for tribal nations to assert this identity. Chickasaw scholar Amanda Cobb Greetham states that "sovereignty manifests an emotional quality, not wholly of the legal realm, that is integrally tied to culture."[58] The following brief text panel conveys both the feeling and tone of this statement, and I quote it in its entirety:

The sovereignty display at the Mille Lacs Indian Museum. Courtesy of the Minnesota Historical Society, www.mnhs.org / Mille Lacs Indian Museum.

Nation within a Nation

"Our sovereignty resides in you, the people of the Mille Lacs Band." Wewinabi (Arthur Gahbow), 1988

Sovereignty means freedom from outside control. Enforcing sovereign rights has been the goal of the Mille Lacs Band for generations.

What rights does a sovereign nation have? Look around the reservation and you'll see the things guaranteed by our rights. Schools. Courts. Clinics. A police force. A tribal government. A network of community programs and services.

Oma eni go kwa kaa ne zi yang chi mi ni
sii akiing. Mi o'ow gi da na kii wi ni naan
We are a nation within a nation. This is our community.[59]

Though never stated explicitly anywhere in the text in this exhibit, those involved in the development process were hoping that, by providing this information, the public would have a better understanding of events covered in the local media about the Mille Lacs Band exercising their rights as a sovereign nation. During the museum-planning process, the Mille Lacs Band filed a lawsuit against the state of Minnesota that asserted their hunting, fishing, and gathering rights on lands ceded in an 1837 treaty. The Ojibwe claimed that they retained these rights under the treaty, and the case went all the way to the U.S. Supreme Court. After several years of appeals, on 24 March 1999, the Supreme Court ruled in favor of the Mille Lacs Band.[60] The topic is never engaged directly, however. The overall tone of the new exhibitions is to minimize controversy and to avoid confrontational topics, and during the planning process, many on the museum's advisory board endorsed this approach.

Powerful visual images of the Mille Lacs Band's sovereign status fill one of the main walls in the "Nation within a Nation" section. Visitors see many expressions of sovereignty: a police car door from the Band's own police force with the tribal seal; a large photograph of the water tower with the tribal seal clearly visible; a car license plate with "Mille Lacs Band of Ojibwe" on it; a slot machine from the Band's casino; a Grand Casino Mille Lacs jacket; and images of the Band's schools and clinics. Near this section, a panel gives the visitor detailed information about the Mille Lacs Band's government structure. A panel on the other side of the exhibit presents images of Band leaders, both past and present, along with quotes from them.

Certainly, this section attempts to complete a historical record of tribal history that has not been documented before. It is a powerful reminder to all visitors that the Band's history does not end with the "closing of the frontier" in the late nineteenth century and the establishment of reservations. The section presents the names and faces of leaders who have made a significant contribution to their own community well into the twentieth century. Here again, one gets the impression that this section—the lives and words of Band leaders—is more for community members than for outsiders.

The center island of the exhibit seeks to clarify some of the difficult concepts around what it means to be a sovereign nation. At the center of this exhibit is a drum with the tribal seal on it. Around the drum are flip-books that pose questions related to sovereignty and then offer explanations to outsiders of often unknown or misunderstood concepts on the legal status of tribal nations. Following are some of the questions:

Do treaties give Indians special rights?
Why are Indian treaties still in the news?
What's tribal sovereignty?
Why are Indian tribes recognized as sovereign nations?
Does sovereignty have anything to do with casinos?

What's self-governance?

How do tribal governments relate to the federal government?

What does "dual citizenship" mean?

What does it mean to be "enrolled in an Indian tribe"?[61]

The sovereignty section of the museum, more so than any other, has a significant amount of literature for the visitor to digest. People are asked to reflect on the complex legal relationship that the Mille Lacs Band has with the federal government, its sovereign status, and its tribal government. This section also directly challenges many commonly held stereotypes about Native people by explaining the Band's sovereign status to the public.

The next section that visitors encounter is called "Making a Living." It provides an overview of the many ways that Mille Lacs Band members have "stayed afloat financially" through changing historical and economic circumstances.[62] Text panels with images of Band members, both historic and contemporary, greet the visitor upon entering this section. The main goal of the section is to describe the labor history of the community and the various ways community members have survived and maintained community cohesion. In the first part of the exhibition, historic images of Band members engaged in more traditional ways of making a living are positioned alongside those of contemporary Band members engaged in new employment activities. This section provides significant coverage of the twentieth-century labor history of the Mille Lacs Band, and it presents various sources of employment on the reservation during the twentieth century, some of which were Band owned and operated.

The section begins with the Mille Lacs Indian Trading Post, a major employer on the reservation from the 1920s through the 1950s. Mille Lacs members began selling their crafts in response to the growing number of tourists visiting the area following completion of Minnesota Scenic Highway 169. "Hanging baskets" along the road, as the Band members themselves recalled, provided community members with a new way to make a living, and tourists got a chance to experience a cross-cultural encounter at Harry and Jeanette Ayer's trading post. Across the country, the development of tourist art on reservations became a method for Native people to carve out ways of making a living during extremely difficult economic times. A quote from then and current tribal chair Marge Anderson provides further context for this new labor practice: "In the summertime, we'd sew baskets and have stands along the highway. We sewed baskets, you know, to survive."[63]

In its survey of early twentieth-century labor history, the exhibit also in-

Photo wall in the "Making a Living" section of the new Mille Lacs Indian Museum, 1996. Courtesy of the Minnesota Historical Society, www.mnhs.org / Mille Lacs Indian Museum.

cludes the history of Mille Lacs Band members who worked in the Civilian Conservation Corps–Indian Division (CCC-ID) during the 1930s. Visitors see images of tribal CCC-ID workers "building roads, repairing houses, and making other improvements throughout Minnesota."[64]

The exhibit goes on to discuss early Band-owned and -operated enterprises, such as its vocational center, which opened in the 1960s, and the Mille Lacs Industries Ladies Garment Division. During this period, the Mille Lacs Reservation Business established several other enterprises, including a machine shop and a marina/tourism complex, both of which are represented.

This section clearly advances the history of the Mille Lacs Band in the twentieth century beyond what is available in the written historical record. By gathering and documenting information on the twentieth-century economic history of the reservation, the museum gives an understanding of Mille Lacs history during a time that is poorly represented in Native American history. As curator Kate Roberts claimed: "I think we probably advanced the historical record a little bit through the exhibit. We were able to put some things down and get some things straightened out in terms of the Band's history that hadn't been published before. Some of the research that we did was pulled together and for the first time presented up in the galleries there."[65]

Roadside stand display in the "Making a Living" section of the new Mille Lacs
Indian Museum, 1996. Courtesy of the Minnesota Historical Society,
www.mnhs.org / Mille Lacs Indian Museum.

The Mille Lacs Indian Museum certainly goes a long way in advancing
the idea that Indigenous people persisted and kept their communities intact
throughout the twentieth century. Even though the curators never specifically mention the stereotypes they hoped to dispel, the astute visitor will recognize the many methods they use to challenge common interpretations of
Native people that predominate in American popular culture. Some of the
exhibit sections, although not visually arresting or stunning, are there specifically to combat painful stereotypes of Native American people that have
existed for centuries.

"Making a Living," for example, challenges the pervasive stereotype that
Native people are dependent on the federal government and welfare programs for their survival. It is no surprise that a community advisory board
comprised of Ojibwe individuals who live and work on a reservation in rural
Minnesota would choose to highlight such a significant part of their experience. Many community members have undoubtedly faced hostilities directed at them by non-Indians because of the non-Natives' limited understanding of the Band's history and sovereign status. This section speaks to
how Band members have survived in spite of policies designed to make them
dependent on the very government that destroyed their traditional econo-

mies. Understanding these historical processes is critical to understanding this fundamental aspect of the Mille Lacs Band experience. Round Valley Native historian William J. Bauer asserts the centrality of this topic to understanding his own tribal history: "Work and labor were fundamental to the way in which Round Valley Indians formed their communities and survived as indigenous people in [the] nineteenth and twentieth century."[66]

"Making a Living" also includes the voices of Mille Lacs Band members who have moved away from the reservation to urban areas to find employment. This is the only section of the exhibition that presents urban Mille Lacs Band members' experiences. Intentional or not, the media section captures the development of a pantribal consciousness in cities by presenting the experiences of tribal members working in urban areas.

For example, Don Pewaush, a Band member and former Minneapolis public school teacher, provides a beautiful and moving discussion of his work with urban Native youth. In the video, he describes the challenges he faces with the youth in providing them with the skills needed to survive in both worlds: "We know that we are all working to save our culture, and at the same time we're trying to get our children to be educated. They have to learn to live in two worlds . . . and it's hard; and it's tough work. . . . Yes, there's a lot of racism yet going on today. We have to deal with our children with that, and work with them, and get them through hard times."[67] He also views his work as beneficial to all tribal communities: "We have so many bright young minds out there that come from different reservations, all our reservations."[68]

Pewaush relays a very moving story about the first time a Native American drum group performed an honoring song at a graduation ceremony—something that had never been done before in the Minneapolis public schools:

We are now doing an honor song at the graduation ceremonies. When we first went out and did this, I was terrified on the inside. But I knew I couldn't show it on the outside. Because the young men that were there, singing for the very first time, [it] was their very first public appearance. And as I looked out into the crowd, I seen very few dark faces—hardly any people of color at all. And it scared me; because I didn't know what kind of a reaction there was going to be. And we came on right after the national anthem. And we sang an honor song in honor of all [the] students graduating. But it was more aimed toward our Native American children. And as we sang that song, I noticed they were getting up. There [are] approximately 350 to 400 students that graduate every year, and that first year there must have been about sixteen Native Americans that graduated. And as we were singing that song, I [saw] them starting to stand up and coming toward the drum. When we got done with the song, just about every one of those Native American children were standing around the drum. And some of them were beaming with pride that they made it, and some of them were silently crying. And I said to myself, "This is what it's all about—to educate our children and get them to feeling good about themselves and moving on."[69]

Through the presentation of the stories of urban Band members, we gain an understanding of the pantribal experience—a major theme in twentieth-century Native history—and the migration of Mille Lacs Band members to the city. Throughout the century, Native Americans moved to cities to find work during hard economic times before the development of casinos and the changing reservation economy. All of the urban Band members' stories emphasize their connections to home and their involvement in the pantribal Indian community in urban areas such as Minneapolis–Saint Paul and elsewhere.

Next to the "Making a Living" section is the "Four Seasons Room," which contains life-size dioramas depicting life at Mille Lacs before the full onslaught of colonization. The "Four Seasons Room" is a reinstallation of the original exhibit that was installed in the 1960s and is the centerpiece of the new museum. From the very beginning of the planning process, the advisory board recommended that it be reinstalled in the new site. The "Four Seasons Room" has always been the most popular exhibition, and audience evaluations at the new museum completed in 1996 confirm that the revised version is as rich and compelling as the first.[70]

This beautiful visual space depicts Ojibwe subsistence activities in each of the four seasons: "hunting and spearfishing in the winter; processing maple sugar in the spring; gardening and berry picking in the summer; and harvesting wild rice in the fall."[71] Even though the use of dioramas to depict tribal life has fallen out of favor in the museum world, the community believed that this section must be reinstalled in the new museum. Many critics have argued that this form of representation reinforces commonly held beliefs that Native cultures were static and unchanging and that they have since disappeared along with the "frontier." Surprisingly, though, many tribal museums, including the Mashantucket Pequot Museum and Research Center, the Tamástslikt Cultural Institute, and the Ziibiwing Center of Anishinabe Culture and Lifeways, continue to develop these types of installations.

Life-sized figures of Band members in the "Four Seasons Room" at the new Mille
Lacs Indian Museum, 1996. Courtesy of the Minnesota Historical Society,
www.mnhs.org / Mille Lacs Indian Museum.

The curatorial team was keenly aware of the drawbacks of this form of
presentation, but they decided to reinstall the dioramas in the new museum
because of the deep connection to the people who developed the original
exhibit. The dioramas includes life-size figures of Band members who posed
for the first installation of the exhibition in the 1960s. Two of the figures in
the room, now deceased, are well-known Ojibwe artists—Batiste Sam and
Maude Kegg. Joycelyn Shingobe Wedll's grandmother, Jennie Mitchell, was
also one of the figures cast. The figure of her is so lifelike that Wedll describes being near that space as "kind of eerie."[72] The exhibit's connection to
the contemporary community is deep. It is, as Nina Archabal described it,
"an icon space."

The dioramas in the new "Four Seasons Room" were painstakingly restored. Beautiful painted murals depicting seasonal landscapes surround the
room, and the original built structures in each of the seasonal spaces have
been refurbished and updated. One can enter this room only with a guide,
and no other area in the new museum has this requirement. The reason for
having a Band member accompany individuals through the space is precisely
to offset the potential misconception that the dioramas fix Ojibwe culture in

a romanticized, static past. Certainly, the new exhibitions surrounding the "Four Seasons Room" emphasize contemporary Ojibwe culture; they reinforce visitors' awareness of the Mille Lacs Band as part of a living tradition. The audience evaluations completed by the Minnesota Historical Society in 1996 indicate that the "Four Seasons Room" remains the most popular section in the new museum.[73]

REPRESENTING THE AYER STORY:
THE RESTORED "TRADING POST" EXHIBIT

As mentioned earlier, the interpretation of Harry and Jeanette Ayer's relationship with the Mille Lacs Band receives scant interpretative space in the redesigned Mille Lacs Indian Museum that opened in 1996. Their story is, however, presented in the "Trading Post" exhibit on site, and this is the only space that clearly reflects more of an outsider's perspective of events at Mille Lacs. The displays in the restored 1930s trading post adjacent to the new museum provide an overview of the Ayers' experiences on the reservation along with specific information on tourism and daily life at the store. All the interpretation in this area is in a more distant third-person voice.

My major concern with the "Trading Post" display is that the curators did not connect the activities of non-Native collectors, such as the Ayers, to the larger colonial project. During the early twentieth century, non-Native collectors like the Ayers contributed to the exploitation of Native people and systematically removed objects from Native communities. Instead of addressing this colonial enterprise and its consequences for the Mille Lacs Band, the exhibit "rehistoricizes" the Ayers and their collecting practices. In other words, the exhibit reframes the Ayers as being "intellectual products of their times."[74] The interpretation in the "Trading Post of Harry and Jeanette Ayer" clearly reflects this type of representation, evident in the following panel:

> What did the Trading Post mean to the members of the Mille Lacs Band? Did the Ayers exploit them, or did it offer a good living? That depends on who you talk to. Some people say the Ayers underpaid Band members for their craftwork, that they were involved in shady land deals, that they had no business being there in the first place. Others say the Ayers were good employers at a time when jobs were hard to come by. Mille Lacs Band members weren't just paid to dress up and dance at the Trading Post. They worked as sales clerks and fishing guides. They

tended to gardens, built the boats, and cleaned the cabins. Exploitation or good business? You decide.[75]

In his 1984 report, George Horse Capture cautioned MHS that, if it decided to tell the Ayer story, it would need to present an Indian perspective in its interpretation, "which would not give much honor to the trader." He further recommended that MHS should "accept the truth or don't attempt to tell the story at all."[76] From the content of the exhibit, it does not appear that MHS followed his advice. It failed to make an important statement on how traders and collectors, such as the Ayers, were linked to the larger colonial process and what their activities entailed for the Mille Lacs Band. Though not all Band members were critical of the Ayers, why did so many continue to hold a negative view of their presence on the reservation decades after the Ayers were gone, as Horse Capture mentions? Given the innovative interpretative strategies that the curators followed in other parts of the museum that presented historical events from a Mille Lacs perspective, it is disappointing that the exhibit fails to provide a more rigorous review of the colonial entanglements that the site embodies. The Minnesota Historical Society's identity is most clearly present in this section of the new site, and one wonders if the Mille Lacs Band of Ojibwe—in a tribally operated and controlled museum—would even bother to tell Harry and Jeanette Ayer's story at all.

THE MUSEUM'S RECEPTION: OPENING DAY AND BEYOND

The significance of the museum is far-reaching, and it has received a great deal of recognition in the museum world. The new site opened on 18 May 1996, and it has been well received by the community, museum professionals, and the public. The museum garnered a great deal of media attention as well, both in print and on television, and the institution was reviewed favorably in both media. In an article on the opening of the new site, journalist Nick Coleman, who followed the museum's three-year exhibition development, described it as "a monument to the triumph of a people."[77]

What is most striking about all of the media coverage is how favorable it has been to the museum. Not one journalist offered a critique of the displays themselves or challenged the presentations in any way. Admittedly, while many reviews have been descriptive and written for marketing purposes, others were designed to provide a more comprehensive view, and those were overwhelmingly positive.

Visitors have responded favorably to the new museum as well. Based on the audience evaluations conducted at the Mille Lacs Indian Museum in 1996, the visitors to the site had a positive reaction overall to the museum exhibitions. At the height of the tourist season, MHS employees surveyed 150 visitors, and all of those interviewed responded favorably to the exhibitions, with the "Four Seasons Room" tour being the most popular. Even though the reviews of the museum were positive, the museum staff was concerned that only a small percentage of visitors interviewed (15.3 percent) were able to articulate the exhibit's main message regarding the cultural persistence of the Mille Lacs Band over the last two centuries.[78]

In an attempt to offset any possibility that the "Four Seasons Room" was undermining the message of twentieth-century survival, the curators developed a new exhibition that linked the themes in the "Four Seasons Room" to other sections in the museum. The staff became concerned that the public's attraction to precontact Ojibwe life depicted in that space was undermining the museum's main message of contemporary survival. They felt that the visitors also needed to "understand the nature of contemporary life within the community."[79] One really needs to consider, though, whether the public's reaction reflects a shortcoming of the exhibitions or, perhaps more likely, the non-Native fascination and preoccupation with Native peoples in the historic past.

On the positive side, many visitors did recognize and appreciate the contemporary themes presented in the museum. Following is a sample of some visitor responses to the question of what surprised them the most at the new museum:

I enjoyed the descriptions of the modern life of the Ojibwe people, especially their governing system.

I was happily surprised at the incorporation of the present day Ojibwe Indians in the exhibit.

Very in depth. Remarkable.

Excellent dioramas and the personal touch—knowing these are about real, often living people and places.

Wonderful exhibit. Much respect was used in putting it together. It is an honest representation of native life.[80]

Even more poignantly, a tribal member expressed feelings of pride to one of the survey takers: "Beautiful, authentic—brings back many good memories

—makes me very proud of our people." Individuals involved with the advisory committee shared this sense of the Mille Lacs Indian Museum as a source of pride for Band members. When asked to describe the significance of the site, Kenneth Weyaus Sr. responded: "There's no words to describe the pride. No words."[81]

The museum also received attention from leading museum professionals in the country, including Richard West, director of the Smithsonian's National Museum of the American Indian. As I explain in this chapter's opening, West acknowledged that the community-collaborative process pursued by MHS helped him chart the course for his work at the NMAI. West had nominated the Mille Lacs Indian Museum to receive an American Association for State and Local History award. In his nomination letter, he offered the museum high praise for the prominence of the Mille Lacs perspective and voice in the exhibitions. "The presence of the Mille Lacs interpretive voice is explicit throughout" and is both "authentic and authoritative," he wrote, "a convincing demonstration of the proposition . . . that good history is not compromised by this kind of inclusiveness but, indeed, can be made sounder, more enriching, deeper."[82]

West went on to praise the exhibitions for successfully incorporating the best of new exhibition techniques, including multimedia and interactive technology, and for their excellence in design. The content of the exhibitions and the coverage they give to the full historical experience of the Mille Lacs people are, he believed, "very successful in making the critical point that Native peoples are as much a part of the present and should not be relegated to some static and often romanticized past."[83]

In 2003, while conducting ethnographic research in the Mille Lacs area, anthropologist Jennifer Stampe decided to return to the survey process and administer a new survey drawing upon the same methodology used in 1996. Stampe wanted to "reevaluate the central finding" and determine if a majority of the visitors did, indeed, miss the take-home message about contemporary life at Mille Lacs.[84] By conducting short interviews with some of the visitors after completing the survey, she found that most visitors had a much more nuanced understanding of Ojibwe history and culture than had been reported in the 1996 survey.

Her new survey brought into full relief the limitations of using quantitative methods alone when trying to assess audience reactions to exhibitions at tourist sites. She encourages the use of interviews and participant observation to properly contextualize their experiences as museum visitors. The information garnered from the 2003 survey, she argues, "cautions against interpreting 'thin' survey responses as uncomplicated evidence of shallow or uncritical responses to tourist sites."[85] It is important, however, to remember that all of the people surveyed in 1996 claimed to have enjoyed their experience at Mille Lacs. While quantitative audience research might be limited—and Stampe's 2003 survey may have complicated our understanding of the messages that visitors take away with them—for me, the most important aspect of the survey data is that visitors found their experiences positive and informative. Every one of those interviewed in 1996 found something compelling about the new Mille Lacs Indian Museum.

AFTER THE OPENING, 1996 AND BEYOND:
THE "ONGOING LIFE" AT THE MILLE LACS INDIAN MUSEUM

While the new Mille Lacs Indian Museum was positively received following its opening in 1996, the postopening life of the museum has not been without disappointments and challenges. During my follow-up site visits to the Minnesota Historical Society in 2001, I interviewed Rachel Tooker, then director of the Historic Sites Department and former Mille Lacs Indian Museum manager, about the status of the museum during a time of transition. Kate Miller, a non-Native woman, had been recently appointed site manager after the departure of two previous site managers, Joycelyn Shingobe Wedll and Sandi Blake, both of whom were members of the Mille Lacs Band. The departure of Wedll and Blake, along with the death of longtime employee and highly respected elder Batiste Sam in 1998, left many at MHS feeling that they had lost their strongest connections to the community. One of the primary reasons given by Rachel Tooker for Wedll and Blake's resignation is that MHS just could not match the Mille Lacs Band in terms of pay in a postcasino world. During our discussion, Tooker emphasized the need to "stabilize the management of the museum," and she spoke about the lack of community involvement at the site. She mentioned the "haltering and faltering" programming efforts, the improvement of which she believed was the crucial next step for the future of the museum. As she explained:

> I think the stories that we developed in the exhibit, what is really successful about that, is that people tend to view the museum as a tribal museum and not a mainstream organization museum. I view that as a real success that we went that far with it that our identity in many ways got lost. That's pretty rare for a mainstream organization to have that happen. But I think now, the carrying through of the programs and

the ongoing life, we have a long way to go in working ourselves into the heart of the Mille Lacs Band. And so, that is what I think is still our challenge, and we haven't solved it. There is still a deep divide, and we will have to work on it. . . . First, we need to stabilize the management there, which has been a real hard thing for us.[86]

As Tooker's words highlight, the postopening issues concern the programming (art classes and workshops, Anishinabe cultural courses for youth and families, community gatherings, public events and performances, lectures, and traveling exhibits, to name a few): Is there going to be an ongoing life at the Mille Lacs Indian Museum? And how extensively will the community be involved? MHS director Nina Archabal shared her concerns with me about the unfinished business and ongoing challenges of the museum. She had hoped that the programming efforts would build upon the momentum that the exhibitions started, but they had clearly stalled: "I have some disappointment, to tell you the truth, about the museum. Not about its content, certainly not the way in which it is regarded by the leaders and people whom I know up there. But the fact that we have not been able to get the kind of leadership we need from the community to make the museum really sing and perform at the level that I think it could."[87]

Certainly, the Minnesota state budget crisis during this period, the departure of key Mille Lacs Band members from leadership positions, and the cuts to the Historic Sites Department, which directly oversees management of the Mille Lacs Indian Museum, all contributed to the "halting and faltering" programming efforts. But, as I consider some of the concerns raised by Tooker and Archabal regarding the ongoing life of the museum, my thoughts return to the deep history of the site. The place is embedded in colonial relationships.

I am reminded, for example, of Thomas Vennum's words in his 1979 report on the Mille Lacs Indian Museum. He mentions that by "accident and bequeathal," MHS became the owners of the Ayer Collection, which he claims is very valuable and also "contains . . . some very sensitive artifacts pertaining to the Ojibwa religion, the *mitewiwin*."[88] In rereading Vennum's comment, I couldn't help thinking how Band members must have felt upon Ayer's retirement in 1959 when this collection of their material culture—some of which is sacred—was given to the Minnesota Historical Society and not to those from whom it originated. Perhaps that is a possible source of the community's ambivalence about this site.

It is true that the exhibitions embody new museum theory and practice and that the Mille Lacs Band's voice is prominent throughout. Even so, an absent-present is here. A historical ambivalence persists that is deeply rooted in the landscape. On one hand, the Mille Lacs Band members were involved with the site. They "made a living" at the trading post and later the museum; they held dance performances; they sold their arts and crafts to tourists at the Ayers' trading post; they posed for the mannequins in the "Four Seasons Room"; and, more recently, they collaborated on a new educational site for their community and the general public. On the other hand, underlying all this, the relationship was colonial. The legacy of the transfer from Harry and Jeanette Ayer to MHS is something that is not easily forgotten or reconciled.

As we know, the Ayers' initial presence at the site and their taking of the land and material culture during their tenure on the reservation is inextricably tied to the colonization process. While more nuanced views of tourism in Indigenous communities are currently being proposed that emphasize Native agency and the ability of communities to adapt to new ways of making a living, we must not forget that this is not a benign process—this production of arts and crafts for the tourist industry on reservations across the country during the early twentieth century. As anthropologist Ann Tweedie reminds us, even when Native people parted voluntarily with objects during this period, "it was often overwhelming economic and social pressures that forced the alienation."[89]

Nina Archabal alluded to the idea of distrust that is part of the deep history of the site and that cannot be easily dismissed, and this distrust remains at times unresolved. She said, "I think unfortunately [that] just as casino gambling doesn't take away hundreds of years of social deprivation and suffering, I would say that ten or fifteen years of good work on the part of the staff members here and good heart does not take away years and years and decades and decades of distrust."[90]

This unresolved issue does not take away from what has been accomplished. It simply indicates that asserting Native voice and decolonizing are processes: they involve many steps and stages. When I worked on this project in 1994 and then again in 1996 when I could view the final product, I really felt that this was one of the finest presentations of Native American history and culture produced in a museum. It reflected the best in new interpretative strategies; it showed keen engagement with the scholarship in Native American studies and Ojibwe history; and it embodied the collaborative exhibition development that swept the field in the 1980s and 1990s. I understood the long and arduous process to bring this project to fruition, and I greatly respected the thoroughness of the endeavor.

But when I returned to the site years later, I found my assessment changing as my own perspective developed. Over the last several years, I have engaged critically with how museums can serve as sites of decolonization and "sites of conscience." While I remain very impressed with the quality of the exhibitions at Mille Lacs, questions arose for me about the interpretative program there. The Mille Lacs Indian Museum is effective on so many levels, yet how successful has it been in offering an analysis of colonialism and its ongoing effects in the community? When that question arises for me, I also wonder, is it even appropriate for me to question the absence of a hard-hitting analysis of colonialism within the exhibition, given that the Mille Lacs Band elders on the advisory board determined the museum's content?

In the decade since this museum opened, at least one Native community has chosen to use their tribal museum as a place to tackle colonialism and its impact on their lives. Addressing historical unresolved grief is one of the primary goals of the Ziibiwing Center of Anishinabe Culture and Lifeways, a tribal museum in Michigan, which I will discuss in a later chapter. Its use of exhibits and programming for decolonizing purposes has served a critical function in promoting healing and understanding across generations in the Saginaw Chippewa community. But this raises the further question, should all tribally authored exhibitions be engaged in the decolonizing project?

While I have yet to fully resolve these questions within my own mind, I do believe that addressing historical unresolved grief should be the primary function of a decolonizing museum practice in a tribal museum. Something does shift in the interpretation when members of the community control a project from the outset.

In June 2010, the current site manager of the Mille Lacs Indian Museum, Travis Zimmerman, shared with me his views of the state of the museum today. A gracious and outgoing person, he conveyed the many plans in the works to bring renewed vitality to the museum following years of changing management and leadership. Museum attendance is down by half—from roughly twenty thousand visitors per year following the museum's opening in 1996 to just ten thousand or so in 2009. One major reason is that the museum is open far less than originally planned. Due to a state budget crisis, the Minnesota Historical Society cut the hours dramatically at Mille Lacs to twenty-five hours per week during the height of the summer season from Memorial Day to Labor Day Weekend.[91] While the numbers may be down at Mille Lacs, the museum still draws a diverse group of visitors hailing from fifty-seven different countries.

When I asked Zimmerman about the subjectivity of the museum, he referred to the museum's status as a hybrid. While it fits most of the criteria of a tribal museum, especially given the first-person voice in the exhibitions, the difference is that it is not tribally owned and operated. He noted that the Mille Lacs Indian Museum has been "adopted as the red-headed stepchild by other tribal museums" because of its unique status as a historic site of MHS that privileges the voice and perspective of the Mille Lacs Band—and that it will eventually revert to Band control.

Currently, plans are under way to make the site more viable and to have the ongoing life that Rachel Tooker (former Mille Lacs manager and MHS Historic Sites Department director) spoke of in 2001. Developing a library for use by students from the Mille Lacs Band school, Nay Ah Shing, and nearby Onamia public schools; starting an All Nations café serving Native American food; hosting book signings and movie nights; digitizing the many hours of interviews with tribal elders in its collection in collaboration with the Mille Lacs Band archives staff for joint use between the two entities; and revising or expanding sections of the exhibit: these are just a few of the plans in the works under Travis Zimmerman's leadership.

Zimmerman also discussed the importance of changing the exhibitions, given that a significant number of tribal members have already seen the galleries. He hopes that changing the exhibits or adding new sections will encourage them to continue visiting. As he observed, "If the exhibits do not change, what would make them want to continue to come back?" At the time of our interview, a new media installation to complement and expand upon the "Veterans" exhibit was in development, which would make it the first new installation since the museum's opening in 1996.[92]

While the ongoing life of the Mille Lacs Indian Museum is a work in progress, I would like to return to the words of Richard West, whose high praise of the Mille Lacs Indian Museum project opens this chapter. I have just highlighted some of the challenges for the ongoing vitality of the museum and its programming efforts. I want to make clear, however, that I deeply value the Mille Lacs Indian Museum project as reflecting what Richard West described: a place that helped him chart the course for another collaborative project between Native people and a mainstream museum, the Smithsonian's National Museum of the American Indian.

The Mille Lacs Indian Museum is a place that presents Indigenous history to the public exceptionally well. It also serves as a site where Mille Lacs Band members can gain knowledge about their history and culture as they educate others. Whereas its subjectivity as a hybrid tribal museum has created challenges for some of its postopening programming efforts, the collaborative exhibitions created there helped set the stage for what would follow in the larger museum world. I refer, of course, to the Smithsonian's National Museum of the American Indian, which opened on the National Mall in Washington, D.C., in 2004—the subject of the next chapter.

three

EXHIBITING NATIVE AMERICA AT THE
NATIONAL MUSEUM OF THE AMERICAN INDIAN

Collaborations and Missed Opportunities

INITIAL IMPRESSIONS: JANUARY–APRIL 1988

In 1988, during the winter quarter of my junior year in college, I served as an American Indian Program intern at the Smithsonian's National Museum of American History. The experience marked my first extended period away from home and my first foray into the museum profession. I was awed by the National Mall museums and spent countless hours wandering the many exhibition halls of the Smithsonian Institution, especially the National Museum of American History.[1] My weekends were spent visiting other well-known monuments and sites in the nation's capital.

I was impressed as well by the large and active community of American Indian political leaders and scholars—the self-proclaimed "real Washington Redskins"—who welcomed me into the city's larger pantribal Native American community. Through my associations with the diverse tribal peoples comprising the Washington, D.C., community, I learned a great deal not only about museum theory and practice at the National Museum of American History but also about the current political struggles facing Native Americans.

Throughout my time in the capital, I heard stories about the possibility of a new Smithsonian museum that would be devoted to American Indian history and culture. Envisioned as occupying the last remaining spot on the National Mall, the site would showcase the vast collection amassed by George Gustav Heye, perhaps the most famous collector of Native American objects in the early twentieth century. The purpose of the new museum would be to serve as an important monument to Indigenous history and memory.

The conversations that took place not only at the National Museum of American History but also at receptions, dinner parties, conferences, and social events within the Native community in Washington captured my attention. I became engrossed in the ongoing political developments concerning the new museum. Not long before, in 1987, Senator Daniel Inouye, chairman of the Senate Committee on Indian Affairs, had introduced a bill (S. 1722) to establish the museum. He had offered testimony for a site that, he said, would honor Indigenous people and correct historical injustices. My supervisor, Rayna Green, had received a copy of Senator Inouye's testimony at her office at the Smithsonian's National Museum of American History, and I quote at length from one of the passages that captured my attention as a young intern:

> Today we are to begin a new chapter in the history of the relationship between the United States and the Indians—a chapter that will begin, we hope, to reverse the centuries of treatment that the Indian people have suffered.... Today, we will consider legislation that will provide... access to the proud culture and traditions of the indigenous people to future generations of Native Americans. There will be a great museum established on the National Mall that will be home to the most priceless artifacts of Indian culture, history, and art. I believe the time has come to honor and remember the greatness of the first Americans, their wisdom, their leadership, their valor, and their contributions to the people of the United States.[2]

When I left Washington, D.C., in late March 1988 to return to the University of Minnesota to finish my bachelor's degree in history, my lasting impression was that the museum was a distinct possibility. Then, in 1989, President George H. W. Bush signed Public Law 101-185, which established the Smithsonian Institution's sixteenth museum. After heated political negotiations, the National Museum of the American Indian (NMAI) was created, and it would include three separate sites: the George Gustav Heye Center in New York City; a new storage facility in Suitland, Maryland; and the National Mall site in Washington, D.C. In 1990, Smithsonian officials appointed W. Richard West, a Southern Cheyenne Indian lawyer, as the founding director of the new museum.

EXTENDED ENGAGEMENTS: SUMMER 2000 AND BEYOND

In the summer of 2000, I returned to Washington for a four-month-long research appointment at the NMAI. A great deal had changed since my initial time in the nation's capital: the George Gustav Heye Center had opened in New York City in 1994; the Cultural Resources Center, a state-of-the-art collection facility, had opened in Suitland, Maryland, in 1999; and plans were under way to open the museum exhibitions on the National Mall site in Washington, D.C.

Things had changed for me as well. In the twelve years since I first visited Washington, I had worked as an exhibit researcher for the Minnesota Historical Society and as an education consultant at the British Museum. Additionally, I had completed my bachelor's and master's degrees in history and had finished all my course work in the doctoral program in ethnic studies at the University of California, Berkeley. My intent for the research visit was to gain firsthand knowledge of the plans to develop the National Mall exhibitions. I was also seriously exploring the possibility of becoming a curator (a term employed by the NMAI, even though the larger Smithsonian bureaucracy did not use it) for one of the galleries just getting off the ground.

During my appointment in the summer of 2000, I worked as a research assistant in the Curatorial Department at the newly opened Cultural Resources Center (CRC) in Suitland, Maryland. The National Mall exhibition plans were well under way, and I was hired to conduct research for the *Our Lives* exhibition, one of three inaugural exhibits scheduled to open in 2004, which would address Native American identity. Great efforts were being taken to represent Indigenous identity in all its contemporary and historical complexity, and the curatorial staff was in the process of selecting fourteen Native communities, seven organizations, and several individuals from across the hemisphere to include in the gallery.[3]

The other two exhibitions—*Our Universes*, focusing on tribal philosophies, and *Our Peoples*, focusing on Native histories—were much further along in development by the summer of 2000. Curators were working with twenty different tribes between the two shows, and the Cultural Resources Center buzzed with activity. Several staff members from these two teams traveled throughout the hemisphere conducting "fieldwork" for the exhibitions, while research staff members at the CRC supported the process on the home front. As a participant observer, I was present during the initial stages of developing the galleries, and this gave me an invaluable opportunity to engage the Curatorial Department staff and tribal delegations as they developed these new "community-curated exhibitions."

My job involved conducting research for *Our Lives* at libraries and archives on the history of American Indian education. I also assisted in conceptualizing this 8,500-square-foot gallery on contemporary Native identity. During my appointment, I participated in exhibition-content meetings for the *Our Lives* gallery, attended Curatorial Departmental meetings, observed a content-development meeting with a visiting tribal delegation (a stroke of good fortune in that typically only the exhibit's curator would be allowed to attend), and entered the daily world of the museum as a staff person. My intent at the time was to document the history of exhibition development and the processes the NMAI used at this important site of Indigenous history and memory. I was also keenly aware of the new museum's significance to the ongoing and changing relationship between Native people and museums.

Before returning to California in 2000, I collected the archival records related to the exhibition process, including planning records and notes from staff meetings and tribal delegation visits. I also gathered secondary sources related to the National Museum of the American Indian, including in-house publications and documents produced by journalists and scholars. In December 2001, I returned to the museum for two weeks as a Native American Visiting Student Fellow under the auspices of the Smithsonian's Office of Fellowships and Internships to conduct follow-up research. During the visit, I interviewed nine key staff members involved in developing the exhibitions and collected additional archival records related to the museum. I particularly hoped to document the evolution of exhibit plans since my first visit in 2000. At the Smithsonian Center for Education and Museum Studies, I also conducted research on the NMAI's history and museum theory in general.

The significant amount of time I spent at the institution—both as a paid staff member in 2000 and as an outside researcher—has given me firsthand knowledge of the culture of the museum. I am grateful to staff members who agreed to participate in the study over the years and who generously shared their time, thoughts, and resources. I am also aware that I was one of the first scholars to have access to plans for the 2004 exhibitions, and I am incredibly grateful to those in the museum who gave me these opportunities.

When I returned to the museum in 2001 after a year and a half away from the project, I witnessed staff changes in both the Curatorial and Exhibits Departments. That the NMAI is a pressure-filled environment is no surprise in view of the difficulties it faces in developing a Smithsonian national museum about such a complex and, at times, challenging subject. In his study of the United States Holocaust Memorial Museum, *Preserving Memory: The Struggle to Create America's Holocaust Museum*, Edward Linenthal describes brilliantly the fifteen-year struggle to build this important national museum of Holocaust history and memory, as various interests attempted/competed to shape its development.[4] The struggle is also seen at the NMAI, which is a highly charged political site in ways similar to the Holocaust Museum. The stakes are incredibly high considering the manner in which museums have misrepresented Indigenous people in the past. The pressure on this site to be, for many, the "museum different" was and remains enormous. The curatorial staff was well aware of the challenges involved, and I had many conversations with various team members who felt the pressure to develop exhibitions that accurately reflected how Native people understood their history, culture, and identity, in the wake of a long history of misrepresentation. In 2001, one staff member conveyed the sheer enormity of the pressure felt given that many of the communities shared intensely painful and searing stories—and it was both an "honor and responsibility" to try and get the story right. The final product must accurately reflect what tribal communities conveyed, this individual stated, and must "be authentic to how they feel, they sense, how they understand their own history."[5] I admired the staff members at the NMAI who took seriously the charge to chart a new museum practice with Native people on the national stage, and I recognized the challenges that they faced in doing so.

Given the long and arduous process of developing exhibitions, I realized that plans for the content of museums change over time. However, I believed it was critical to document the process under way at the museum—to explore the emergence of this new "Indian museology" at the self-proclaimed "museum different." My earlier examinations proved important to my future analysis of what finally appeared on the exhibition floor following the museum's official opening on 21 September 2004. I have since returned to the museum for numerous research visits. In addition to publishing exhibition reviews of their galleries,[6] I have served as the sole editor for a special journal issue and as the coeditor of a book that both focus on the museum and its impact.[7]

What follows is an analysis of my multilayered engagement with the Smithsonian's National Museum of the American Indian—both its early history and its evolving exhibition-development philosophy. Finally, I provide an analysis of the exhibits that opened on the National Mall in 2004, giving particular attention to the *Our Peoples* gallery, which focuses on tribal histories. Following the lead of another early researcher of the NMAI, Judith

Ostrowitz, I, too, "trace relationships between ideals and reality through observation on final forms."[8]

THE GEORGE GUSTAV HEYE COLLECTION AND
THE MUSEUM OF THE AMERICAN INDIAN

When one traces the genealogy of the Smithsonian's National Museum of the American Indian, the story always begins with the large-scale collecting practices of George Gustav Heye in the early part of the twentieth century. While much of this story has been told before, some details bear repeating here. During his lifetime, Heye collected "all things Indian" from across the Western Hemisphere. Eventually, his collection would total more than 700,000 pieces.[9] He later established the Museum of the American Indian (MAI) in New York City at the Audubon Terrace on 155th Street and Broadway to showcase his vast and important collection, while also maintaining a storage facility in the Bronx. Scholars have documented the significance of the collection, praising it for its diversity and scope and for including pieces that "represent both the highest artistic expressions of Indian cultures and the evidence of everyday life."[10] It is recognized as one of the finest collections of Native American objects in the world.

Throughout the MAI's early history—most notably during George Gustav Heye's tenure at the museum—the emphasis was not only on acquiring objects but also on documenting and researching the materials.[11] The mythology surrounding Heye's collecting practices has depicted him as an insatiable and eccentric individual, obsessed with amassing enormous quantities of Native objects with little regard for research and documentation. In recent years, this image of Heye has been complicated by the work of anthropologists Ira Jacknis and Ann McMullen. In their projects, Heye emerges as less of an "obsessive," manic collector of Native materials and more of a complex individual. He is seen as being equally interested in preservation, research, and developing a museum that rivals other anthropology museums of the time. McMullen argues that the contemporary renderings of Heye's career, some of which are produced by the NMAI, do a disservice to his legacy and our understanding of the collections. As she states: "He is not remembered as a man who funded countless expeditions and excavations, who funded research and publications, or who assembled a professional staff the likes of which few museums have ever seen. Most of all, he is not remembered as a man who built a museum that rivaled its contemporaries in scope and scholarly production."[12]

While both authors make unique contributions to complicating the story of George Heye, one element of the Heye story is not dismissed: the needs and interests of Native Americans were not considered primary during his tenure at the MAI. This is certainly reflected in the MAI's mission statement: "This museum occupies a unique position among institutions, in that its sole aim is to gather and preserve for students everything useful in illustrating and elucidating the anthropology of the aborigines of the Western Hemisphere, and to disseminate by means of its publications the knowledge thereby gained."[13] As envisioned by Heye, the museum was to be distinct from other New York museums as well as natural history museums established in the United States, including the American Museum of Natural History. However, the MAI was similar in that people outside Indigenous communities would produce the scholarly knowledge about Native Americans.[14]

During the institution's seventy-plus-year history, the lack of Native involvement was evident in all aspects of the museum: exhibitions, collections care, education, and administration. Eventually, Native American museum leaders and scholars would serve as trustees for the institution, beginning with the appointment of George Abrams (Seneca) and Vine Deloria Jr. (Standing Rock Sioux) in 1977.[15] While serving as vice-chairman of the board of trustees in the 1980s, Deloria would later play a critical role in lobbying for the transfer of the museum to the Smithsonian.

The noncollaborative working relationship with Native people was evident in the MAI's exhibitions, which reflected the museum display strategies of the time. Culturally insensitive and older types of object-based ethnographic displays dominated the museum. As one scholar claims, the "exhibitions looked like storage facilities."[16] Of significant concern, one of the first exhibits visitors encountered upon entering the museum featured Iroquois False Face Society masks—ceremonial objects that the Haudenosaunee leaders requested be taken off display in museums in the 1980s. When the Smithsonian Institution took over the museum in 1989, the masks were finally removed, along with a disturbing display case of seventeen Native American scalps.[17]

Over the years, the MAI was plagued by inadequate exhibition and storage space and by the economic decline of the neighborhood surrounding the museum. Because of the magnitude of the collection and the inadequate exhibit area available, less than 1 percent of the collection was on display.[18] The deteriorating neighborhood at 155th and Broadway in New York made it dangerous for tourists to visit the site, so attendance rates for the museum became incredibly low.

The story of George Heye, his massive collecting enterprise, and the private museum he later built followed a historical trajectory similar to that of the Southwest Museum in Los Angeles, which became part of the Autry National Center in 2003.[19] Both collections needed a wealthy institution to "rescue" them. This story line, however, is more dramatic for the MAI. As Ira Jacknis writes, "All museums have a life history, with ups and downs, but the Heye's history was particularly severe and dramatic: a rapid and great high and then a protracted low, followed by a radical transformation."[20] In the MAI's case, the "radical transformation" would be its identity change from a private museum to a national public institution.

Fewer than fifty thousand people a year visited the MAI in the year before its transfer to the Smithsonian in 1989.[21] The collection of priceless artifacts was in grave danger, and plans were under way in the 1980s to locate a more permanent home for the collection. In his testimony at the congressional hearing to establish the NMAI, Senator Daniel Inouye described the conditions of the collection at the Bronx storage facility:

> When I left . . . I was stunned, I was shocked and I was nauseated. There was a collection of the greatest magnitude, priceless in nature, and because of the lack of funds kept in the condition which obviously would have led to the final deterioration of this collection. In a room about half this size were about 200 buffalo robes. Any one of them would have been the center piece in any museum. They were covered with plastic bags that you find in a dry cleaning shop. And that is not the way to store buffalo robes. And in other rooms, you had Navajo robes by the dozens just folded and stacked, and masks of great sacred value hanging all over the walls.[22]

Several options were explored to rescue the collection, including a possible merger with the American Museum of Natural History. Billionaire H. Ross Perot approached the MAI with an offer of $70 million for the collection and a plan to move it to Texas. These options and many others were rejected, as the Heye collection "became the prize in an odd tug-of-war between the cultural capital in New York and the national capital in Washington D.C."[23] Negotiations between the museum and the Smithsonian began in the 1980s, but it was not until 1989 that the enabling legislation finally passed. The National Museum of the American Indian Act not only established the NMAI but also provided for the repatriation of human remains held by other Smithsonian museums. Roland W. Force, director of the MAI from 1977 to 1990, claimed that during his tenure at the museum, he engaged in a thirteen-year struggle to find a new home for the collection and an adequate exhibition space. The political battles that ensued were long and arduous. He recalled, "I could not have anticipated that the Museum [of the American Indian] would be engaged in protracted struggle with borough, city, state, regional and national political figures."[24]

Vine Deloria Jr., a Native political activist and scholar who served on the MAI's board of trustees for roughly two decades, testified during the 1989 hearing for the establishment of the new museum. In his written testimony, he claimed that the MAI's collection "is as significant to Native Americans as the Elgin marbles and the Parthenon are to the Greeks, as the Museum of Chinese History and the Forbidden City are to the Chinese, as the pyramids and their contents are to the Egyptians."[25] He also linked the new museum and its educational mission to the larger American Indian self-determination movement that began in the 1970s. The museum would be "absolutely essential to give American Indians a tremendous boost in the progress we have already made in a lot of other areas," he said.[26] Deloria believed that controlling the means of representation is a powerful step in exercising tribes' sovereign rights.

During his testimony, Senator Inouye stressed the need to rescue this great and important collection to benefit the further study of American Indian history and culture. Furthermore, he believed that the site could educate the general public about the great contributions that Native people have made to American society. These contributions include, for example, the Native influence on the Founding Fathers and the American system of government. Acknowledging these contributions through a national forum could challenge the commonly held view that the continent was a cultural backwater before the Europeans arrived.[27]

Additionally, Senator Inouye discussed the high rates of unemployment and alcoholism in Native communities throughout the United States, arguing that the museum could serve as a place to reaffirm Native dignity—to give Native Americans "a sense of identity and a sense of pride that we have denied them."[28] From the very beginning, the discourse around the museum among those who supported the Heye collection's rescue by the Smithsonian framed its importance both as a tool of education and as a source of pride for Native communities.

In her excellent article tracing the complex negotiations to establish the NMAI and the tensions that arose with the Smithsonian's National Museum of Natural History, anthropologist Patricia Pierce Erikson reminds us that establishing the NMAI was a watershed moment in the changing historical relationship between Native Americans and museums. The enabling legislation did more than just rescue the Heye collection. As Erikson states:

> In the end, the negotiations to create the NMAI determined the future deposition of not only the enormous Heye American Indian collection, but also the National Museum of Natural History's Native American human remains and funerary materials. Furthermore, the creation of the NMAI influenced the future deposition of Native American human remains, funerary materials, and cultural patrimony in museums across the nation. Thus, the creation of the NMAI marks one of the critical moments in rising Native American influence in a national arena.[29]

Through the complex dynamics just described, the Museum of the American Indian—previously a private institution—was transformed into a Smithsonian national museum devoted to American Indian history and culture and situated on the last remaining spot on the National Mall. The exhibitions at the new site and how they were created formed a critical part of this transformative process.

CHALLENGING CURATORIAL AUTHORITY: THE DEVELOPMENT OF EXHIBITIONS AT THE NMAI'S GEORGE GUSTAV HEYE CENTER

In order to understand the uniqueness of the exhibits that the NMAI developed on the National Mall in 2004, one must examine the museum's exhibition-development philosophy and its emphasis on creating a new Native museological practice. The NMAI is committed to developing interpretative programming and exhibitions that reflect its commitment to tribal communities, as articulated in the museum's mission statement. Its influence on the museum field will be immense, according to Gerald McMaster, a Cree artist and formerly the NMAI's deputy assistant director for cultural resources: "I think in terms of scholarship, in terms of museology, I think we will give people a lot of material to write about in the future. A lot of material to speak about, about an Indian museology, and I think we have really taken it away from certain anthropological paradigms and even art paradigms by really constructing and shifting more to a model of working with Indigenous peoples that is really significant."[30]

The early stages of this development were reflected in the inaugural exhibitions at the George Gustav Heye Center (GGHC). In 1994, the museum opened at the Alexander Hamilton U.S. Custom House in New York City with much publicity and great public and scholarly interest. The GGHC marked the opening of the first of the three sites of the NMAI. Its three inaugural exhibitions—*Creation's Journey: Masterworks of Native American Identity and Belief, All Roads Are Good: Native Voices on Life and Culture,* and *This Path We Travel: Celebrations of Contemporary Native American Creativity*—were developed in cooperation with the museum staff and Native individuals. A great deal was made of the museum's new interpretative strategy: to transfer curatorial authority to Indigenous people and thereby enable Native Americans to tell their own stories. Founding director Richard West believed this was essential to carrying through the mission of the museum. As he stated, "Native peoples are entitled to a participation, and, indeed, arguably to a primacy of voice, in the representation and interpretation of Native cultures at the museum."[31]

In the early 1990s, the actors involved in shaping exhibition content and developing the philosophical underpinnings of the new exhibitions were the museum's senior staff, including W. Richard West, James Volkert, Elaine Gurian, Rick Hill, and senior advisors to Rick West, Native artists Lloyd Kiva New and Arthur Amiotte, along with many other Native educators and intellectuals.[32] James Volkert, former head of the NMAI Exhibits Department, described the early days of development of the new exhibition philosophy:

We were looking at the renovation of the Custom House, and so the notion of what this museum's exhibitions ought to be were birthed then. The group working on it was pretty much me and Elaine Gurian, Lloyd Kiva New, and Arthur Amiotte. Arthur and Lloyd were senior advisors to Rick [West] at that point in the process. We made trips out to the Southwest, and they would come here and so forth. But in that process, we shaped the three opening exhibitions: *Creation's Journey, All Roads Are Good:,* and *This Path We Travel.* That was a very conscious decision for those three exhibitions. They were set in that sequence around the galleries.

The first one, *Creation's Journey,* it was really intended that this was not only a path for visitors but a path that this museum was embarking on—that is why the metaphors in all the titles and all that. My partner in all of these was Rick Hill. By then we had an exhibit staff. We started working on *All Roads Are Good* first, because the intention was to change the nature of where the authority of the museum comes from. Because even at 155 Street [the old MAI], there were Native people involved who came in to visit, but the authority of the museum still rested with the museum—as with every other museum at that point.

[We] consciously set out to change the nature of that. The most basic question you can ask around the authority of the museum is who gets to pick the stuff when you talk about an exhibition. In talking with Lloyd and Arthur about that, we decided to simply change the rules.[33]

According to Volkert, *All Roads Are Good* represented the new direction for the museum—a transfer of curatorial authority to Native people. Beginning in 1991, the museum invited twenty-three Native selectors to survey the collection and choose objects that had great meaning for them as Indigenous people—spiritually, culturally, personally. The selectors chose more than one thousand objects for inclusion in the exhibit, and their reflections on the pieces were included in the exhibition text.

The new strategy met with some resistance from the MAI's older museum staff, some of whom participated in the exhibit's early planning stages. Questions over authority and who has the right to speak arose as discussions evolved:

We had a meeting out at the research branch with the then curatorial staff of the museum. It is important to understand that one of the things that Rick [West] was trying to do was to move this institution to a different place, and, in any institution, there is an inertia or resistance to it. . . . We met with the curatorial staff and presented this idea: what would happen if twenty-three people whom we called selectors came to the research branch [and] could look at and talk about anything that interested them? There was a reaction to that, because they were not academics; they were not scholars; and they were artists and musicians and all kinds of different folks. So we talked about it, and the questions that came back—even from our own curatorial staff—were interesting.

The first intention was, shouldn't we put our best stuff out? And we said no. Then it became really interesting. One of the curators—I will never forget this—who is not on staff now, asked, "What if they all pick baskets?" So, there was this anxiety. If you invite strangers, essentially, no matter what you say about Native people at that point in time, there was still this anxiety and kind of patronizing attitude that said, "Yeah, but they may not pick the right stuff." So, Elaine [Gurian] said—and I will never forget this—"Well, then we will just have a wonderful basket show." Through a series of conversations, we ended up doing that, and it was the first project that the museum really did. . . .

Ultimately, *All Roads* came out of that, and in looking at *All Roads*, it was important that the visitor got the sense of who these people were as individuals—not speaking for their tribes, speaking for themselves about things that interested them. . . . The range of what the museum could do had to be embodied in that show. . . .

People thought it was disjointed. People thought it was superfluous in some ways and so forth. And that is all fine. But it was important for the museum to change the way it did the work, and that is really what that show was all about.[34]

To change how the museum "did the work" became the overarching goal for the new staff involved with the NMAI. The first challenge for the curatorial team became how to transfer authority to the Native selectors, whose commentary on the objects formed the basis of the text. Written in the first person, the exhibition text was taken from the recorded thoughts and comments of the selectors who were inspired by their visits to the collection space. The next challenge—and what became the central question for the museum—was how to make this new multivocality legitimate and, at the same time, authoritative.

This central question led to the development of *Creation's Journey*, an exhibit that highlighted the masterworks of the museum's collection. Representing tribal nations from throughout the Western Hemisphere, the 150 objects exhibited were some of the finest works in the George Gustav Heye collection. They were selected for their uniqueness, beauty, and their dialogic potential.[35] The show was designed to challenge the anthropological and art historical presentations that had predominated in the past and to include Indigenous reflections on the significance of the pieces:

All of *Creation's Journey* was just a prelude to *All Roads*; the whole show was a prelude. It started with a series of questions that said—talked about—"What is the meaning of objects?" and those sorts of things, and "How do we read objects?" The whole show was very carefully structured to be a set up for *All Roads*. . . . So, that is why, in that first section, there were three duck decoys. Our curatorial staff selected the objects for *Creation's Journey*. Rick Hill structured them into a story. They picked these decoys, and, truth be told, they were really selected for a masterpiece—the very best objects in the collection.

So, Rick looked at all this stuff and put this show together, and that is why . . . the duck decoys were presented, each in a different setting. One was presented as fine art, one was presented as ethnography, and one was presented as anthropology—side by side. So visitors could begin to see [that] how a museum presents something affects how you perceive it. If they present it as fine art, you read it as fine art, no matter what is said around it. If you present it . . . in a little tableau with reeds and water and how it was used, you read it as ethnography, no matter what you say about it as being fine art. What surrounded those objects were anthropological voices. . . .

Then the question was asked, "Okay, we have the anthropological voice and the fine art voice; we have always looked at Native materials these ways. What is missing?" What was missing is a Native perspective. That is why you pass through the structure [within the exhibit] and, from that point forward, you begin to see Native takes on these same objects.[36]

The third and final exhibition, *This Path We Travel*, was an installation of the work of fifteen Native artists. It featured various mediums, including "sculpture, performance, poetry, music, and video." The group met in Calgary, Hawaii, Phoenix, and finally New York City. The artwork completed by the group in New York formed the basis of the exhibit. The show addressed the following themes: "the creation of the Indian world," "the sacred transitions of people, animals, and places," "the profane intrusions into sacred thought," and "the world view of the future."[37] The artists agreed that individuals would not take credit for the show, and labels were not included in the exhibit. Designed to highlight the contemporary achievements of Native artists, the show appeared disjointed at times and received a great deal of criticism. One reviewer wrote, "Suffice to say, its hodgepodge of fake mesa-walls, video monitors inside clay pots, a raised burial platform and slogan-eering platitudes cross the line between art installation and theme park."[38] These criticisms were not lost on the curatorial team, as Volkert explained:

From my standpoint, most people didn't like the show, though they remember the schoolhouse clearly. But they didn't like it as an exhibition, because it didn't look like an exhibition. . . . But it was important at that point that we push beyond what people's expectations for the museum were, and so I liked the fact that it didn't look like a museum exhibition. Ultimately, it was not successful as an exhibition, though, because it was so far away from what people expected. . . . We had to push out to that edge first, otherwise you cannot creep out to the edge incrementally. . . . We all took a lot of flack for that show. I still think it is probably the strongest piece of work this museum has ever done, because it was so outside of the bounds of how a museum could operate.[39]

This Path We Travel exhibit at the National Museum of the American Indian, George Gustav Heye Center, 1994. Courtesy of the National Museum of the American Indian, Smithsonian Institution.

The NMAI's new exhibition philosophy received a great deal of attention, and several scholars and journalists have since critiqued its new interpretative strategies. In her review essay "A Different Sort of (P)Reservation: Some Thoughts on the National Museum of the American Indian," Allison Arieff questions whether self-portrayal constitutes a significant departure from traditional museum practice and whether the NMAI succeeded in challenging the status quo. Recognizing the problems in trying to be too many things to too many people, she claims that, while "walking through the exhibition space, I felt I was thrust in the middle of dueling museological paradigms—unequal parts art, ethnographic, history, technology, and children's museums."[40]

She further claims that the NMAI's rhetoric advanced the "notion of a generic or 'normal' Indian, and this has the effect of replacing one stereotypical representation with another—homogenizing an inherently heterogeneous group of people."[41] Additionally, she felt the museum failed to address complex issues—reburial and repatriation, for example—in any of the three exhibitions. She contends that the exhibits perpetuated century-old stereotypes, such as the primitive/noble savage, evidenced in the tendency to overemphasize Indians' relationships to the land. According to Arieff, the lack of discussion on contemporary issues, like urbanization, failed to address the complexities of contemporary Indian identity. In her view, the museum also did not include enough work by contemporary Native artists, highlighting instead historic objects in the galleries.

In another review essay, noted historian Richard White challenges the museum's desire to transfer curatorial authority to Indigenous people. He, too, questions whether self-portrayal constitutes authority, and he challenges the primacy of Native perspectives in the museum. He claims that "identity does not bestow knowledge. Identity is itself a contestable and unstable notion. The false claims of earlier generations of scholars and curators are not necessarily corrected by replacing them with Indian voices."[42] According to White, the exhibitions were uneven at best. He argues that the multivocal interpretative approach ended up making the exhibits seem "confused and confusing."

Like some other scholars and museum professionals, White appears to have been unsettled by the authoritative Native voice in the exhibits. For example, he critiques the moccasin display arranged by artist Gerald Mc-Master in the *All Roads Are Good* exhibit as not providing enough information about the objects themselves. McMaster claimed that the display was a "metaphor for the diversity and creativity of indigenous people." It was an art display, not a standard museum ethnographic presentation. Providing detailed historical or ethnographic information on the specific moccasins was not the intent. Nonetheless, White takes issue with the selectors' presentations in the exhibit for what he claims was their "erasure of original meanings, this willed ignorance of Indian objects."[43] White seems to view the information as not being sufficiently scholarly and seeks to delegitimize the significance of multivocality and the primacy given to the Native voice and perspective at the NMAI.

In her introduction to the *All Roads Are Good* exhibition catalog, Clara Sue Kidwell, former assistant director for cultural resources at the NMAI, states: "The reasons for the [Native selectors'] choices do not necessarily reflect the standards of aesthetic or historic value that might inform displays in an anthropology or history museum. Rather, objects become expressions of distinct ways of seeing the world, an entree for the viewer into a different cultural understanding of the collection."[44] The stated intent of the display—an intent clearly expressed in the exhibition catalog—was to privilege Native cultural understanding. This decision is what Richard White called into question.

Moccasin display arranged by Gerald McMaster in the *All Roads Are Good* exhibit
at the National Museum of the American Indian, George Gustav Heye Center, 1994.
Courtesy of the National Museum of the American Indian, Smithsonian Institution.

Founding NMAI director Richard West anticipated the criticism. He recognized that the central question would become whether the Native voice or interpretation was more valid than an ethnographic presentation. In a speech given at the annual meeting of the American Association of Museums in 1997, he claimed that both were equally valid but that his museum would give primacy to the Native perspective. He made this choice fully aware that those who used to control the representation of Native peoples would be the ones most threatened by the privileging of Native voices and perspectives.[45]

The museum's ambitious attempt to achieve this new Native multivocality was critiqued by many as failing to address the needs of the audience.[46] As articulately as the development team may have described the philosophical and methodological underpinnings of the project, if the messages were lost on visitors, their curatorial goals could be undermined. A reviewer with the *New York Times* recognized the beauty of the more than five hundred objects on display but felt they were "sabotaged by an overproduced installation and by a curatorial philosophy that too often favors political grandstanding and feel good sentiment."[47] In her review of the NMAI, Margaret Dubin includes commentary from visitors who expressed confusion over the display techniques. One visitor felt compelled to write, "The presentation was horrendous—very cramped, chaotic media blitz, no sense of scale, not enough space, and information incomplete."[48]

In their NMAI review essay, Patricia Penn Hilden and Shari Huhndorf argue that, while the NMAI embraces a new museum theory and practice that seeks to challenge ethnographic display practices of the past, the master narrative of conquest and colonization was nonetheless reinscribed within the museum site: "We discovered that the displays . . . merely replicated—though with more sophistication and considerably more obfuscation—all the tired clichés long familiar to 'Indian Museum' visitors. In other words, nothing about the newly refurbished Alexander Hamilton Custom House muted the customary triumphal sounds of the victors' celebratory choruses."[49] In their analysis, the three inaugural exhibitions failed to provide sufficient context on the history of colonialism and, in some places, perpetuated stereotypes by "pandering to New Age consumers."[50]

Their essay concludes with self-reflective questions about their own failure to appreciate what the museum offered them as the "authentic voice" of Indigenous people. The NMAI's literature—produced both before and after the GGHC opening in 1994—forcefully asserts the NMAI's efforts to include Indigenous people in all aspects of museum practice: selecting objects, choosing exhibit themes, writing museum labels, and participating in fund-raising. Hilden and Huhndorf wonder about their own lack of appreciation for these efforts: "Why did it sadden us? Who were we to reject it?"[51] But reject it they did. They, too, challenged the idea that the NMAI embodies a truly revolutionary museum practice—that it decenters Western authoritative knowledge and places Indigenous voices and perspectives at the center.

In my conversations with staff in 2000 and 2001, the exhibition and curatorial staff revealed that the multitude of concerns expressed about the New York site informed the decision making for the National Mall site. They were keenly aware of many of the shortcomings that scholars and journalists had raised and took steps to try to address specific issues, such as voice, thematic content, translation, and the process of collaboration.

For example, one of Allison Arieff's major criticisms is that "the NMAI veers dangerously close to projecting a pan-Indian nationalism. . . . In its efforts to instill Indian pride, and to bring a greater understanding and tolerance to the non-Indian public, the museum more often than not glosses over tension and difference."[52] Whereas the Heye Center exhibits were perceived as blurring the distinctions between tribal communities, the plans for the National Mall site included tribally specific sections that each respective community would curate.

The staff members interviewed for my study in 2000–2001 believed that this new directive of working closely with tribal communities would be an important new step for the museum. Not only would the content of the exhibitions be more tribally specific, but also the process would build ongoing relationships with Native communities. This approach is central to carrying out the overarching mission of the NMAI. Bruce Bernstein, then assistant director for cultural resources, reflected on the NMAI's evolving exhibition philosophy:

> I think we have learned a lot in ten years. I think that [today], having full partners and not consultants, these [mall exhibits] are big thematic exhibitions, whereas [the GGHC exhibits] were much more about individuals. *All Roads* [is] about individuals talking about great stuff, so you have individuals talking about their own tribes—their own cultures and backgrounds and objects. And you have other people picking things out because they think it is a beautiful object. Although it is not related to their traditional culture, . . . it is related to what they see. I think we've learned from that, and hopefully we developed out of a continual learning experience.[53]

THE NMAI'S NEW "INDIAN MUSEOLOGY":
DEVELOPING COMMUNITY-CURATED EXHIBITS

Following the opening of the George Gustav Heye Center in 1994 and even before, discussions were under way about what to include in the National Mall exhibitions. During my four months at the museum in 2000, I observed a particular emphasis emerging from exhibition planning: a desire to promote more tribally specific presentations and less of a pantribal view. The exhibits would focus on three critical areas: tribal philosophy, history, and identity. These three areas were seen as interrelated, though they would be explored separately in the exhibits. Twenty-four communities from across the Western Hemisphere were selected to develop the exhibitions in cooperation with the curatorial staff at the NMAI. Whereas individual tribal people were given primacy of voice at the GGHC exhibition, tribal communities would have primacy of voice at the National Mall site. As I will discuss in a moment, the museum struggled with how to achieve this goal—different methodological approaches—but the clear consensus was that the Native community voice would be central.

While more specific discussions about the content for the National Mall exhibitions began in 1994, the overall layout of the museum had already been set in the early 1990s. The layout was summarized in *The Way of the People*, which became the fundamental planning document for the three NMAI facilities, and it included preliminary discussions about exhibit content based on extensive consultation with Native people.[54] Following additional conversations with advisors, a "mall exhibition master plan" was published in 1995. It identified three thematic areas for the inaugural exhibitions: "spirituality; lifeways; [and] history."[55] A revised version of the plan appeared in 1997, based on further consultations with artists, scholars, museum professionals, and Native leaders.

Plans for the three exhibitions would evolve further under the leadership of Craig Howe (Lakota), who advanced a more tribally specific focus for the permanent exhibitions. In 1999, Bruce Bernstein and Craig Howe, the deputy assistant director for cultural resources at the time, developed the methodology for the galleries that the staff in the summer of 2000—and beyond—adhered to. The guiding principles for all three of the exhibits were defined as follows:

> *Community: Our Tribes Are Sovereign Nations.* Stress that Native rights and issues are community-based, and that tribal communities possess unique rights and inherent powers. . . .

Locality: This Is Indian Land. Show the interrelationship between geographical landscape, spiritual tradition, and community identity. The focus is on particular geographical places and their inextricable relationships to indigenous spiritual traditions of the Western Hemisphere.

Vitality: We Are Here Now. Present native cultures as living cultures that continue through time and space. The focus is on the continuities within Native communities today.

Viewpoint: We Know the World Differently. Develop interpretations from interdisciplinary viewpoints, but with indigenous worldviews always central. The focus is on Native philosophical systems, the distinct worldview of each and the Native languages that transmit this information.

Voices: These Are Our Stories. Include stories from multiple and divergent perspectives, but with Native voices always central. The focus is on Native individuals and their personal stories.[56]

The exhibition statement goes on to say, "Our tribal ancestors are the mentors, curators, developers, and designers of [the] exhibition."[57] The twenty-four communities featured in the three galleries represent tribes from throughout the Western Hemisphere. The staff went to great lengths to select communities from a carefully designed map that divided the hemisphere into four separate zones. To increase the representation of tribal communities, the museum planned to rotate by bringing in new communities every three or four years. Each tribal group had five to ten members working with the NMAI curatorial staff to develop the exhibits.

Since 20 percent of the museum's collection comes from south of the U.S. border, the staff decided that Indigenous communities from Mexico and Central and South America should be included in the exhibits in roughly that proportion. The staff acknowledged that the exhibits could present only the tip of the iceberg in terms of the diversity in languages, histories, and cultures of Indigenous peoples living in this hemisphere. Even so, a methodology was in place to ensure some geographic, historic, and cultural diversity.

The *Our Universes* gallery was designed to be the first of the three shows the visitor would encounter upon entering the exhibition space. The 8,500-square-foot gallery would be devoted to tribal philosophies as they "are communicated in . . . languages, ceremonies, art and everyday life."[58] The take-home message developed by the curatorial team and the various community advisory boards was, "Our ancient philosophies are the foundation upon which our community identities are built."[59] The curatorial staff identified eight different communities for this gallery. All of them have annual ceremonies based in traditional knowledge that involve built structures, which are replicated in the exhibit. The eight communities are Yupik, Ojibwe, Lakota, Hupa, Tewa, Maya, Quechua, and Mapuche.

In my interview with Emil Her Many Horses, lead curator for the gallery, he described the layout of the gallery as it was being formalized in 2001:

> *Our Universes* gallery is arranged along the solar year. If you looked at the gallery, the pathway of the gallery, which we call the path of observance, it is actually the solar year told by the night sky, the constellations that you see in the night sky. One of the things about it is the constellations that we have selected are the constellations that can be seen by both the Northern and Southern Hemisphere, because what became very important was to try to figure out how to incorporate the Native people from the Southern Hemisphere. The gallery is divided, marked by solstice, equinox, solstice, equinox. The eight groups that are represented are selected because each one has an annual communal ceremony at some time of the year. And it has a built structure, and that built structure somehow represents the ordering of their cosmology or their universe. . . . When that annual community ceremony is held, [that is where they are] placed throughout the solar year [in the gallery].[60]

This gallery was created—as was the *Our Peoples* gallery, which I will elaborate upon soon—through a five-stage process that Craig Howe developed. Her Many Horses described the methodology as it unfolded for *Our Universes*:

> We began doing our own research first . . . and we built the bibliography, and then we saw who was publishing heavily on these communities. If we had a question about one, if we weren't sure about it, we actually flew in an academic person and presented the idea to them. And if they said, "Yes, that sounds like a great idea" or "That will work," [then we continued]. They often gave us a community contact. Then the academic person, we usually dropped them away; they still served as some kind of consultant. But . . . we didn't want to have heavy anthropological research presented; we wanted Native voice.
>
> So, we contacted a community person through the recommendation of the academic person, and then the community person . . . referred us to people [who] they thought would be good for us to work with from

the community. Because we are working with philosophy or spirituality a lot of time, we work with the spiritual leaders from those communities. . . . Once we have identified them—the people that we are going to work with—we go into the communities and do these presentations and ask them if they want to be involved. . . .

The first phase was getting their approval for them to work with us, and fortunately, they all did. In the first phase, we began to do some of the preliminary interviews and began to talk about the kind of framework—what ceremony could fit in and what it would represent.

In the second phase, we brought everyone here, because they were moving the collections down from New York [the Bronx storage facility]. And so, as they moved them down, we told them [which] groups we were working with. So, as those collections came down, they were all laid out here, so when the groups came, they could look at everything and decide what they wanted to include in the exhibition. We continued to talk during that time about the content.

When that phase was completed, we did a content presentation back to them with object schematics [and] with a framework of what we thought we heard them say. So, we went back into the communities and presented that. And [when] they approved that . . . —from that content approval—we turned that material over to our designers. . . .

In stage four, the designers . . . will come up with some sketches . . . and then they would develop a model. And we would take the model back to the community, and then the community looks at it and approves it, makes recommendations as to what they think. If there are any changes, then we come back and we meet about that . . . to present what we have heard. . . .

The final phase will be developing all the text panels, labels, and media. And that fifth stage eventually ends with the final approval of the project.[61]

The main objective of the *Our Universes* exhibit, according to the curatorial staff, is for people to realize that Native American philosophies are complex and they form the basis of how Native people see the world. This is the essential place to start, because Native philosophies and spiritualities have been the most misrepresented aspects of Indigenous life. The desire to challenge stereotypical understandings of Native worldviews was not lost on Her Many Horses:

I hope people will see the complexity of these Native groups—that their philosophies, their spiritualities are very, very complex—and [their] relationship to the world about them. There is nothing simplistic about them. They're all very spiritual people [working with the museum]. And some of the concepts that they want to present—what can I say?—these are men and women who have lived their whole lives this way—spiritually, following their Native traditions. And they are very knowledgeable about the traditional culture that they have and practice.[62]

For me, one of the most striking aspects of this gallery—even more so than the other two galleries—is that it contains information that tribal communities in recent years have been reluctant to display. Their reluctance is no surprise. Tribal sacred ceremonies have been exploited, and spiritual practices misrepresented. Disrespectful, distorted, demeaning, pejorative, and dehumanizing treatments have dominated the earlier exhibitions of Indigenous peoples produced at museums throughout the world.[63] However, in the *Our Universes* gallery, the NMAI, in cooperation with the spiritual leaders from each tribal group, was allowed to feature the very ceremonies—with the objects associated with them—that other museums have been asked not to represent or display.

In the case of the Lakota, the museum and the community advisory board decided to represent the Sun Dance ceremony, complete with a built structure and the objects in the collection that are related to the ceremony. The Sun Dance is a "microcosm of the Lakota Universe." The objects that the community selected for display from the NMAI collection represent the significance of the ceremony for Lakota people.

The Hupa decided to present the Jump Dance, the White Deerskin Dance, and the Brush Dance ceremonies, which are held every autumn. Contemporary issues around the struggle to continue these ceremonies would also be presented. For example, the exhibit would point to the fight that the Hupa face each year with the Bureau of Reclamation to "have the water levels in the Trinity River increased so that [they] may conduct their Boat Dance, which is an integral part of the White Deerskin Dance."[64] The exhibit would also present the ongoing struggle with Christian churches, which have continually pressured the community to cease these ceremonial practices.

I was at the museum in July 2000 when the Hupa delegation visited Washington, D.C., during stage two of the process: they came to select the objects to include in the gallery. As I mention earlier, only the curator who was developing the gallery usually attended the meetings with visiting tribal delegations. Because of the highly sensitive nature of the material discussed and the need to develop a good working relationship with the communities, the belief was that work on the issues should be conducted with only the curator and perhaps one other NMAI representative.

However, this decision also reflected an ongoing institutional divide between the Curatorial Department (those working on the exhibits directly with the communities, and the department in which I worked) and the Exhibits Department, which I will elaborate upon in a moment. James Volkert referred to the meetings as a "sequestering" of the communities by the Curatorial Department, which he claimed hindered the exhibition's development in the end.[65] In my interview with Bruce Bernstein, he described the difficulties that arose during the first meetings with the tribal delegations and the challenge of establishing trust with the communities:

> The first day was always the same with the group. Whichever one of the eight groups, it was always the same. It was really messy. They hadn't really worked together as a group perhaps, and we have never worked with them as a group, so it was all over the board. Inevitably, they would go back to the hotel that night, they would decide, and they would come back the next day, stand by the board or the big pad, and they would draw out their cosmology. The discussion then was not about what their cosmology is or is not, but what they wanted to tell the world about their cosmology. The conversation was most often in their own language. We were set way back. We sat on our collective hands and lips, because it was not our privilege to be in that conversation. They needed to work out what they wanted to tell the world about cosmology.[66]

To achieve the "museum different" relationship with Native peoples, the Curatorial Department needed to establish trust with tribal representatives and to reinforce the idea that the exhibitions would give primacy of voice to the communities themselves. During each of the delegation visits, the department hosted a reception for the tribal visitors and the museum staff. The Hupa appeared very pleased and excited to be at the museum, and they expressed surprise at how much authority they were given in determining content.

A few days earlier, the Hupa delegation had toured the Smithsonian's National Museum of Natural History (NMNH), and they were clearly angry at the museum's demeaning representation of their community in one of its exhibits. Developed in the middle part of the twentieth century, the NMNH exhibit was a diorama scene depicting historic Hupa life. It would be closed in May 2004, shortly before the NMAI opened. The objects on display were separated by category, and the exhibit did not convey the meaning of the objects to the Hupa, nor did it include their relevance for tribal members today. Hupa spiritual leader Merv George later commented that he overheard visitors at the museum comment that "this is how they used to live," as if the community had ceased to exist. Certainly, by keeping Hupa culture frozen in time and by not addressing the continuing cultural traditions of the community, this presentation reinforced the "vanishing Indian" stereotype. In the exhibits for the *Our Universes* gallery at the NMAI, the museum would attempt to convey the opposite—the ongoing cultural traditions and experiences of Native peoples.

For their section, the Anishinaabe (Hollow Water and Sagkeeng Band) from Manitoba chose to emphasize a spring ceremony of a highly sensitive nature. The "teaching lodge" to be featured in the spring equinox section included information that had never been displayed before, certainly not in a manner that was being developed in cooperation with the community's spiritual leaders.[67] The tensions surrounding this type of representation and the implications for the tribal people involved were not lost on the Curatorial Department. All the parties acknowledged the highly charged and sensitive nature of the presentations and the possibility that Anishinaabe from other bands might object to the displays and protest them. Emil Her Many Horses explained:

> This is something that even the groups discussed themselves. That they knew they were going to be presenting things that maybe other [tribal] people would disagree with. So, it really became a thing of building a relationship with them in which we said—and they even said it themselves—that people will dispute what we are saying. Or people will criticize what we are doing. So, it became really important to stick with that particular group and continue to work and develop that relationship with that particular group, even though they knew there eventually might be some criticism. But these were the things that they really wanted to present. In the case of the Anishinaabe, they knew that there was going to be some disagreements with some of the other groups [Anishinaabe bands], but that is what they wanted. So we had to honor that . . . [and] say, "Okay, if that is what you want to present, then we will do that."[68]

Tribal philosophies are embodied in ceremony, and the groups represented in the *Our Universes* exhibit were choosing to present their histories as peoples to the world. The Indigenous knowledge and worldview conveyed in the exhibitions reveal a great deal about tribal ways of knowing. That tribal people themselves were choosing to represent these at the NMAI was significant. In my interview with him, Gerald McMaster spoke about the importance of honoring the communities' desires to portray their ceremonial lives:

> It is the measure of our success in working with Native peoples. I go back to the beginning of that trust relationship with Native peoples, being transparent with Native peoples, being responsible and showing that they have agency and authority. . . . It's so important to our work that we can help them establish a relationship where they don't mind— "Yeah, put it on"—I mean, "That is who we are, but we know how you are going to treat it, and you will allow us to tell the story, and we will only tell so much" or whatever. As opposed to [us] saying, "This is how they do it."[69]

The second gallery, *Our Peoples*, would become a permanent 8,500-square-foot gallery devoted to presenting tribal histories. The original plan was to feature twelve different groups from across the Western Hemisphere. During my visits in 2000–2001, the exhibit plan included five components: the introduction, moorings, tribal histories, issues, and the conclusion. The gallery would begin with an introductory section, which would feature a presentation of the Choctaw origin story. The intent was to let people know that "it is not history from the point of European contact, but that Native peoples have histories that are culturally sovereign in a sense, and you do not need to have Europeans to tell you one's own history."[70]

On leaving the introductory area, visitors would then encounter one of six moorings. These are geographic spaces from across the hemisphere where two distinct tribal communities have been affiliated during their history. These moorings would convey that "places are part of history and history is part of place." In 2000, plans were under way to include six moorings, which together would feature twelve tribal histories: Seminole, Eastern Cherokee, Chiricahua Apache, Tohono O'odham, Nisga'a, Tahltan, Blackfeet, Kiowa, Nahua, Huichol, Tapirapé, and Urubú Ka'apor.[71] Each tribe would depict ten to twelve events in a 300-square-foot space, and the events would include the epitomizing moments that define who they are as a distinct people. Recognizing that most tribal histories are concerned with place and that a people's identity is tied to what happened in those places, the curatorial team sought to move away from a Western academic, linear cause-and-effect representation of Indigenous history.[72] Similar to the process used in creating *Our Universes*, a five-phase process involving the tribal communities in all aspects of development was used to create *Our Peoples*. The tribes were actively involved in conceptualizing the exhibits, determining their content, selecting objects, designing the displays, and developing scripts.

The plan was that as visitors walked through the mooring sections running north to south in the gallery, they would encounter five issue stations in the center of the gallery that would address the impact of colonization in the Western Hemisphere. Both historic and contemporary challenges to Indigenous sovereignty would be presented. These included land and resource rights: minerals, water, demarcation of lands, timber, and hunting and fishing.[73] In 1999, just before my research visits to Washington, the much-publicized issue of Makah whaling arose and was to be included in this section. Given the politically charged nature of the Makah controversy, however, this decision was later changed and issues facing the Inuit were featured instead.[74]

One of my earliest responses to this gallery, though impressive in scope, was that the nature of the presentation was confusing. I worried about how the museum would frame the histories told by the communities in their respective sections. *Our Peoples* was encompassing so much information that visitors could easily be overwhelmed by the complexity of it all. The exhibit was part natural history, part history, and part ethnography—all happening in the same place. What surprised me most was the sheer volume of information that would be covered: contemporary political issues, geological and geographical data—the flora and fauna in the tribal regions—and tribal histories. The plans felt too confusing, with no overriding take-home message.

Certainly, the needs of the audience had to be addressed as well. How could a generally uninformed public be able to grasp the complexity of the American Indian historical experience? For visitors to begin to appreciate the significance of what they saw, the events that the communities wanted to depict required an interpretation of the larger, broader themes in American Indian history. The events also called for a discussion of ongoing colonization and its effects throughout the hemisphere. The tribal stories and histories needed the wider context to be understood, yet this context seemed to be missing.

My other concern was that *Our Peoples* would end up being received in the same manner as the GGHC's 1994 inaugural exhibits had been—"too many voices speaking at once," as one of the staff members told me when we discussed the NMAI's evolving exhibition development methodology.[75] At the time of my research trip in December 2001, the curatorial team was reevaluating the scope of the gallery and was attempting to address these types of concerns. They eventually hired Comanche writer Paul Chaat Smith and Tuscarora artist and scholar Jolene Rickard to develop the NMAI-curated section of the *Our Peoples* gallery.

The final inaugural exhibition was *Our Lives*, which would address the contemporary experience of Indigenous people and includes eight different tribal communities. In 2000–2001, this gallery was farther behind in development than the others and featured only one community from south of the U.S. border. The communities featured in this exhibit are the Yakama Nation (Washington State); Saint-Laurent Métis (Manitoba, Canada); urban Indian community of Chicago; Kahnawake Mohawk (Quebec, Canada); Igloolik (Nunavut, Canada); Pamunkey Tribe (Virginia); Kalinago (Carib Territory, Dominica); and Campo Band of Kumeyaay Indians (California).

The *Our Lives* gallery examines these tribal communities' "relationship to their families, communities, homelands, and heritages" and explores how Indians "reconcile their tribal philosophies and histories to carve a unique identity today."[76] Some advisors to the gallery have included José Barreiro, Inés Hernández-Avila, Craig Howe, Truman Lowe, Gerald McMaster, Tessie Naranjo, Martin Oliver, and Ruth Phillips.[77] Serving as a curator for *Our Lives*, Cynthia Chavez Lamar worked closely with the communities in developing the community-curated sections of the gallery. Gabrielle Tayac and Jolene Rickard served as curators for the NMAI sections.

The process of developing the content for the exhibitions has not been without criticism. What does it mean not only to transfer curatorial authority but also to claim to let communities curate? As in every undertaking of this magnitude, disagreements abound about how to follow through on the curatorial directives. A staff member interviewed in 2001 questioned whether this was truly a new direction in museology and if the museum had provided enough benefits to tribal communities for their involvement with the NMAI:

The way that I see the work being done right now is that, in certain ways, I don't see it as very different from traditional museum development with Native peoples. Sure, they are involved, but I see them as just an information resource—like a book you pull off a shelf and you open, and there is the information on the Indian community. Okay, let's pull people to the table, talk to them, they are just like the books. We are the experts. We put together the exhibition, and all you guys have to do is tell us what you want.

So, in that way, sure, there is reciprocity to the extent that maybe we're implementing their ideas. But I think the reciprocity needs to go further. We need to be able to give back some kind of better learning opportunities, because we're this museum and we have all these people here with tremendous amounts of experience. And we go to these communities and ask people to put together exhibitions for us. Sure, it is just conceptually, but they don't have, they are not at the same knowledge level as us. So, why can't we do a better job at teaching them before we actually ask them to do something for us?[78]

Others have questioned whether the galleries were truly community curated and if it was accurate to state that the exhibitions were "without the filter, without the interpretation of the NMAI."[79] James Volkert, who was instrumental in developing the GGHC exhibits, raised concerns about whether the museum could fully claim that the exhibits were tribally controlled and curated. He believed that the NMAI needed to be more straightforward about its role in the process and should have taken more responsibility for its involvement in shaping the exhibits.

I think it is important for this museum to be a player, to be a partner in this process, to offer what we can offer. To not simply say, "You guys decide, you, the community, decide; we will do whatever you want to do, whatever you say, that's it. That is what we are doing." Well, that is not really true. We are not really doing that anyway. We are really shaping it, we're just saying we're not. My sense is [that] we need to be a little bit more up-front about the museum's role in making this stuff happen. I think it is right—the way we are doing it with the community—and so forth. I also think that we have a responsibility to be the bridge between the community and the visitors walking in the museum. We want people to get it. . . .

So, if we say you guys decide design—you guys decide this, and you guys decide that—we are not fulfilling our responsibilities completely, because that's our job. Our job is to do a design that communicates what you want to say to this group of people who we know over here. . . . It should certainly feel right and appropriate and all that stuff, but it's not fair if we were to say to the community, "Tell us what it should look like." It is just not fair. So, we are working through all of that. That point—and it is a somewhat contentious point in the museum—has been the cause of some difficulties over the past couple of years. . . . It has to do with that particular point, I think, as much as anything else.[80]

Volkert raised an important issue concerning the museum's role as a bridge between the communities and the public. He also identified the need for the museum to take a more active role in translating ideas in a manner that the audience can retain. Once again, the needs of the audience are critical. The projected attendance rates for the NMAI were high—more than 4 million people per year—hence the educational opportunities were and continue to be enormous. However, in my interviews with curatorial staff as well as during my tenure at the museum, the needs of the audience did not seem to be a primary concern.

Moreover, the staff members who were developing the galleries during the conceptualization phase were not working with an exhibition or education specialist. This struck me as odd, given my previous work experience at the Minnesota Historical Society (MHS) in the mid-1990s. At MHS, exhibit-development teams brought together a diversity of museum professionals, including exhibit curators, designers, graphic designers, researchers, production leads, as well as educators. These individuals were present from the outset.

In recent years, the museum profession has undergone major developments in addressing audience awareness. An entire new cadre of specialists has emerged to help museums make their exhibits accessible to the viewing public. In the early 2000s during the planning stages for the NMAI's exhibits, the annual meetings of the American Association of Museums—the largest museum organization in the country—devoted a significant number of sessions to exhibition-development techniques. In the old way of constructing exhibitions, an academic curator worked exclusively on content. This approach has changed dramatically. Today's curators work with a heightened awareness of the audience and of how visitors are likely to receive and experience exhibitions.[81]

I naturally recognize the complexity of this paradigm shift within the museum profession—the shift to addressing the needs of the audience—as well as the contests and conflicts that arise as a result. Still, it struck me as somewhat surprising that the needs of the audience were not being discussed at the NMAI. The museum's Curatorial Department seemed preoccupied with developing exhibitions that would reflect the community's perspective. They seemed to view themselves as mediating solely between the tribal communities and the museum. Mediating further with exhibition audiences—and needing help in doing this—did not seem to be of great concern.

My earliest impressions of the struggle within the museum between the Exhibits and Curatorial Departments over who should maintain control of the exhibition-development process are reflected in Jennifer Shannon's ethnography of the *Our Lives* exhibition. She states that the curators deferred to communities "for exhibit content and cultural expertise, and they saw their role as facilitators and advocates working in communities as requiring specific skills. The Exhibits department, on the other hand, viewed the Curators as not providing enough expertise, or museological guidance, to the communities to develop the best exhibition possible."[82]

Shannon goes on to argue that the crux of the issue was, "for Exhibits, . . . the power to make the exhibit a representation of Native life that is accessible to the audience (and in so doing benefits the reputation of Native communities)[;] for Curatorial it was the power to maintain a faithful representation to the wishes of the communities as to how they want to represent themselves (and in so doing maintain ethical relationships with Native communities)."[83] Shannon's depiction of the tensions between these two departments is certainly what I witnessed. Moreover, these conflicts were never resolved; the struggles continued until the museum's opening in 2004.

Shannon's argument reveals embedded assumptions made by both departments that are worth questioning. First, must it be either-or? In the minds of many at the museum, one almost had to choose between developing exhibitions that reflected Indigenous voices and perspectives and creating an exhibition that considered the needs of the audience. But is this binary or polarized choice necessary? Both approaches reflect values important to cutting-edge museum work. One wonders how the Native communities themselves might respond. If they had been asked from the outset whether they wanted to work with exhibition developers who were skilled in translating ideas into three-dimensional exhibits, might they have said yes? Is it perhaps a bit paternalistic to assume that members of a community advisory board are not invested in making sure that their messages reach their audience, which is comprised of both Native and non-Native individuals? Why would they not want their intended messages to be disseminated as clearly and effectively as possible within the exhibition space?

Second, isn't it possible that curators can be committed to both: to pursuing their work with the needs of the audience in mind and to privileging the perspectives of the community? Recently, Paul Chaat Smith reminded me of a critical lesson in exhibition development: "I learned that a kick-ass museum exhibit is [as] difficult to create as a great rock tune or a great novel."[84] I concur with this statement, as I learned early in my career that the process of developing a museum exhibit is long and arduous. Working from the best of intentions, well-trained academics or researchers may believe that they can change the manner in which Native people have been (mis)represented in the past by shifting authority away from anthropologists and museum curators to the community. This is unquestionably movement in a good direction. As a Native scholar and community member, I applaud this shift. Yet, by itself, this shift will not guarantee an effective exhibit. The process of translating great ideas into three-dimensional spaces requires the fine art of exhibition development. Instead of excluding those who have mastered this art, curators can create "kick-ass museum exhibits" by working in full collaboration with them.

I learned this lesson while I was at the Minnesota Historical Society. I watched as skilled exhibit curators, such as Kate Roberts, Brian Horrigan, and Marx Swanholm, took the research I had collected and transformed it into engaging, multilayered, audience-aware, and historically relevant exhibitions. While at the NMAI, I worked with a curatorial department that demonstrated an admirable commitment to rigorous, collaborative methodology with Indigenous communities. However, the curators seemed reluctant from the outset to engage the exhibition-development process in a way that involved others, most notably those who had developed the GGHC exhibits.

CONCLUDING IMPRESSIONS OF EXHIBITION PLANS: 2001–2002

My research visit in December 2001 gave me the opportunity to meet with several curators and other NMAI staff. At the conclusion of this trip, I spent a day touring the United States Holocaust Memorial Museum—my third visit to this powerful site. After another thought-provoking and moving experience, I wrote the following thoughts on the NMAI's plans for the inaugural exhibitions on the National Mall. I quote at length from my field notes and the brief essay I drafted shortly thereafter on my impressions:

In their philosophy and scope, the museum's exhibitions hold the promise of offering new interpretations of Native life. Allowing tribal communities to have curatorial authority makes a presentation of Native American history and culture possible on a scale never seen before. To allow Native communities to speak for themselves on their philoso-phies, histories, and identities will advance the historical record. It will also challenge commonly held stereotypes of Indian people predomi-nant in American culture.

The curatorial staff involved in the project have asserted that the Na-tive voice is fundamental to the development of the exhibitions and that the three inaugural exhibits will reflect Native participation. This im-portant site of tribal history and memory will provide an opportunity to correct historical wrongs through the telling of Native histories in a national museum. The Holocaust Museum—another national mu-seum located in D.C.—is a powerful testimony of Holocaust history and memory and conveys a story that clearly challenges visitors as it forces them to confront inhumanity on a scale so large that it is, at times, dif-ficult to comprehend.

The Native American story is tragic as well. My concern is that our stories will come across as more benign than those at the Holocaust Museum. Will the new museum challenge people to reflect on the atroc-ities committed against Native people and on those responsible for such actions? The new museum needs to challenge the very core of American consciousness. American identity is defined by what took place on the frontier and the supposed disappearance of the Indian is central not only to the idea of America but also to what it means to be an American.

People need to know that they did not invade virgin lands. Amer-ica was not a cultural backwater. Indigenous people were here; they achieved great civilizations. Their world began here—in North Amer-ica. We were not only here then, but we are still here now. If we celebrate only survival and benign histories—if we present stories in ways that fail to carry out the full force of their educational responsibilities—do we do a grave disservice to tribal peoples?

In his work *Preserving Memory: The Struggle to Create America's Holocaust Museum*, Linenthal traced the ongoing controversies over specific story lines presented at the Holocaust Museum. Whose stories would be told, and who would tell them? By contrast, the NMAI staff agrees for the most part to privilege Native voices and to allow com-munities to drive the content. In my experiences at the NMAI, the idea of turning curatorial control over to Native peoples has not been heav-ily criticized by staff members. Instead, the struggles have been over choosing the best methods to carry out that objective.

It will be interesting to see how the desire to showcase and privilege

Native voices might influence the audience's understanding of American Indian history and culture. The challenge is clear: to offer new interpretations and to critique the old assumptions and beliefs about the Indigenous experience that are so deeply embedded in the American historical consciousness. Will the NMAI's goals to transfer curatorial authority to Native voices—to have them do the telling—really offer new understandings?

The importance of this national site to changing the relationship between Native Americans and museums cannot be underestimated. Collectively, it will be our site of tribal memory—and tribal voices will tell the story.

As I reflect on my observations years after writing them, I realize I was concerned early on about the absence of a hard-hitting analysis of colonialism and its ongoing effects. I was also concerned about the needs of the audience: would visitors "get" the exhibits' messages? Would their awareness of Native people and issues change? Three years later, in September 2004, I would face the "final form" and assess whether the NMAI had addressed these issues.

CRITICAL REFLECTIONS ON THE GALLERY SPACE: 21 SEPTEMBER 2004 AND BEYOND

With these concerns in mind about the NMAI's evolving exhibition-development methodology, I engaged the final product: the inaugural exhibitions that opened on the National Mall in September 2004. Ira Jacknis has argued that, in many respects, a museum is "synonymous with its exhibitions." Exhibits are "a tangible and visible expression of a museum's fundamental concepts and values."[85] In the analysis that follows, I offer my reflections on the galleries, giving particular attention to the *Our Peoples* gallery, which focuses on tribal histories.

Since the NMAI's opening, its community-based approach for the Washington, D.C., site has been the topic of much discussion. The endeavor—both method and outcome—has been widely praised and equally critiqued. Several scholars and journalists have applauded the ambitious new "Indian museology."[86] In their view, the galleries—told from the perspective of Indigenous communities themselves—offer a complicated, nuanced, and ultimately effective presentation of Indigenous philosophy, history, and identity.

But for many, something is missing. Voices from all cultural and professional backgrounds have expressed dissatisfaction. These individuals view the exhibits as ineffective and vastly disappointing. For them, the final product is confusing, negating, and lacking in historical context.[87]

The NMAI emerged from a growing movement within museums to fundamentally change how museums do their work. For example, exhibits are more thematic than object based. They include more storytelling, especially in the first-person voice. Museums use collaborative methods that bring "source community" perspectives to the forefront and they decenter the authority that museum curators once held. As I walked through the NMAI, I saw these important new directions in the museum world on full display: state-of-the-art film presentations, first-person-voice text panels, large images of Native people everywhere, emphasis on twentieth-century survival, and more thematic and storytelling exhibitions than object-based exhibitions. In other words, I saw all of the markers of a museum that has embraced the new exhibition practices of the past several decades.

But I had hoped for more. Where were the moments of wonder and the places that touched my heart? Where was the larger understanding of history—of colonization and of what Native peoples have faced for centuries? I had worked behind the scenes, and I knew the depth of information that the communities had shared with the museum. I had also seen the U.S. Holocaust Memorial Museum and observed audiences taking in intensely challenging information. Compared to what I believed could have been done, the final form fell short. Through the various stages of translating the ideas, stories, and memories to the built structure of the exhibition itself, the power of some of these narratives just got lost.

When I was at the NMAI previously, I had reviewed some of the information that the communities had shared with the museum. The depth, quality, and power of what they shared repeatedly moved me, both intellectually and personally. When I later saw what was done with this information, I felt considerable sadness: the dynamism was gone. Museum ethnographer Jennifer Shannon writes of an NMAI curator's concern about the translation process that sheds light on this issue: "Without the intimate knowledge of the gallery landscape—its history and creation stories—known only to those who had 'been there,' the experience might seem like watching someone's 'wedding videos.'"[88] As a result, the exhibitions could be "boring and tedious to view."[89]

I fully acknowledge that the museum advances an important collaborative methodology in its exhibitions. However, my impressions of the outcomes— the inaugural exhibitions themselves—focus on three main areas of concern. First, its historical exhibits fail to present a clear and coherent understanding of colonialism and its ongoing effects. I am disappointed by the lack of emphasis on truth telling. At this site, the NMAI could finally tell the difficult stories to a nation that has maintained a willed ignorance of ongoing colonization over the past five hundred years. Unfortunately, my concerns in 2000–2001 that the museum might shy away from telling the hard truths came to pass.

Second, I argue that the museum conflates an Indigenous understanding of history with a postmodernist presentation of history. The result obscures the power of the museum's take-home message and compromises the museum's claim that the exhibits advance an Indigenous way of knowing.

Finally, some scholars now assert that this institution is a decolonizing museum. More, they claim the NMAI is a site of reconciliation between the U.S. government and Indigenous peoples. I contend that these assertions are seriously premature and co-opt the language of decolonization.

THE ABSENCE OF THE HARD TRUTHS: MISSED OPPORTUNITIES

Several scholars have given considerable attention to the NMAI's silences around the subject of genocide, the hard truths of colonization, and colonization's lasting impact on Indigenous communities. I notice these silences as well. Indeed, I am profoundly disappointed about the museum's missed opportunity to truly challenge the American master narrative. Instead of engaging in truth telling, the exhibitions articulate an abstract historical message that is confused and confusing. By so doing, it fails to hold those who walk through this museum accountable for the colonization of Native peoples. For a national museum of such prominence to reinforce the nation's historical amnesia is tragic, and that this site has such potential to create new understandings of American history makes the tragedy only greater.

Other scholars have argued that the museum does, in fact, include these stories.[90] According to them, the stories are told implicitly. They justify this choice by suggesting that it reflects an Indigenous way of knowing and teaching. The stories are there, they assure us; the museum just presents them in a manner that makes the visitor work for them. But is this an effective way to present Native American history and culture to a nation and a world that cling to a willed ignorance of Native history? Will the low-key approach shift the views of a society that harbors so many damaging stereotypes about who we are as Indigenous people? Will subtle messages about genocide challenge a nation that has defined itself by "playing Indian"?

In *Our Peoples*, glass cases are filled with stone figures, gold, swords, treaties, Bibles, and guns. But I did not see the hard-hitting images, stories, and statistics of genocide and other crimes of colonization that explained to visitors the significance of these objects. As Myla Vicenti Carpio argues, a storm display in *Our Peoples* problematically uses an event caused by *nature* as a metaphor for what happened to Indigenous people at the hands of the U.S. government and its citizens.[91] Tragically, this museum fails to tell the painful stories that every Native nation carries, and it obscures a message that should have been portrayed powerfully and prominently.

In comparison, the U.S. Holocaust Memorial Museum did not sacrifice the specifics of the difficult and painful history of the Jewish holocaust. It did not obscure the specifics of the Jewish people's past or try to frame the violence they suffered at the hands of the Nazis as a force of nature—a storm. Nor did it try to make a larger theoretical argument about how history is constructed. The curators present the specifics in a moving narrative that does not surrender coherency to make some sort of relativistic argument in the service of postmodernism.[92]

The most prevalent stories at the NMAI are those emphasizing Native survival—"survivance," and this emphasis does, indeed, tackle head-on the "vanishing race" stereotype that dominated earlier museum representations. But the museum fails to provide the fundamental context for survival. To understand survival and Indigenous agency (another popular theme in the museum), one must have a clear understanding of what we were up against— the government policies and campaigns designed to destroy us. The more painful stories of the last five hundred years of colonization are excluded or, if they are there, do not figure prominently. I agree with the American Indian Movement activists who criticized the museum for not telling the story of the American Indian holocaust along with our stories of survival. As they stated, "The museum falls short in that it does not characterize or does not display the sordid and tragic history of America's holocaust against the Native Nations and peoples of the Americas."[93]

The museum's silences around the tragedies that took place were, again, not an oversight but intentional—a conscious choice. Founding director Richard West defends this choice by saying that the period of tragedy is only a small portion of our time in the Americas: "Here's what I want everyone to understand. As much and as important as that period of history is . . . it is at best only about 5 percent of the period we have been in this hemisphere. We do not want to make the National Museum of the American Indian into an Indian Holocaust Museum."[94] However, if this painful period makes up "only about 5 percent" of the broad sweep of our history, as West claims, where is our earlier history? The museum offers no extensive treatment of our pre-Columbian past in any of the galleries. Although West seems to imply that the thousands of years before contact are critical and that the museum will give equal emphasis to the entire span of our history (not just the last five hundred years of colonization), those earlier periods are not reflected on the exhibition floor. The time-depth argument is important, and it could serve as the principal illuminator of our deep history in these lands. But our ancestral past is not presented prominently at the NMAI in any of the three inaugural exhibitions.

Furthermore, while it is accurate to say that the past five hundred years do not constitute the entire span of Indigenous history, this period has had a disproportionate impact on our communities and cultures. And its impact on our communities continues. Colonization is not over, nor has the holocaust in the Americas ever been fully recognized. The continuing legacies of these policies in Indian Country are very much a part of our contemporary experience and lives continue to be lost because of them. The period may have been short relative to deep ancestral histories, but it has had the most devastating impact.

ABSTRACTION, POSTMODERNISM, AND AUDIENCE CONFUSION

One of the most interesting arguments made by several scholars is that the museum is advancing an Indigenous way of knowing in the exhibitions—an "Indigenous museology." If the more subtle messages are not coming across, they contend, then non-Natives and even some Native people are simply not working hard enough to understand them.[95] They argue that the exhibitions are designed to be challenging, that they reflect engagements with both postmodernist and postcolonial critiques, and that they embody decolonizing strategies.

I agree that many of the very thoughtful displays at the institution are there to challenge us, and they also provide visitors with new insights by presenting Indigenous knowledge from the Indigenous perspective. But why is this new knowledge system at work in the institution not clearly conveyed? Given that the public carries so many stereotypes about who we are as Native people, isn't it critical that the exhibits engage those issues right away? Reviews of the exhibitions indicate that visitors often leave feeling overwhelmed, confused, and frustrated by the display techniques. If the museum is to challenge stereotypes that have long dominated the representation of our histories and cultures, then content, design, text, and images must be clear, consistent, and coherent.

The museum's failure to tell the more painful stories of colonization combined with the curators' inability to convey their ideas clearly to the public persists throughout the *Our Peoples* gallery. Eight community-curated sections plus sections curated by NMAI staff focus on tribal history. Given this subject, *Our Peoples* is critical to changing public misconceptions about Native peoples. And the importance of the NMAI-curated section titled "Evidence" in particular cannot be emphasized enough. Curator Paul Chaat Smith has stated that the content covered in this section "is the *raison d'etre* for the existence of the museum itself" and comprises roughly half of the gallery space in *Our Peoples*.[96] This display section is meant to tell the "biggest untold story of all": that contact between vastly different worlds changed everything.[97] The exhibit deals with the aftermath of "contact"—disease, warfare, dispossession of lands and resources—and the role that Christianity played in the process. "Evidence" is a heavily object-based exhibit—yet without any labels associated with individual objects.

At the entrance to the gallery, the word "Evidence" is emblazoned on a large frosted glass wall with objects buried underneath, designed to suggest that the exhibit itself is an "excavation site . . . where history is buried, lost and found."[98] From there, visitors find a case with the large black numbers "1491" filled with figurines that are there to supposedly represent the diversity of tribal nations before contact. Next are cases filled with gold and other riches of the Americas, symbolizing the great wealth in abundance throughout the hemisphere. From there, visitors see weapons, such as swords and guns, which one could assume were used to plunder these resources. Behind the gun display is a case filled with Bibles, and around the corner is a case filled with treaties. The guns, Bibles, and treaties form the storm installation. These objects represent the forces—guns, Christianity, and foreign governments—that all tribal nations in the Western Hemisphere faced after invasion.

Some have argued that all of these "symbols of power" are just meant to overwhelm visitors. This is perhaps why the curators chose not to provide labels with identifying information, such as tribal affiliations, provenance, and dates.[99] In her review essay, Gwyneira Isaac argues that this gallery reflects an engagement "with [the] postmodern discourse on the history of colonialism—a discourse that stems from the academic critique of how history is created, constructed and controlled."[100] She further states that "in *Our*

View of the guns that appear in the *Our Peoples: Giving Voice to Our Histories* exhibit at the National Museum of the American Indian in Washington, D.C. Photo by Walter Larrimore. Courtesy of the National Museum of the American Indian, Smithsonian Institution.

Peoples [curators] Jolene Rickard and Paul Chaat Smith do not want us to learn the details of Native American history, they want us to question our ethnocentric ideas about history itself."[101]

This may be a valid role for a museum. However, it took Isaac—a highly trained academic—two different encounters with this institution to come to these conclusions about the exhibit's intended meaning. Should an exhibition require a person to be well schooled in postmodernist theory to engage effectively with the displays? It is one thing for a curator or academic to understand an abstract, theory-laden argument behind an exhibit; it is another thing entirely to convey this message to the public in an engaging, moving, and compelling manner. A majority of the estimated 4-plus million people coming to this museum annually have only one opportunity to engage with the exhibition—only one. Moreover, they do not bring with them an extensive background in either postmodern theory or museum training. "Evidence" was created to prepare visitors for the eight community-curated history presentations that follow in the *Our Peoples* gallery. Its task was to set the context and to frame what the communities chose to present. Was this the most effective way to achieve this goal?

The decision to pursue an abstract story line driven by a postmodernist critique was, in my view, a poor choice for the museum. Abstraction is not

Bible case in the *Our Peoples: Giving Voice to Our Histories* exhibit at the National Museum of the American Indian in Washington, D.C. Photo by Katherine Fogden. Courtesy of the National Museum of the American Indian, Smithsonian Institution.

an effective method of presentation for a museum in general. However, using this method to try to educate a nation out of its willed ignorance of its treatment of Indigenous peoples and away from the policies and practices that led to genocide in the Americas: this is bound to fail for all but a few museumgoers. Our survival, as many people have argued, is one of the greatest untold stories. Yet, to tell this story in all its power and import, we must also tell the specifics of this difficult and painful history.

To illustrate my point about the dangers of representing history in the abstract manner that the NMAI chose for the "Evidence" gallery, I would like to share an encounter I had in front of the gun display in October 2005. My impressions of that display remain the same as they did on the first night that I walked through this exhibit in September 2004. As a Native woman, historian, and museum professional, I found this case highly problematic. I was seriously worried whether the intended message of the display would reach the audience. For example, would the audience read the display as another depiction of Indigenous people as warlike savages engaged in a futile battle to evade encroachment on their lands? Or, just as problematically, would audiences read it as a glorification of weaponry? Suffice it to say, such takeaway

Treaty case in the *Our Peoples: Giving Voice to Our Histories* exhibit at the National Museum of the American Indian in Washington, D.C. The guns, Bibles, and treaties all form the storm installation. Photo by Walter Larrimore. Courtesy of the National Museum of the American Indian, Smithsonian Institution.

messages fail to convey the broader meanings of invasion and genocide and the devastating impact that guns have had on Indigenous peoples.

Whenever I return to this gallery and stand in front of the gun case, I always notice who is standing with me. On every one of these occasions—numbering more than twenty now—I am almost always standing with men. Time after time, they stare with awe and intense concentration on the case densely packed with guns. From my vantage point, it looks as if they are focusing on the objects themselves, instead of on reading the text panels. Those panels might have given visitors the context that other scholars claim is there: that these guns were used against Native people as one of the three forces they faced after invasion and, at the same time, that Native people have "transformed the tools of colonialism into the instruments of integration, empowerment, and even liberation."[102]

On one particular October afternoon in 2005, one year after the museum's official opening, I stood in front of the case with several middle-aged men and two young schoolboys, both around ten years of age. The boys were chatting excitedly to each other and pointing to various guns in the case. Their animated conversation was interrupted abruptly when a middle-aged

Storm installation in the *Our Peoples: Giving Voice to Our Histories* exhibit at the National Museum of the American Indian in Washington, D.C. Photo by Walter Larrimore. Courtesy of the National Museum of the American Indian, Smithsonian Institution.

woman told them loudly that they were not to be there. At this point, I decided to go over and introduce myself to the woman. I explained that I was a historian conducting research on the museum, and that I couldn't help overhearing their conversation. I mentioned that I had heard her say that they shouldn't be there, and I was wondering why. She proceeded to tell me that she was their teacher, and the school has a policy that forbids the children from entering this gallery to view the gun case. Somehow, though, they manage to hear about it anyway, and many are determined to find it. At this moment, one of the boys asked her, "If you could have any one of these guns, which one would you choose?" She quickly responded none and told them that they must return to the group. That the children were banned from viewing the case while on a school field trip because of the violence that these guns embody speaks volumes. The experience offers a display—a spontaneous microexhibit in response—about the dangers of using "implicit" means to make a point to the general museumgoing audience.

I think this encounter is revealing. It shows what can happen when curators choose an abstract, object-based exhibition with very little contextual information to convey a complex history. The text that is included does not connect the abundance of visual information to a larger narrative of systematic violence against Indigenous people. I worried on several occasions whether the larger argument that the curators were trying to make would be lost on visitors. Given the many misconceptions that the general public holds about Native people, the great risk is that the intended messages would be "hijacked"—that is, read "on the basis of . . . misinformation and stereotypes."[103]

And this is precisely what happened. The intended arguments that I assume the curators attempted to convey appeared to be entirely lost on the people I spoke with that day. I remain greatly concerned that the curators' intended messages will continue to be hijacked and read within ethnocentric narratives. According to Claire Smith, the absence of labels in this installation is strategic. It reflects an Indigenous way of imparting knowledge, where knowledge has to be earned. As she argues: "People have to work at understanding the exhibits- and perhaps this is the point. They have been given the power to determine what is important for themselves, and this will vary according to each individual. . . . This is an Indigenous, not a Western, route to knowledge."[104]

Not only is this a problematic and essentialist argument, but it also presumes far too much about the knowledge base of visitors. What happens when the visitors who are supposed to come to their own conclusions bring with them deeply embedded myths and stereotypes about Indigenous communities? What happens when the audience is completely unaware that another knowledge system exists or is at work in the museum? Audience evaluations will help demonstrate what visitors are taking away and whether they do, indeed, understand the knowledge system at work in the museum.

I would like to cite an example from the work of Oxford University anthropologist Laura Peers, who conducted an impressive ten-year ethnographic study on living history sites in the Great Lakes region. In *Playing Ourselves: Interpreting Native Histories at Historic Reconstructions*, she critically examines the complex process of representing Native American and First Nations history at reconstructed historic sites. This is the first major study to focus exclusively on Indigenous interpreters who work to incorporate Native themes into the programming at historic sites. Peers's study captures the complexities of their roles and how these histories are negotiated and produced. Her study also provides insights into the impact of the sites on shaping the public's understanding of Native American history.

One of the most important conclusions that Peers draws from this study is the problem inherent in not providing enough context for the visitor. For many who show up at these sites, what they encounter is new information about the Indigenous past and present. The history of the site is revised in ways that challenge prevalent attitudes rooted in the American master narrative, including stereotypes about Native people, history, and cultures. Yet master-narrative conditioning and filters do not fall away readily, and their influence persists in shaping the perceptions of visitors. As a result, Peers discusses how the revisionist messages presented at these sites can, even with the best of intentions, be hijacked. For many visitors, the take-away message can be contrary to or even the opposite of what those managing the site hoped to convey.

A case in point is a new interpretative strategy developed at Colonial Michilimackinac in Michigan. The site is a reconstructed eighteenth-century fur-trade post. The manager at this site wanted to include a war post as part of the interpretation. The intended message was a more nuanced argument on "the participation of the upper Great Lakes Indians in the American Revolution . . . [and] to explain how Michilimackinac functioned as a recruitment and staging center for Indian warriors in the 1770s."[105]

Even though the intended message is historically accurate and appropriate for this site, the interpreters Peers interviewed claimed that this more nuanced, revisionist message was not received as such: "Most visitors did not have this knowledge . . . and often made comments indicating that they associated it with stereotypes about savages, scalping, and the warpath, as well as with the much-emphasized 1763 Ojibwa attack on the fort."[106] The well-intentioned idea was designed to combat stereotypes and to challenge visitors to new understandings, but many visitors recast it through the stereotypical narratives that they brought with them to the site. As Laura Peers argues, "While the stories suggested by artifacts are crucial, it is dangerous to let them remain implicit, for—as with the war post—they can be 'read' by visitors as easily within misinformed narratives as they can within intended ones."[107]

Peers's study acknowledges the embeddedness of the many myths and stereotypes concerning the Indigenous past and present that visitors bring with them; she emphasizes throughout her study that these stereotypes, this cultural baggage, must be challenged explicitly. There is danger in letting messages in exhibitions remain implicit, especially given how misunderstood and misrepresented Indigenous communities and our history have been. Interestingly, the video in the NMAI's "Evidence" section acknowledges this very point. In *Making History*, narrator Floyd Favel movingly tells visitors that we as Native people have long had our histories framed and powerful representations formed by forces not of our own making. As he states:

"The subjects here, us, have been portrayed from the outside. Our stories told by others to explain or justify their own agendas. Or we've been considered people without a history. The truth is we care passionately and have fought at great cost to reclaim knowledge of the past. We are left then, with this paradox: for all our visibility, we have been rendered invisible and silent. A history-loving people stripped of their own history."[108]

Disappointingly, though, the history that is conveyed in the rest of the "Evidence" section does not fulfill the video's promise and fails to provide a hard-hitting analysis of the forces associated with the colonization process—forces that have sought to silence our versions of the past. The death caused by guns and swords, the forced conversions and abuse at the hands of Christian churches, the devastation that resulted from European diseases (some deliberately spread), and the colonial policies and practices of foreign governments that broke treaties and attempted to destroy our worlds: these realities were not explicitly told. Unless visitors knew about these human-caused catastrophes beforehand, they could potentially leave as unaware of them as when they arrived.

As it is, visitors walk past cases of guns, swords, Bibles, and treaties. They encounter an abstract, object-driven display that fails to connect these objects of power to the forces of power that devastated our worlds. The museum has missed an important opportunity to make explicit how colonization operates and what it has done to Indigenous peoples throughout the hemisphere.[109]

DECOLONIZATION AND RECONCILIATION: BEGINNING WITH TELLING COLONIZATION'S HARD TRUTHS

What is at stake in not speaking the hard truths? The museum has long stood by its story: contemporary survival is what Native people asked to be represented in the exhibits, and the NMAI's curators honored their request. And, yes, the message that "we are still here" is important to convey. But if the hard truths of colonialism are not also told, this message loses its most important context. Visitors miss the primary reason the message of survival is so amazing and worthy of celebration. We did survive a holocaust in North America, and even though the U.S. government refuses to take responsibility for this act, we as Indigenous people must name this history for what it was: genocide.

Apache scholar Nancy Mithlo bravely calls into question our failure to face this history. Emphasizing our survival without sufficiently explaining what we were surviving endangers our self-knowledge. She states: "Couldn't the concept of the holocaust museum be just as appropriate for recognizing the genocide of American Indians? Why are we always celebrating the survival of Native American culture, instead of truly understanding just how much we have lost and how we have lost it? It is this type of representation I am interested in and as far as I know, no museums are talking about my people truthfully in this manner."[110]

My desire to complicate the discourse on the NMAI over the years stems from my concern that scholars co-opt the language of decolonization when they assert that this institution is a decolonizing museum. In an essay published shortly after the museum's opening, Australian archaeologist Claire Smith argues:

> As a National Museum charting new territory, the NMAI is leading a nation down a path of understanding and reconciliation. . . . A cultural and spiritual emblem on the National Mall of Washington, D.C., the Smithsonian's National Museum of the American Indian exemplifies decolonisation in practice. Through being consciously shaped by the classification systems, worldviews and philosophies of its Indigenous constituency, this new national museum is claiming moral territory for Indigenous peoples, in the process reversing the impact of colonialism and asserting the unique place of Native peoples in the past, present and future of the Americas.[111]

Smith asserts that the NMAI "exemplifies decolonisation in practice . . . reversing the impact of colonialism," yet she ignores the absence of a clear and consistent discussion of colonization throughout the museum. Such a discussion is critical, for, as Waziyatawin Angela Wilson and Michael Yellow Bird argue, "The first step toward decolonization . . . is to question the legitimacy of colonization."[112] The NMAI's silence around the history of colonialism throughout the Americas fails to challenge the public's steadfast refusal to face this nation's genocidal policies. Yet these policies not only had but also continue to have a devastating impact on Indigenous people. The NMAI's silence does not help Native communities combat this legacy today. It does not help them recognize how colonialism has affected all areas of their lives, nor does it help them embark on the necessary changes to move toward decolonization and community healing.

I also question Smith's assertion that the NMAI is "leading a nation down a path of understanding and reconciliation." This seems presumptive. The U.S. government has never formally apologized to Indigenous people, nor is a reparations process in place. In her essay "Performing Reconciliation at the National Museum of the American Indian: Postcolonial Rapprochement and the Politics of Historical Closure," Canadian scholar Pauline Wakeham highlights how the NMAI's opening ceremonies "bypassed any performance of apology for colonial injustices and moved straight to a joyous, depoliticized celebration of reconciliation."[113] Her argument focuses on the museum's opening ceremonies, yet I would argue that the desire to move to a "joyous, depoliticized celebration of reconciliation" permeates the entire institution. It is certainly reflected in its exhibitions. In all three of the permanent galleries at the NMAI, the exhibits fail to explicitly address the hard truths of colonization. With this silence, the museum sends the implicit message that colonization's brutal realities are a closed chapter in our history.

To be clear, I am not discounting the role that Native American knowledge systems have played in influencing aspects of the NMAI's development. Nor am I dismissing the museum's important collaborative methodology with Indigenous communities throughout the Western Hemisphere. The NMAI represents the most ambitious collaborative project to date. Collaboration and the inclusion of Native voices in all aspects of museum practice reflect the most important new direction in the last thirty-plus years of our relationships to mainstream museums. But these changes alone are not decolonization.

While I fully acknowledge these steps, my goal is to raise awareness of the complicated identity of the NMAI. The NMAI reflects a still-evolving relationship between Indigenous peoples and museums. I therefore caution against referring to the NMAI as a decolonizing museum or as a form of "museological reconciliation." To do so is highly problematic. Precisely as Pauline Wakeham argues, such a view "lends itself to complicity with and co-optation by the state for the purposes of staging postcolonial rapprochement via the cultural milieu of museums."[114]

As the NMAI charts its future course, the institution must take seriously the calls for historical narratives that challenge deeply embedded stereotypes and colonizing mind-sets. The assumption of Native disappearance in the wake of westward expansion in the nineteenth century is but one of many stereotypes to be challenged. Certainly, the nation's willed ignorance to face its colonialist past and present must be challenged as well. Truths need to be told specifically—and outright. Presenting the colonizing forces in our history through a passive voice—subtly and implicitly—is not effective, as my encounters in front of the gun case suggest.

W. Richard West has stated that this museum "make[s] possible the true cultural reconciliation that until now has eluded American history."[115] But how can this "cultural reconciliation"—or any form of reconciliation, for that matter—be achieved without first recognizing what actually took place? Reconciliation cannot be set in motion, as scholar Rebecca Tsosie has argued, "without an acknowledgement of responsibility for the historical wrongs and their continuing effect."[116]

The messages coming from the museum are that the historical traumas we have suffered as Indigenous people are a closed chapter. Yet what process brought closure? The U.S. government and its citizens have not formally acknowledged—much less apologized for, rectified, or repaired—the harms perpetrated against Indigenous peoples. Nor have we as Native communities had a forum in which to tell these painful stories.

This institution and its exhibitions could provide such a forum. Yet, to do so, the museum must describe the genocidal acts committed against Indigenous peoples and must name the specifics of a shameful history that those who have benefitted from Indigenous suffering should be held accountable for. It must tell the truth to a nation and a world that have willfully ignored this history and tried to silence our versions of the past. Without these actions, this museum on the National Mall in Washington, D.C., will remain a museum that serves the interests of the nation-state.

If we assess this museum in relation to the growing movement for decolonization—for which telling the truth about our past and present is critical—this museum falls short in its mission. It does not move us forward in our efforts for decolonization and reparative justice. If this institution is to make a positive difference in the lives of Native peoples, it must use this national space as a place for education, commemoration, and truth telling.

I am left with the question, then, of how museum exhibitions can effectively disrupt colonial constructions of Native history and culture, engage in truth telling, and honor Indigenous understandings of history and contemporary survival. I believe I have found a place that is very successful in achieving these complex goals and that models a decolonizing museum practice in a tribal museum, the Ziibiwing Center of Anishinabe Culture & Lifeways, the subject of the chapter that follows.

four

THE ZIIBIWING CENTER OF
ANISHINABE CULTURE & LIFEWAYS
Decolonization, Truth Telling, and Addressing
Historical Unresolved Grief

THE ZIIBIWING CENTER: INDIGENIZING MUSEUM PRACTICE

I first visited the Saginaw Chippewa Indian Tribe of Michigan's Ziibiwing Center of Anishinabe Culture & Lifeways in May 2006 while attending a tribal museum development symposium on their reservation. Since my first viewing, I realized that this community center embodies a decolonizing museum practice and creates an engaging learning experience for visitors. The 34,349-square-foot facility includes a state-of-the-art research center, changing exhibition gallery, meeting rooms, a gift shop, tribal collections storage, and a 9,000-square-foot permanent exhibition space that features the history, philosophy, and culture of the Saginaw Chippewa community—told from their perspective. This cultural center, though unique in content, grows from an emerging movement of large-scale tribal museum development over the last twenty years. This movement includes places such as the Museum at Warm Springs (Warm Springs, Oregon), the Tamástslikt Cultural Institute (Pendleton, Oregon), and the Mashantucket Pequot Museum and Research Center (Mashantucket, Connecticut).

I encountered the Ziibiwing Center at a critical moment in my thinking. As previously mentioned, I had been pondering the potential of museums to serve as sites of decolonization and how Indigenous history and memory might be represented in exhibitions. This center, more than others I have visited, engages directly with the theoretical concepts of historical trauma

Interior entryway of the Ziibiwing Center of Anishinabe Culture & Lifeways. Courtesy of the Ziibiwing Center of Anishinabe Culture & Lifeways, Saginaw Chippewa Indian Tribe of Michigan, Photography by Penrod/Hiawatha Co.

and historical unresolved grief. While I define and contextualize these concepts in chapter 1, I think some of this information bears repeating here. Lakota scholar and social worker Maria Yellow Horse Brave Heart developed these theories based on more than twenty-five years of direct-practice experience working with Lakota and other Native American communities. Brave Heart defines historical trauma as a "cumulative emotional and psychological wounding, over the lifespan and across generations, emanating from massive group trauma experiences."[1] Historical unresolved grief is "the impaired or delayed mourning" that is a consequence of the many traumas that Indigenous people have faced as a result of colonization.[2] This psychological pain leads to the "historical trauma response," which gives rise to the many social problems that continue to plague Indian Country, including "substance abuse . . . self-destructive behavior, suicidal thoughts and gestures, depression, anxiety, low self-esteem, anger, and difficulty recognizing and expressing emotions."[3]

Along with other colleagues, Brave Heart established a nonprofit organization, the Takini Network, to address many of these problems, most notably through an intervention program called the Historical Trauma and Unresolved Grief Intervention (HTUG). HTUG seeks to address the ongoing legacies of historical trauma in Indigenous communities. A central goal of this distinguished program is to assist Native people in understanding the historical events that led to Native communities' unresolved grief. In other words, it builds a critical understanding of the colonization process. To help communities process their grief and to assist the healing process, the program goes on to foster a reattachment to traditional Native values by incorporating tribally specific ceremonies and cultural teachings.[4] Yet this healing process must begin with addressing the historical process of colonization and the toll it has taken on tribal people and communities. Naming the specifics of the difficult history of U.S.-Indian relations, Native people and communities can begin to frame their history within the context of colonization.

The literature on historical trauma and historical unresolved grief has had a major influence on the Ziibiwing Center team, evident in their exhibitions and cultural programming. In her application in 2008 for an award from the Harvard University Honoring Nations program, which recognizes and honors Indigenous nation-building efforts, current Ziibiwing director Shannon Martin articulated the staff's engagement with these theoretical concepts powerfully and eloquently. In her essay responding to the question of how each applicant's program assists in making tribal governance efforts more effective, she wrote about the problems and challenges that the Ziibiwing Center addresses:

> Numerous studies indicate troubling statistics for American Indian people: high suicide rates and high mortality rates, prevalent substance abuse, diabetes, and heart disease. In our research, we reviewed studies that directly correlate these systemic problems to inherited grief or multi-generational historic trauma as a result of colonization, forced relocation, and boarding schools. At the Ziibiwing Center, we acknowledge this history and work with our community to move in positive directions to heal the age-old wounds. The issues may seem . . . complicated, but we believe that by providing entry points for our people to gain access to our true history, culture, and language, we can, so to speak, turn back time.[5]

The Ziibiwing Center actively engages the theoretical concepts of historical trauma and historical unresolved grief to begin the healing process for Native people. By so doing, it reflects the finest in twenty-first-century tribal museum practice. The Ziibiwing team's choice to design the site around assisting the community in healing "age-old wounds" is perhaps the center's most significant role. This focus exemplifies its subjectivity both as a cultural center and as a site for community empowerment and decolonization.

In the sections that follow, I will discuss how this exemplary tribal museum developed and the impact of its exhibitions and programming on visitors, on the community, and on Indian Country as a whole.

ORIGIN STORY

From the outset, the Ziibiwing Center of Anishinabe Culture & Lifeways has been a tribally controlled project. The origin story of the museum begins with the formation of the Ziibiwing Cultural Society (ZCS)—a collective of concerned tribal members who came together in 1993–94 to address issues related to the Native American Graves Protection and Repatriation Act (NAGPRA). NAGPRA passed in 1990 and provides a legal means for Native individuals and tribes as well as Native Hawaiian organizations to reclaim Native American human remains, sacred objects, funerary objects, and objects of cultural patrimony from museums and federal agencies. The law also provides protection for Indigenous burial sites discovered on tribal and federal lands in the United States. NAGPRA is highly significant as human rights legislation, and the law requires museums and federal agencies to compile inventories of their holdings and to notify tribes of the human remains and objects in their collections.

Following passage of the law in 1990, inventories from museums and federal agencies began flooding into the office of Ronald Falcon, who at the time was the tribal chairman for the Saginaw Chippewa reservation. These inventories included lists of human remains and cultural objects that were identified as being possibly affiliated with the Saginaw Chippewa Indian Tribe. Falcon's sister-in-law Bonnie Ekdahl decided to take a leadership role in gathering members of the community together to address the issue, and close to fifty people showed up for the first meeting in late 1993. She described her reasons for sharing the information contained in the inventories with tribal members:

> It was really shocking to see the lists of human remains. It was really horrifying. You hear about those things, but to actually see the evidence, and the proof, and the admission, I guess, by all those institutions of learning, that they had these people . . . who were our ancestors. So, that was enough catalyst for me, and for a lot of other people, to say, "Well, let's try to do something." But then, part of doing something is, you can't just go out and retrieve and demand without having a plan for what you are going to do when you bring them back. There were

all the artifacts . . . and then the bodies, the people themselves. So we started out by just having a general session. . . . About fifty people came, and we sat down and just did a kind of a strategic plan. A brainstorming session for the first steps of a strategic plan. Like, what did people think? What should the priorities be? What did they want people to know about? And it kept coming up—a cultural center. So, if we are going to do that [request repatriation], then we are going to have to have someplace to put these things. But, always knowing that we weren't intending on keeping them. We were going to put them back into the earth. To restore basic human dignity.[6]

The Saginaw Chippewa Indian Tribe sanctioned the Ziibiwing Cultural Society as a tribal organization in 1994, and NAGPRA-related issues were central to its formation and work from the start. In 1995, the Nibokaan Ancestral Cemetery was established on the Saginaw Chippewa reservation to rebury the ancestors and funerary objects reclaimed under NAGPRA. In 1996, the Ziibiwing Cultural Society successfully negotiated for the return of 108 ancestral remains from Michigan State University. This repatriation served as the opening chapter in the ZCS's work on repatriation. Since 1996, close to 400-plus ancestral remains and 65,000 associated funerary objects have been reburied in the Nibokaan Ancestral Cemetery.

While NAGPRA-related work defined the early years of the organization led by Bonnie Ekdahl, the ZCS initiated efforts to build credibility within the community by expanding the organization's role. During the mid-1990s, the Saginaw Chippewa were in the midst of planning for their major gaming facility, the Soaring Eagle Casino and Resort, and the ZCS became involved with the tribal gaming operations in several key ways. First, Ekdahl and the ZCS board offered to assist with the design of the casino after a non-Native architectural firm submitted preliminary design plans that turned out to be stereotypical and kitschy. Tribal member Paul Johnson characterized the early designs for the tribal casino as "a monument to loggers."[7] The ZCS decided to step in and assist by drawing upon the talents of gifted artists in the community, including Daniel Ramirez, who created beautiful Anishinabe designs that were later incorporated throughout the casino complex.

During this period, the ZCS also offered to help run the gift shops located in the casino. This served two central purposes. One was to provide a place for tribal artists to sell their arts and crafts, thereby supporting these efforts within the community. Second, the gift shops created an income generator for the ZCS that would later play a critical role in its becoming a viable tribal cultural center. By serving as a facilitator and bringing community artists to the table to assist in the design of the casino—and later to run the casino gift shops—the zcs situated itself as a valuable source of information in the community. Its work with the tribe's gaming enterprise gave it a significant position in the community as a source of cultural knowledge. As Bonnie Ekdahl stated, "We kind of came in through the side door and became part of that world, with the arts, and the stores, and the enrollments, and then they started looking to us, like, oh, they can help us. They'll help us. Because there is always a need for cultural information. So we became that [source]."[8]

At this time, the zcs worked with James McClurken, a historian hired by the Saginaw Chippewa to conduct research for a land lawsuit. The zcs received copies of all the historic documents he collected while he was conducting his research at libraries and archives across the country. It then made these documents available to tribal members who wanted to see them. Enrollment issues in the community were heating up during this period, because gaming successes were producing per-capita payments to enrolled Saginaw Chippewa tribal members.

The biggest milestone for the project came in 1996 with an award of $3.5 million. The award enabled Bonnie Ekdahl and the zcs board to build a permanent staff. With the award came the responsibility to develop something, as Ekdahl explained. With adequate staff, the zcs was able to hold ongoing meetings with community members, to update tribal council members on recent acquisitions of research documents, and to form plans for a cultural center. But Ekdahl exercised caution. She had to decide when to push and when not to request support from the tribal council. She stated:

> You're going through every two years, the tribal elections, so there were some years when we just kind of flew under the radar, because there were opponents on [the] council who didn't support Ziibiwing. So, then we didn't go there and demand any decisions from them, because they weren't going to be favorable. So, recognizing all of that, you had to have your timing down. Sometimes people didn't appreciate that part— the way that I made those decisions—but I knew that if they already were grumbling about us, then why would they vote to give us more money, or whatever we needed? So, if you don't ask, then you don't get denied. So we just kept planning, planning, planning.[9]

Tribal member Paul Johnson was brought on board in late 1996 as a planner. He played a critical role in helping both to develop a mission statement for the zcs and to gain staff enthusiasm for the project. He brought years of experience in community organizing and strategic planning to the table, following a successful career working with the Michigan Education Association and other state government agencies. Both Paul Johnson and Bonnie Ekdahl served as the administrative leads in bringing the Ziibiwing Cultural Center to fruition.

It is important to acknowledge, however, that the Ziibiwing Center staff, both past and present, hold a collective sense about Ziibiwing's creation. It is a "community project"—a "we" effort instead of an individual one. As Johnson stated: "It's a 'we' concept, so it is all of us together. And that's what the philosophy of this place is."[10] This collective approach is certainly reflected in the zcs's emphasis on collaborating with the community as it developed plans for all aspects of the center, including the building design, exhibitions, and programming. While NAGPRA issues brought this grassroots organization together, the zcs eventually expanded its role to providing critical resources and services to the community. Tribal members could see that a team was getting things accomplished.

In 1998, the architectural firm Dow Howell Gilmore Associates was contracted to design the building. Throughout, however, Bonnie Ekdahl and Paul Johnson maintained complete authority over the outside contractors. While the staff may have contracted with outside firms to build the cultural center, they exercised great care in selecting firms that would be able to work effectively with the tribe. Ekdahl cited her previous experience working on other building projects funded by the Saginaw Chippewa where she witnessed non-Native contractors taking advantage of the tribe. She vowed that she "wasn't going to let that happen here."[11] After a lengthy and extensive vetting process, the following outside contractors were hired by the Ziibiwing team to assist in developing the museum: André and Associates (exhibit design firm), J. R. Heineman & Sons (general contractors), Maltbie (exhibit fabrication and installation), and Monadnock Media (multimedia development).

In 2000, the tribal council awarded an additional $6.5 million for completion of the cultural center. Added to the previous award of $3.5 million, this gave the zcs a budget of $10 million. Construction began in May 2002, and the Ziibiwing Center of Anishinabe Culture & Lifeways opened its doors in May 2004. The opening ceremonies celebrated the culmination of years of community-collaborative research that led to the center's creation. In my conversation with Bonnie Ekdahl, she expressed pride in the diverse range of tribal members from different families who attended the inaugural festivities. It was a fitting tribute to the collaborative process that the team had followed, seeking to include the perspectives of as many Saginaw Chippewa tribal citizens as possible.

I asked Ekdahl about the process the zcs used to establish community involvement and support as well as how it developed a museum that represents all the families in the tribe, not just certain families on the reservation. She emphasized the importance of the commonsense yet rigorous approach of holding ongoing meetings with people. The zcs engaged tribal members in conversations about what they hoped to see in the galleries and what was working or not working with existing plans. The team also made collective decisions about which one of them was the most appropriate person to do a job. As Ekdahl stated:

> You've got to be strategic about who asks, and how you ask. . . . You have to have a lot of people from the community. Maybe not necessarily sitting on a committee, but informally, just talking to different families. You just have to take the time to do that, and I think that's why this one ended up so powerful. . . . People always ask me that [about how to achieve community support], and the only thing I can say is that you have to talk to the people. And if it's not you individually, you have to align yourself with people who can.[12]

A number of individuals worked on the teams that Ekdahl assembled to develop the exhibitions in collaboration with the citizens of the Saginaw Chippewa Indian Tribe. Charmaine Benz (Saginaw Chippewa) and Shannon Martin (Gun Lake Pottawatomi) conducted the research and wrote the text. Gilbert Williams served as the multimedia developer with Shannon Martin's assistance. Curators Patrick D. Wilson and William Johnson (Saginaw Chippewa) selected objects and artifacts for inclusion, while Anita Heard (Saginaw Chippewa) and Amanda Falcon Agosto (Saginaw Chippewa) handled the images and primary source documentation reproduction.

THE *DIBA JIMOOYUNG: TELLING OUR STORY* PERMANENT EXHIBITION: DECOLONIZING MUSEUM REPRESENTATIONS

Leading museum professional Kathleen McLean states that exhibitions are central to a museum's identity, as they "are the soul of a museum experience for the millions of people who visit them, as well as for many of the people who create them."[13] *Diba Jimooyung: Telling Our Story* is a permanent exhibition that reflects the rigorous, collaborative, and commonsense approach of those involved in creating it. The *Diba Jimooyung* exhibition incorporates some of the most current and innovative exhibition strategies. Specifically, it is more thematic than object centered.[14] It includes film presentations and multimedia that are state of the art. It uses a considerable amount of storytelling and first-person voice, and, most significantly, its emphasis is on twentieth-century survival within the context of what Native people have survived in the first place. The museum provides an engaging and in-depth presentation of Saginaw Chippewa history and culture in the *Diba Jimooyung* exhibit.

The range of topics covered in the gallery includes precontact Anishinabek history and seasonal living; tribal creation stories and the oral tradition; first contact with Europeans; the lasting legacies of colonization; and contemporary issues, such as language-revitalization efforts, protection of tribal sovereignty, gaming, repatriation efforts, and reclaiming and revitalizing Saginaw Chippewa culture and identity today.

Here, I will highlight the Ziibiwing Center's treatment of two themes that I believe represent the best interpretative strategies in museum exhibitions and reflect a decolonizing agenda. First, by framing the entire exhibition within the context of the tribe's oral tradition, its representation of history reflects more closely an Indigenous understanding of history, as opposed to a postmodern sense of history. Second, its ability to speak the hard truths of colonization in its exhibitions addresses the legacies of historical unresolved grief.

As Indigenous peoples, we have long since established that we have a different way of understanding history from non-Native people, and the most important difference is our adherence to the oral tradition. As Waziyatawin Angela Wilson states, "We have our own theories about history, as well as our own interpretations and sense of history, in which our stories play a central role."[15] At the Ziibiwing Center, what happens on the exhibition floor privileges the oral tradition, which provides the overarching framework for the visitor to engage with Anishinabe history and culture. Through its presentation of the oral tradition within the exhibits, this museum engages the best in emerging scholarship in Native American history, which seeks to "position oral traditions as vehicles to create histories that better reflect Native people's perspectives on the past."[16]

The exhibitions highlight the Seven Prophecies/Seven Fires of the Anishinabe people, which are part of their oral tradition. The museum is organized around the prophecies, and this is a very effective and intimate manner in which to narrate their history. As visitors travel through the center's 9,000-square-foot exhibition, each of these prophecies is introduced on text panels. Visitors then hear the prophecy, which is spoken first in Anishinabe and then in English. The prophecies provide the narrative thread that connects the contents of the museum and conveys an understanding of Anishinabe tribal philosophies and spirituality.[17]

By representing historical events within the context of the prophecies instead of through a rigid adherence to the specifics of U.S.-Indian relations, the museum engages an important decolonizing strategy: it privileges the oral tradition and Indigenous conceptions of history. The historical material is there, but it is presented in a tribally based framework for understanding history that illustrates the themes of the prophecies. The tribe's history within the fifth prophecy, for example, is its time of separation and struggle during the nineteenth century. How the museum treats this period within the oral-tradition framework is, as I will elaborate upon in a moment, powerful for both visitors and the Saginaw Chippewa community.

The Ziibiwing staff's desire to use the prophecies as the overarching narrative structure gives the museum a culturally rooted way both to honor a tribal understanding of history and to provide a well-organized structure through which the visitor can engage the material. The oral tradition gives this museum an organized presentation all the way through. Not only is the presentation definitely clear and coherent, but it also introduces the visitor to new knowledge by how it is organized.

The uniqueness of the Ziibiwing approach—looking to oral tradition for the guiding narrative structure for the museum—both builds and expands upon the efforts of other sites that I have visited and studied. For example, at the Mille Lacs Indian Museum the exhibition narrative is clearly informed by oral histories of past and present band members, several of whom are quoted throughout the museum. However, the museum is not organized to follow the oral tradition as its overarching framework.

I make this observation, not to diminish or disrespect the choices of the Mille Lacs Band advisory board, but to contextualize the significance of the choice of the Ziibiwing Center's staff to use the prophecies as the organizing structure for the museum. I have witnessed changes in tribal museum development over the last fifteen years, and it is important to acknowledge these changes. In the case of the Mille Lacs Band, the decisions of the advisory board were based on their own unique identities and circumstances. They were working in collaboration with the Minnesota Historical Society at a particular moment in time, and their choices served their interests and the needs of their intended audience, as previously discussed. In the case of the Ziibiwing Center, by contrast, the staff felt it was appropriate to share their oral tradition and spirituality. As one staff member recognized, "We tried something that we felt was very daring and unusual, but made sense to us."[18]

NARRATING THE HARD TRUTHS OF COLONIZATION

The second theme evident at the Ziibiwing Center that makes its narrative strategy so effective is its direct presentation of colonization. The community's desire to build this museum had everything to do with wanting it to be a site of "knowledge making [and] remembering"[19] for its members. It wanted the center to be a place where the difficult stories could be told. As the Ziibiwing staff stated: "Years of multi-generational trauma, experienced as a result of years of oppression and alienation, have left our community with many blanks in our communal history and memory. We felt by building this facility and acknowledging our past, it would allow us to begin a healing process for our community and the communities that surround us."[20]

By narrating their history in this museum, the Saginaw Chippewa did not shy away from speaking the hard truths of colonization and the lasting legacies of those truths in their community. A significant amount of floor space is devoted to emphasizing their survival within a colonial context, and this message directly challenges the stereotypical displays produced in the past that emphasized Native disappearance in the wake of westward expansion. In telling the story of survival, the museum does not shy away from telling the difficult stories of land theft, disease, poverty, violence, and forced conversion at the hands of Christian missionaries. Its unflinching treatment of colonization provides the context that makes the survival of the Saginaw Chippewa so amazing and worthy of celebration. And it devotes a considerable amount of floor space to addressing important contemporary issues and tribal survivance. Because it allows no silences around the forces that sought to destroy the Saginaw Chippewa—because it tackles head-on the very painful aspects of the tribe's history—it is then able to address the ongoing legacies of historical unresolved grief that are so prevalent throughout Native America.

With these two key themes in mind about why the narrative strategy chosen by the exhibition developers is so effective—privileging the oral tradition and speaking the hard truths of colonization—I will now give a detailed walk-through of the permanent exhibition, *Diba Jimooyung*. As I have mentioned, the Ziibiwing Center's use of the Seven Prophecies creates a coherent overarching narrative structure that guides visitors through the museum's material. Accordingly, I will use these prophecies to structure my discussion of the exhibition and its impact.

WALK-THROUGH

Upon entering the exhibit, visitors are introduced to the idea that the Anishinabe understanding of history will guide their experience in the gallery. A large diorama of an ancient petroglyph site, complete with two life-size mannequins carving teachings in stone, conveys the idea that Anishinabe history is deeply rooted in place and on the landscape. Text panels explain that the petroglyphs represent the Saginaw Chippewa's "ancestors' collective oral memory, wisdom, and spirituality."

Ezhibiigaadek Asin
Written on Stone

Ezhibiigaadek asin have always existed in Anishinabek history.

Our ancestors lived and were defined by their spiritual and physical world. Many Anishinabek believe that ezhibiigaadek asin are teachings and instructions given to us by the Creator. Carved generations ago, ezhibiigaadek asin represent our ancestor's collective oral memory, wisdom, and spirituality. The same ezhibiigaadek asin imagery can also be seen in our sacred wiigwaas (birchbark) scrolls, earth mounds, and rock paintings. Our ancestors' teachings still benefit us today. Ezhibiigaadek asin are reflections of the love our ancestors had for us, 21st century Anishinabek, knowing that one day we would see and learn from them.

You are seeing the way in which our ancestors may have carved ezhibiigaadek asin.[21]

The petroglyphs section sets the appropriate tone for the rest of the museum and conveys a significant take-home message: the teachings in the exhibit reflect the Saginaw Chippewa's traditional means of "knowledge making and remembering" and are part of the Anishinabe past. These petroglyphs speak of their ancestors' care in preserving knowledge—"shooting knowledge" into the future. The Ziibiwing Center takes its place in this ongoing process of simultaneously creating, preserving, and disseminating knowledge about the Anishinabe past and present.

While the text does not mention this specifically, the display is a replica of the Sanilac Petroglyphs site, located near present-day Bad Axe, Michigan, in

Diorama of an ancient petroglyph site at the entrance to the *Diba Jimooyung* exhibit. Two life-size figures are seen carving teachings in stone. Courtesy of the Ziibiwing Center of Anishinabe Culture & Lifeways, Saginaw Chippewa Indian Tribe of Michigan, Photography by Penrod/Hiawatha Co.

the eastern part of the state. Two tribal members posed for the life-size mannequins featured in the diorama. The staff followed this practice throughout the exhibition, using contemporary tribal members as the models for all the mannequins placed throughout the galleries. Because the Anishinabe people consider the Sanilac site sacred, the developers went to great lengths to protect the integrity of the site by not providing an exact replica of its petroglyphs. The museum's diorama includes some of the images at Sanilac, but not in the same configurations.

One of the images is of Ebmodaakowet, the archer, a pictograph figure with an arrow. The text panels state that the figure symbolizes the commitment that the Saginaw Chippewa's ancestors made to pass knowledge on to future generations. Additional images include a spiral that reflects the "circle of life"—a symbol of the journey individuals take in both this life and the next as well as of their "connection to all of creation." In a move that reflects the community-center nature of this institution, one panel near these figures invites hands-on learning: "Our teachers tell us to touch and place our hands on the teaching. By doing so, we are letting our spirit connect with the spirit of the teaching."

The beginning of the gallery focuses on precontact life. It is here that the visitor is introduced to the Anishinabe understanding of history and to the idea that their oral tradition will provide the overarching framework for the *Diba Jimooyung* exhibition. Specifically, the Seven Prophecies/Seven Fires of the Anishinabe people provide the organizational structure; each of the seven prophecies is tied to a unique part of the exhibition. Visitors hear the first three prophecies in the seasonal diorama gallery. This is a beautiful space depicting subsistence activities through the four seasons that includes a replica of a birchbark spring teaching lodge at one end of the gallery and a winter lodge at the other.

The spring teaching lodge has the objects and articles typically found in these spaces. Here, the visitor is introduced to the first prophecy/first fire. This prophecy directed the Anishinabek people to move away from their homelands on the east coast to avoid death and destruction and to find a new home where "food grows on the water"—a reference to the wild rice that is abundant in the Great Lakes region where modern-day Anishinabek people reside. An additional text panel in the spring lodge introduces visitors to the Anishinabe traditional religious practice, the Midewiwin, and gives information about the teaching lodge they are standing in. The following text panel provides further context:

Kinoomaagegamik
Teaching Lodge

The kinoomaagegamik (teaching lodge) provides the setting for life-long learning.

Our ancestors lived a very spiritual way of life long before the arrival of the Light-Skinned people. The Midewiwin (from the heart way of life), our original spirituality, taught us how to live with and honor all of Creation through ceremonies, prayers, songs, stories, and wiigwaas (birchbark) scrolls in the kinoomaagegamik. The Midewiwin way of life remains intact and is still practiced by many Anishinabek. Today, Anishinabek of all ages gather in teaching lodges to learn about our original spirituality.[22]

The space also features objects used in a traditional teaching lodge, and a drawing identifying the specific items on display indicates that they are all replicas. One of the most striking features of the Ziibiwing Center for me is the willingness of this community to share aspects of their spirituality with visitors. In my visits to other tribal museums in the United States— the Makah Cultural and Research Center, the Museum at Warm Springs, the

Mille Lacs Indian Museum, the Mashantucket Pequot Museum and Research Center, and the Tamástslikt Cultural Institute—I have not seen an exhibition in a tribal museum that explicitly discusses tribal philosophy and spirituality. What makes this center so compelling is the community's willingness to discuss this central part of their identity. Anishinabe spirituality is reflected in the Seven Prophecies/Seven Fires framework, and the text panel provides contextual information on the Midewiwin. Keenly aware of the long history of appropriation and misrepresentation of Indigenous spirituality, the Ziibiwing team nonetheless decided to go ahead with plans to present this aspect of their identity. As Bonnie Ekdahl stated: "That's what we believe. Why shouldn't we put it in there? . . . Somewhere in my training, working with the elders, there was always this thought that our purpose, and why we are part of this earth, is to take care of the earth. . . . The way our beliefs are and the teachings are. They are something that the rest of the world needs to know about. And this was a way to make it happen."[23]

The second and third prophecies instructed the Anishinabe to continue moving westward and are introduced in a diorama space that covers roughly one-fourth of the entire *Diba Jimooyung* exhibition. Banners overhead include the names of the seasons in both Anishinabe and English. Life-size mannequins modeled after contemporary tribal members are placed near a sugar bush camp in the spring section and are shown harvesting wild rice in the late summer and fall. An Anishinabe hunter stands in front of a deer in the winter scene. This is a beautiful section, and the exhibition developers went to great lengths to include appropriate plant species and objects, such as baskets, canoes, and other items suitable for each season.[24] Most notably, artist Jan Vriesen's stunning backdrop for the diorama brings each respective season to life. Text panels nearby explain the objects and activities that the visitor is viewing. During the planning stages for the museum, community members requested significant coverage of precontact Anishinabe culture, and this section addresses this need to represent life before the "Chimoko-man arrived."

Although museum studies scholars have critiqued the use of dioramas to depict precontact tribal life as keeping Native cultures "frozen in time," several tribal museums have continued to use them. According to a Ziibiwing Center tour guide, the Saginaw Chippewa community chose this type of presentation to break free from another problematic display strategy: placing objects on pedestals in glass cases. The goal was to create an open, visually appealing space that captures seasonal activities and sites for traditional teachings. Furthermore, by offering rich explorations of the group's contemporary experiences, later sections of the museum effectively challenge the idea that Saginaw Chippewa culture is static or frozen in time.

The fourth prophecy concerns initial encounters with Europeans. It is introduced after the visitor has engaged with substantial information on Anishinabe precontact culture and lifeways. Images of early contact, painted by Robert Griffing, and maps of European contact sites line a hallway ending at a case with fur-trade-era objects, including trade silver, copper items, metal axes, and furs. Sounds of water and of sails are heard overhead as visitors move through this space. Text panels emphasize that the Anishinabe "lived peacefully with the Light-Skinned people for about 200 years," but their world changed dramatically with further encroachment on their lands and lifeways. The objects and images in the showcase speak to this period of coexistence and Anishinabe adaptation. Mannequins wearing articles of clothing and ornamentation made possible by trade, including cloth shirts, bandolier bags, and beaded moccasins, are placed near images of furs trapped by the Anishinabe for trade.

The "Effects of Colonization" gallery presents the period of the fifth prophecy, which foretold that many Anishinabe would abandon their culture, spirituality, and language during years of great struggle and collective hardships. The exhibits focus on the tragic period in Anishinabe history that included loss of land, disease, poverty, violence, and forced conversion at the hands of Christian missionaries. The design elements in this section illustrate physically the sense of intense pressure—the walls begin to narrow, giving the impression that the world is closing in on the Saginaw Chippewa. The gallery relates a painful story by layering information, including voice-overs and images, to provide an auditory and visual break from the emotional stories that visitors are reading. The maps, text panels, and images of ancestors and treaties provide context for the devastating period on display.

In this section, the truth-telling aspect of the museum comes to the fore. No silences protect the forces that tried to destroy the Anishinabek people. For example, the following text panel placed near the beginning of the section names the brutal realities of the period. Notice its use of the active voice:

Gichi Ogimaa Do Naakonigewinan
The Laws/Rules Made by the Government

The United States government implemented many policies that were destructive to our way of life.

Government policies included ruthless efforts to remove the Anishinabek from their lands. Genocide, smallpox, and forced removal were ways to secure the highly valuable and fertile grounds of the Michigan Territory. For the Anishinabek who would not move, the government brought an era of cruel acculturation through the establishment of government and missionary schools.[25]

The museum also does not shy away from speaking about the devastating impact of alcoholism. It describes alcohol as a "weapon of exploitation" and tells how it was used during the treaty-making period. The following text panel is placed near a replica of a treaty table:

Waawiindimaagewinan Gii Zhichigaadek
When the Promises Were Made

This is how a treaty signing may have looked.

An interpreter, hired by the government, "translated" the negotiations between the two nations. Many gifts were brought to the treaty table as "gestures" of goodwill, including alcohol. Alcohol was a foreign substance to the Anishinabek and we had no context for its use. It was intentionally used as a weapon of exploitation.[26]

The use of audio in this section is extremely effective. In one area, visitors hear voices reading some of the documents featured on nearby text panels. As visitors walk through this space, they hear the words of government officials, such as Lewis Cass and John Hudson. Listening to the angry, racist opinions of the colonizers is very difficult, yet the exhibit is strategically designed so that no one can miss hearing their words. One may choose not to read a text panel, but visitors cannot avoid hearing words repeated overhead many times as they move through the space. Hearing Cass and others express such deep-seated hatred for the Anishinabe people is a difficult and emotional experience—one that the museum insists that visitors confront.

Audio is also strategically used in the area of the gallery that focuses on the boarding school experience, as voices of children and military drills are heard overhead. This area is located behind the treaty table display and includes an overhead banner that reads "What Is Done to Us" in Anishinabe and English. On one side of a small pathway are life-size images of children in marching-band uniforms. They stand behind a text panel that provides context on the history of the boarding school experience and the devastating impact of these sites of forced assimilation and cultural genocide. Children

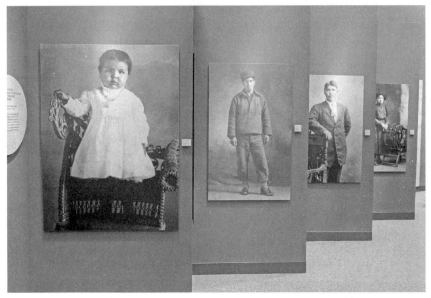

Images of ancestors in the "Effects of Colonization" section of the *Diba Jimooyung* exhibit. Courtesy of the Ziibiwing Center of Anishinabe Culture & Lifeways, Saginaw Chippewa Indian Tribe of Michigan, Photography by Penrod/Hiawatha Co.

as young as five and six years of age spent nine months in residence at the schools. During these long months, they were forbidden to speak their tribal languages. The Ziibiwing team describe the tragic legacies of the schools within their community today and their direct impact on the kinship relationships within the tribe: "The effects of this policy were felt generations later, as we never learned how to parent due to this family disruption."

Across from the text panel and images of the children is a replica of the exterior building of Mount Pleasant Indian Industrial Boarding School. This federally run boarding school opened in the early 1890s, and members of the Saginaw Chippewa community were forced to attend. Visitors can look into the windows and view a range of objects on display related to the tribe's experience, including scrapbooks, trophies, school uniforms, and an Ojibwe spelling book. The exhibit also features images of the brick school building, graduating classes, sewing classes, sports teams, and a striking image of a large group of uniformed children outside the school in 1893. The curators are careful to acknowledge that Native responses to this school are ambivalent: "Some Anishinabek recall fond memories of the Mt. Pleasant Indian School." Still, the overall message of this section is one of great loss and dev-

Treaty-signing installation in the "Effects of Colonization" section of the *Diba Jimooyung* exhibit. Courtesy of the Ziibiwing Center of Anishinabe Culture & Lifeways, Saginaw Chippewa Indian Tribe of Michigan, Photography by Penrod/Hiawatha Co.

astation as children were taken from their families and subjected to government assimilationist policies designed to separate them from their culture, identity, and spirituality.

This section's description of the intergenerational trauma that Anishinabek people experienced during this period connects the social problems of today with what happened in the past. This has a powerful impact on community members. The community is not afraid to acknowledge that the problems that they still must confront are a result of colonization. I greatly respect their willingness to speak of what we as Indigenous people know but are somewhat reluctant to talk about within a museum context. All too often, we are concerned about coming across as if we are subscribing to the language of victimization. Perhaps the more legitimate concern that many of us have is that this information could potentially reinforce stereotypes. Such concerns prevent us from speaking the hard truths about our present social problems and connecting these issues to the colonization process. In an effort to "acknowledge our past . . . and begin a healing process for our communities and the communities that surround us," the curators at the Ziibiwing Center state:

Gichi Aakoziwin Miinawaa Nibowin
Great Illness and Death

Government policies resulted in profound health problems for the Anishinabek.

The Anishinabek fell into poverty and despair from our loss of land and livelihood. The settlers brought diseases for which the Anishinabek had no immunity or cure. Many villages were completely wiped out by these new sicknesses. Tuberculosis and mass burials were common. The Anishinabek suffered greatly and we still suffer the effects of this era today. Due to the poverty that we have endured, health problems such as diabetes, tuberculosis, heart disease, and alcoholism still plague us.[27]

During the planning process, the curators conducted audience evaluations with community members and museum professionals to assess the effectiveness of particular sections. The feedback on the "Effects of Colonization" gallery indicated that this "was a very painful and emotional era for people to visit, see, and hear."[28] In light of this information, the curators decided to provide a place where people could collect their thoughts and have a moment of reflection after witnessing the painful truths presented in this section. In an attempt to provide a healing space so as to "not leave . . . open wounds in the hearts of our people,"[29] the exhibition team developed a gallery entitled "Blood Memory." This unique exhibit is very effective, engaging, and profoundly moving.

Visitors engage with this section even before they leave the "Effects of Colonization" area. The sound of a heartbeat and a beautiful song sung by three women from the community pull the visitor forward toward the healing space. The exhibit is an open, inviting, circular area, with benches nearby for people to use to rest and collect their thoughts. The following text panel introduces the concept of blood memory to visitors:

Mindjimendamowin
Blood Memory

Blood memory is an inherent connection we have to our spirituality, ancestors, and all of Creation.

Blood memory can be described as the emotions we feel when we hear the drum or our language for the first time. The Creator gives these emotions to us at birth. We use these emotions or blood memories to understand our heritage and our connection to our ancestors. Blood memory makes these connections for us.

Today, many Anishinabek use their blood memory to relearn our language. Our beautiful and descriptive language is deeply rooted in the land and our connections to it. As more and more Anishinabek recall their blood memory, our language and our spirituality will be spoken for the next Seven Generations.[30]

Included in the "Blood Memory" space is a showcase with beautiful objects that have been made by tribal individuals. These objects are meant to convey an important take-home message: even through the darkest and most painful period in their modern history, the Saginaw Chippewa's ancestors managed to create works of great beauty. The display case "Creating Beautiful Things in Difficult Times" features beautiful beadwork items, including bandolier bags, vests, belts, and leggings with labels identifying specific objects.

The idea that these objects embody the strength and resiliency of their ancestors reflects an important point made by art historian Ruth Phillips: "Historical objects are witnesses, things that were *there, then*. They bear their makers' marks in their weaves, textures, and shapes, and have a compelling agency to cause people living in the present to enunciate their relationships to the past."[31] The relationship to the past embodied in the Ziibiwing Center's objects connects contemporary tribal members to their ancestors and artistic traditions. It conveys an important message of tribal strength, which is a part of their modern identity as Saginaw Chippewa.

By presenting examples of their rich artistic tradition in this manner, the museum is providing a unique perspective on early twentieth-century material culture. I have seen many museums present these types of objects in a way that challenges age-old "art versus ethnographic" categories or that demonstrates cultural continuance by placing contemporary objects nearby. However, this is the first place I have seen these sorts of objects presented explicitly to illuminate survival during the "crying time." Their presence reminds tribal members of their ancestors' strength and endurance. As Bonnie Ekdahl claimed, the central goal of this section is "to convey to [visitors] that despite all of this heartache, and this tragedy, and this loss, that there was still this powerful resiliency in our people during that period, which is why we are here today."[32]

From the outset, the "Effects of Colonization" and "Blood Memory" gal-

The "Creating Beautiful Things in Difficult Times" case features beadwork items, including bandolier bags, vests, belts, and leggings. This case is part of the "Blood Memory" section of the *Diba Jimooyung* exhibit. Courtesy of the Ziibiwing Center of Anishinabe Culture & Lifeways, Saginaw Chippewa Indian Tribe of Michigan, Photography by Penrod/Hiawatha Co.

leries stood out to me as both unique and pathbreaking. They reflect a decolonizing agenda, given the clarity and depth of the historical treatment of the Saginaw Chippewa's difficult history. During my interviews with the Ziibiwing Center staff, I asked about the development of these sections, as I have not seen another tribal museum address the legacies of historical unresolved grief so completely and directly. In my interview with Bonnie Ekdahl, the center's founding director, she described the evolution of the "Blood Memory" section based on the exhibition team's conversations with the community. Throughout the planning process, the staff followed a community-collaborative model of exhibition development. Members of the Ziibiwing Center staff would meet with community members to get feedback on specific sections and their effectiveness. During these gatherings, the team would place chairs around a room to give the tribal members a sense of how the space would be laid out, including pictures of the objects and text panels.

In my interview with her, Ekdahl movingly described the impact of the "Effects of Colonization" gallery on tribal elders during one of these planning meetings. The elders' emotional reactions made them realize the need for a healing space:

> What we learned is that when they came through the effects of colonization, it was so heartbreaking for them to look at the facts. Because, you hear the stories from your grandmothers or your grandfathers, or your parents, but then when you come to realize that it was a strategic assimilation process, and there were government policies that mandated the way that they treated our people, and the development of the schools, the results of the schools, all of that. It validated all of that history for them. And they would cry. We had this one emotional grandmother that came through, just started crying. I remember that part so well. She said, "Now I know what happened. Why my mom did what she did." So then, we knew we had to be responsible.
>
> And I remember saying, "We have kind of a mental health issue." That is what I called it at first. When you stir up all that emotion, shouldn't we have some kind of responsibility to bring them back down ... or help them to resolve it? So, we thought about that, because it was traumatic. A traumatic realization that those people didn't know. And those people are the ones that we are counting on to always guide us. But they were victims of the process—of that history. And we were seeing it from a bigger picture. You know, when you have to put all those things together and then you see the results on the individuals, it's real powerful, about the messages that you can actually leave with people who don't know.[33]

For Ekdahl, it was a "traumatic realization" that the elders did not know the full extent to which the suffering of their relatives was part of a U.S. government policy of assimilation and cultural genocide. This painful not-knowing certainly shows what colonization does to our communities. It also demonstrates why truth telling is so important for both Native people and the general public. Her statement reminds me of the words of Choctaw historian Jacki Rand. In her article critiquing the exhibits at the National Museum of the American Indian for their failure to address the painful history of U.S.-Indian relations, Rand wrote: "Experience, personal and otherwise, has shown me that it is not just white Americans who need to grasp the full scope of Native history. Native people can also benefit from a more just and accurate depiction of their past. No one can understand the experience of twentieth- and twenty-first-century Indians without understanding the U.S.

laws and policies that radically reshaped their lives."[34] During the periods foretold by the fifth and sixth prophecies, the Saginaw Chippewa suffered immensely at the hands of the U.S. government. By engaging in truth telling about this painful period, the community was able to move forward in their healing efforts.

I recognize, however, that engaging in truth telling is not an easy process, and this history proved challenging at times for the Ziibiwing team members I spoke with. The process of researching this history, engaging with it directly, and wrestling with how to most effectively present the complicated and painful experiences meant that the staff had to live very closely with the material for many months as they developed the galleries. In my interview with him, Curator William Johnson described his own process of coming to terms with the painful history addressed in the "Effects of Colonization" section and the impact on him personally:

> Learning about the struggles of our ancestors was really difficult. Knowing that my own grandmas and grandpas had to go through the effects of assimilation was very difficult to deal with. . . . Because, a lot of times, we didn't really come to that gallery with a whole lot of knowledge, so we were learning it firsthand as we were creating it. Just being able to swallow it for the first time was one of the most difficult things that we had to deal with. . . . The story is told in a matter-of-factual way, but the hope is that it would provide a little healing for the community after they visit that particular area. Luckily for us, it worked. The people are able to come to the "Blood Memory" gallery and sit and contemplate what they just went through. And it's not unique that we see people sitting in there, in that area, who are crying, and maybe a little of the healing can begin now. But, it was a rough, rough gallery to have to put together. And like I said, if for every time that we used profane language while we were putting it together, if we had a dime for every time that we said a swear word, we could probably have funded the building ourselves. I say that in all sincerity, because it was real hurtful stuff. And it's stuff that we learn continually all the time, so it's not like it was just a one-shot deal.[35]

In my mind, the "Effects of Colonization" gallery along with the "Blood Memory" gallery represents one of the most effective methods that a tribal museum can use to assist community members in the truth-telling and healing processes. The Ziibiwing Center does not shy away from telling the difficult stories. But alongside these stories, it also provides a healing place where tribal members can gain strength from understanding and reclaiming their rich, cultural inheritance and identity.

The healing space of "Blood Memory" also introduces the first part of the seventh prophecy/seventh fire. This prophecy conveys the uplifting message foretelling that the Anishinabe people would return to their culture and seek knowledge once again from the elders—that they would reclaim their language, history, and identity. The Anishinabe believe that this period began in the 1960s. During the larger Native American self-determination movement occurring at that time, their tribal nation along with other Native peoples engaged in various forms of activism to protect Indigenous culture, lifeways, and sovereignty. The remaining areas of the museum focus on a range of contemporary issues, including language-revitalization efforts, asserting tribal sovereignty, gaming, repatriation efforts, and reclaiming and revitalizing Saginaw Chippewa culture and identity today.

The curators devote considerable attention to highlighting "Anishinabe Strengths" in the time of the seventh prophecy/seventh fire. One area focuses on the ongoing efforts of their community to preserve their language. Images of youth at language camps are placed near language-interactive screens, where visitors learn the Anishinabe translations for terms such as "birchbark," "tree," "stone," "rope," and "teaching lodge." Another showcase highlights Saginaw Chippewa basketry, featuring the Red Arrow family. Text panels convey that basketry is both an art form and a way that tribal members made a living throughout the twentieth century.

Yet another compelling section focuses on the tribe's youth. It features a lovely mural that fourteen young people, ages fourteen to seventeen, developed during the summer of 2002. A nearby showcase presents a video that they produced about their lives today. The mural incorporates images that represent the issues important to them. The words "Anishinabe Pride" are prominently placed on the mural, and a large representation of the Saginaw Chippewa tribal seal divides the historic and contemporary images.[36] The mural has a floral border design, reflecting the Anishinabe artistic tradition. A panel nearby offers context for each of the images represented.

Like their elders, the youth were not afraid to reflect on both the positive and negative influences in their community. Their mural has images of the drum, medicine hoop, eagles, and the hatchet, which symbolize tribal strengths. But their mural also includes a symbol that they refer to as "Ugly Face," which represents the struggles in their community with drugs and alcohol. Including the panel that explains the mural symbols aids visitors in their appreciation of the piece and gives them a sense of the issues important to Saginaw Chippewa youth—something unique to the Ziibiwing Center. Most tribal museums do not have youth-curated displays, and these areas go a long way toward conveying a richer sense of both community and a multi-generational presence.

Tribal museums across the country devote a section of their exhibits to honoring veterans, and the Ziibiwing Center is no exception. The *Diba Ji-mooyung* permanent exhibit includes a case featuring objects and photographs from Saginaw Chippewa veterans who served in many branches of the U.S. Armed Forces as part of the "Anishinabe Strengths" section. But even here, what the Ziibiwing team does is unique. It extends the definition of a modern-day warrior to include not only veterans of the military but also those who fight for the well-being of the community as well. A panel states: "Many Anishinabek are on the battlefield everyday fighting to protect the land, the waters, or for our people's way of life. Those who protect our tribal traditions like fishing and hunting, or those who work to prohibit toxic waste sites on reservation lands can also be seen as warriors."

The Ziibiwing Center, similar to the Mille Lacs Indian Museum that opened in 1996, devotes considerable floor space in its contemporary galleries to sovereignty issues. This is a fairly recent development and perhaps one of the most significant contributions of Indigenous exhibit-curation methods in tribal museums. Exhibit curation by Native communities in their own galleries emphasizes twentieth-century survival and sovereignty. This focus clearly departs from early ethnographic and historical exhibitions that were typically object based and not conceptually driven. When earlier exhibits did decide to address thematic issues, contemporary topics such as sovereignty were typically ignored. By contrast, the Ziibiwing Center's coverage of sovereignty is extensive. Ziibiwing curators devoted considerable attention to defining sovereignty as inherent and not as something "granted to tribes." They also incorporated a discussion of the community's ongoing efforts to maintain and assert their sovereignty today.

Particularly moving in the "Spirit of Sovereignty" section is a wonderful film focusing on contemporary identity. At the theater's entrance, overhead banners list the names of the three bands that constitute the modern Saginaw Chippewa Nation: Zaagiinaa Anishinabek—the Original People of the Zaagiinaa Band (the Saginaw Band), Waabziin Ziibii Anishinabek—the Original People of Swan Creek (the Swan Creek Band), and Makade Ziibii Anishinabek—the Original People of Black River (the Black River Band). The film presents the voices of community members to convey the message that "our collective history is rich in the oral tradition and helps us to continue to be strong in spite of adversity and oppression." Community members share the challenges and hard work they face in retaining their culture and language. One interviewee sums up the take-home message of the film: "I am proud to say that I am Saginaw Chippewa. It is my whole identity."

Visitors also learn about important leaders in the tribe's history. A row of five bronzed, life-size mannequins are modeled after those who fought for the rights of the Saginaw Chippewa people from the nineteenth century to the present day. Audio plays overhead, and each of the mannequins lights up when a direct quote from one of the leaders is spoken. In many instances, family members read the words of their relatives in the "Parade of Activists" installation.

Near the area featuring exemplary historic and contemporary Anishinabe leaders is a wall display devoted to the history of gaming in the Saginaw Chippewa community, which is also part of the "Spirit of Sovereignty" section. Sandwiched between a brightly colored slot machine and a large picture of the tribe's Soaring Eagle Casino and Resort is a text panel that provides the context for gaming on the reservation. It explains why tribes generally are able to have gaming facilities. As the panel states, "Gaming is allowed on federally recognized reservations because of our sovereign status as a separate nation." The public harbors many misunderstandings about Indian gaming. For example, many non-Native people mistakenly view gaming as a special privilege for Native peoples and do not understand that gaming occurs because of the unique relationship that American Indian tribes have with the federal government. Clarifying this from the outset is therefore critical. The section provides additional information on the community's early forms of gaming. Car bingo started in the 1960s, for instance, and is depicted in a painting of a bingo game during this period. While the staff mention briefly that gaming supports the tribe's infrastructure and programming, it would have been nice to include a greater discussion of how this state-of-the-art cultural center is also due in part to their gaming success.

The Ziibiwing Center is filled with unique touches. It treats topics in ways that I have not seen elsewhere—ways that are critical to changing the historical relationship between Indigenous people and museums. One critical issue it takes up, for example, is repatriation. Given the central role that repatriation played in establishing the center, it does not come as a surprise that the curators would include a discussion about this somewhere within the galleries. Because the subject is so important to Native peoples and given Anishinabe views on the rights of their dead, I would like to highlight the excellent text produced by Shannon Martin and Charmaine Benz. They address the

The sovereign status of the Saginaw Chippewa community is explored in the "Spirit of Sovereignty" section of the *Diba Jimooyung* exhibit. Text panels in this case recognize the important leaders in the community who have fought to preserve their rights, and objects and images representing their sovereign status are featured, including the tribal flag. Photograph by the author.

significance of the Native American Graves Protection and Repatriation Act passed in 1990. The text panel is well written, and I include it in its entirety:

Aandjinigookiigaazawaat Gewe Anishinabebanik
The Reburial of the Anishinabe of Long Ago

We believe our ancestors deserve the right to remain undisturbed in the earth.

Unfortunately, our relatives have been unearthed from their graves to be examined and researched. Their remains and sacred funerary objects become the property of various museums and institutions where they are stored, put on display, or studied.

Until the Native American Graves Protection and Repatriation Act (NAGPRA) was passed by congress in 1990, we had no recourse in bringing our ancestors home and putting them back in the earth. The NAGPRA gives federally recognized tribes the right to repatriate, or to return, burial remains and associated funerary objects from the various public museums and institutions of this country.[37]

This space also covers the statewide coalition of federally and state-recognized tribes in Michigan, called the Michigan Anishinaabek Cultural Preservation and Repatriation Alliance (MACPRA). The coalition works to protect cultural resources as well as to repatriate ancestral remains and funerary and sacred objects that are currently housed in museums and federal agencies across the country. The space includes a photo of MACPRA representatives and their logo, along with an explanation of the symbols reflected in the design. The logo includes the four sacred colors of the Anishinabe—yellow, red, black, and white—in a circle. A turtle facing downward symbolizes "how our ancestors are repatriated under MACPRA and given a proper burial." Across the turtle, two pipes symbolize the unity of MACPRA. Below the turtle at the bottom of the circle are seven feathers, which symbolize the Seven Grandfather Teachings that guide them.

Near the logo and its description is a copy of the "Anishinabeg Consensus Statement on Repatriation of Native American Human Remains and Cultural Items." This forceful statement written on behalf of all the tribes in the alliance speaks to their unity as members of the Three Fires Confederacy[38] and expresses their unified commitment to work for the return of their ancestral remains and cultural items. Most significantly, it clearly asserts that the tribes have the authority to determine the cultural affiliation of objects and ancestors in museums and federal agencies. This issue is central to their ongoing repatriation work today, which I will discuss more fully in the following section. The "Anishinabeg Consensus Statement on Repatriation," though lengthy, is disappointingly small visually. But for those knowledgeable about the issue, the "Spirit of Sovereignty" section provides further context. This is an example of how effectively layered the Ziibiwing Center exhibition is. Even if visitors moving through the space read only the introductory panel, they still gain some understanding of the issues. Those interested in more information can read the MACPRA consensus statement in full. It offers visitors insight on how this important statewide coalition of tribes is working to challenge the museums and federal agencies that "have made it very difficult for tribes to repatriate our ancestral remains and objects."

The *Diba Jimooyung* exhibit concludes with an area called "Continuing the Journey," situated near the ancient petroglyph site where the visit began. Visitors hear audio of a young boy's voice describing the Seven Teachings of wisdom, love, respect, bravery, honesty, humility, and truth. These core tribal values are etched on stones below seven original pieces of artwork in a dimly lit corridor. Text panels nearby explain that the original teachings were given to the tribe by the Creator. They emphasize that these values need to be followed if the world is to survive: "If we apply the Seven Teachings to our daily lives and learn from the Seven Prophecies, we can create a better world for the next Seven Generations."

The panels state that, according to oral tradition, we are now in the time of the seventh prophecy/seventh fire. During this time, we face a choice between a path of "desecration" and a path of "compassion." If we choose the path of "compassion," we will enter the period of the eighth prophecy—a time of peace for all humanity. Connecting core Anishinabe tribal values to universal ones, the message encourages all visitors to reflect on their lifestyles. Although museum representations have long stereotyped Native spirituality, the gallery's organization and final take-home message reflect the Saginaw Chippewa's willingness to share aspects of their spirituality with visitors. The Ziibiwing Center sensitively incorporates aspects of Anishinabe philosophy and spirituality that effectively convey the uniqueness of the tribe's worldview and knowledge system, and it is a fitting way to end a thought-provoking and engaging museum experience.

PROGRAMMING

The Ziibiwing Center is much more than an exhibition space. This is critical to recognize, for, as Patricia Pierce Erikson argues, "No matter what museum you look at, the exhibition galleries are only one expression of the institution's identity."[39] The Ziibiwing Center is perhaps most significant as a place for cultural preservation and revitalization. The programs it offers complement the spirit and intent of the gallery: to provide a safe place for community members to learn about their culture, identity, language, and history. As current director Shannon Martin stated, "'The Diba Jimooyung—Telling Our Story' permanent exhibition is what we created, and from this groundbreaking exhibit, we built everything around its message."[40]

The center sponsors exemplary cultural educational programs that reflect the decolonizing vision of the galleries. These programs include the Cradleboard/Dikinaagan Project, Plant Medicine Walk, Anishinabemowin Club, Lil' Language Warriors Club, Anishinabe Performance Circle Class, Regalia-Making, Song and Dance Presentations, Mother Earth Day Activities, Wild

Rice Day Activities, Monarch Butterfly Day, Community Projects, Speaker's Bureau, and a Promotional "Road Show" Booth.[41]

My first introduction to the Ziibiwing Center's excellent cultural programming was in 2007. I attended the Anishinabe Performance Circle Presentation—a special event where young people performed their recently acquired dance skills for the community. Their pride in their newly developed dance abilities was evident at the performance. Equally touching was the large number of adults from the community who came to watch the children perform in the busy days before Christmas. For the tribal youth, the performance was a culmination of twelve to fourteen weeks of preparation; they attended classes in which they learned not only music and dance but also the Anishinabe language and oral tradition. Most significantly, the classes helped the youth develop leadership skills as well as a commitment to carry their cultural teachings into the future. Herself a student and teacher, Ziibiwing assistant director Judy Pamp explained that the goal of the Anishinabe Performance Circle program is to provide an opportunity to demonstrate that learning the Anishinabe culture is a lifelong process. It also seeks to prepare children "to step up when it's their turn to carry on these cultural teachings."[42] This program and others like it make it abundantly clear that the center is a site of community revitalization, knowledge making, and cultural sovereignty.

The Ziibiwing Center, along with other agencies and programs in the Saginaw Chippewa community, has engaged in efforts to protect and promote the Anishinabe language. The language is featured prominently in the *Diba Jimooyung* exhibit. Text panels are presented in both Anishinabe and English, and audio zones feature the Anishinabe language. The center's mission calls for ongoing efforts to preserve the language. One early initiative was the Anishinabemowin Club, a language program that served close to eight hundred people each year. A fluent Anishinabe speaker provided instruction to adult learners in the community, and one of the overarching goals of the program was to create an atmosphere that promotes language acquisition while ensuring a safe place to learn.

Language-revitalization efforts in Indigenous communities across the country remain a challenge. Not only has the colonization process led to the loss of languages, but also Native people have internalized colonization's negative messages that devalue their languages. Boarding schools, combined with the stereotypes of Native languages perpetuated in American popular culture, have led to ambivalence about the need for Indigenous languages today. Tribal nations across the country are working tirelessly to challenge these perceptions.[43] The Saginaw Chippewa community has been successful in tackling perhaps the biggest hurdle, namely, to reestablish a deep respect for the language and a desire to reclaim it. Referring to the community's renewed commitment to learn the language, Judy Pamp stated, "It's no longer a smothering ash for the desire for the language and the value of it. It's a full-blown flame now."[44]

Another innovative project that the Ziibiwing Center recently sponsored exemplifies its commitment to community healing and empowerment. The center organized events for the 2009 Wellbriety Journey for Forgiveness on 17 June 2009. Don Coyhis of White Bison (a Native-run nonprofit organization) initiated the Wellbriety Journey to raise awareness throughout Indian Country about the trauma Native people endured during the boarding school era and the tragic legacy of this history in our communities today. White Bison coordinated a 6,800-mile walk to boarding school sites across the country, and the Ziibiwing Center collaborated with the organization to address the difficult history in its community of the Mount Pleasant Indian Industrial Boarding School. The Wellbriety Journey program brought into further focus this painful chapter in Saginaw Chippewa history, which the "Effects of Colonization" section in the permanent exhibition presents so well.

The Ziibiwing Center staff sponsored several events in conjunction with the Wellbriety Journey to promote awareness, dialogue, and healing for survivors of the boarding school and their descendants. These events included a Three Fires Confederacy 5-Mile Forgiveness Walk to the Mount Pleasant Indian Industrial Boarding School site, guest speakers and panel discussions, a jingle dress healing dance and other healing ceremonies, and, finally, a "Healing the Circle" concert that featured Kevin Chamberlain and Ulali. Close to nine hundred people attended the events, and several tribal members continued on the Wellbriety Journey to Washington, D.C., to advocate for a formal apology from the U.S. government for the boarding school system. These types of events reflect the Ziibiwing Center's ongoing commitment to community revitalization and healing. Its commitment is the hallmark of this organization's work, building on the historical themes and content presented in the "Effects of Colonization" and "Blood Memory" galleries. The decolonizing agenda of truth telling as a means to healing and empowerment, which the *Diba Jimooyung* permanent exhibition addresses so powerfully, is carried forward in programming efforts such as these.

The most important aspect of the cultural programming at the Ziibiwing

Center is that it recognizes the fact that Indigenous communities have been forcibly separated from the knowledge about their language and cultural practices. All of the center's programming builds on the idea that people should not feel bad or blame themselves for what they do not know about their past. The center is a safe place for tribal members to learn, and its programming invites tribal citizens to reclaim knowledge without chastising them for what they do not know. It provides access to knowledge that, in the past, families most likely transmitted to new generations. The Ziibiwing Center embodies the community's culture-based response to changing circumstances—their resolve to adapt to circumstances caused by colonization.

This spirit of inclusion is powerfully reflected in the Cradleboard/Dikinaagan Project—another cultural programming initiative developed by Judy Pamp. The project is a collaborative effort with two other Saginaw Chippewa tribal programs, the Nimkee Clinic and the Seventh Generation. It provides instruction on how to construct and use cradleboards as well as on cultural teachings around gender roles. When I interviewed Judy Pamp in December 2007, the community had made close to sixty cradleboards based on these classes. The Ziibiwing Center's identity as a living cultural center is apparent from the important role the project has played in addressing specific cultural needs in the community. The center is responsible for reviving Anishinabe teachings on child rearing through this cultural practice, from which individuals have been separated due to the processes of colonization. The Ziibiwing Center gallery raises the issue of how the boarding school experience disrupted traditional child-rearing practices and, as a result, left some survivors unable to parent effectively. The Cradleboard/Dikinaagan Project addresses this issue head-on. In my interview with Pamp, she described how she came to realize the need for this type of cultural programming at the Ziibiwing Center—that the center could take the lead in reintroducing the use of cradleboards to Anishinabe mothers:

I found out I was going to be a grandmother for the first time, [and I thought] . . . we've gotta get ready! One of the things that I asked my daughter is, we have always used the cradleboards in our family. Is that something that you feel comfortable enough that you would choose? Because, if so, we have a lot of work to do. We've got to get moving on this! She actually said, "Yes. Most definitely." So then I asked her if she wanted to use hers, . . . or would she like to design one for her child herself. Because this is something that becomes a family heirloom. She wanted to make her own. I said, "Not a problem." . . . We always joked that her and I are very slow beaders. So, everywhere we went we had to be beading, and working on this. Carrying it wherever we went. When we were out in the community, people started to see it. "Oh, what are you making?" So we'd start talking about it, and they'd say, "Wow, we haven't seen cradleboards in this community in a long time." And it hadn't really dawned on me that I hadn't seen them, because I, myself, had only been back about ten years. So then I start watching, and they're right. . . . You didn't see it. So, just talking to friends in the community, they said, "Wow, why do we use the cradleboard?" One of the things that I hadn't quite realized is . . . I was given stories with these, but I didn't realize they were teachings. You just did them. . . . And I remembered the stories, and that [the teachings] answered the questions of why: the health benefits, [and] the bonding. They're just such new spirits to the physical world. They're not sure they want to be here, so we've got to keep them close and show them how much love there is here, and that it's okay, and we're going to guide them. We're just a guide, we're not even technically "The Parent"; we're the guide, and we're . . . to help them feel comfortable enough to stay here, and get their footing. . . . I guess I had never really thought of me having the teachings, because I hadn't had to pull them out again until now.[45]

During ongoing conversations with members of the community, including a friend working in the tribal Healthy Start Program, Pamp realized that others would be interested in learning what she had learned from her family—both how to make cradleboards and the cultural teachings associated with them. So, in collaboration with other Saginaw Chippewa tribal programs, she decided to offer classes on the use of the boards, gender roles, and parenting.

Constructing cradleboards is a long process. Men complete certain parts of the board, such as the design and crafting of the handles, head, and foot bowls. Women work on designing the covering. It could be beaded, or it could include fabric that needs to be sewn. Working on the cradleboards creates spaces for conversations among those engaged in the preparation. As Judy Pamp mentioned, the cradleboard-making process traditionally "created an opportunity for both the man and the woman to learn about what was to come, and how to guide that new spirit, and how to provide support for one another while they went through this."[46] She wanted to bring this opportunity back into the community, and she did it in collaboration with the other tribal programs that could offer the resources and reinforce the cultural teachings.

The Ziibiwing Center staff's commitment to developing the cradleboard courses reflects the beautiful philosophy captured in "Blood Memory"—the idea that the center is a safe place for tribal members to learn their culture. Responding to the realities that community members face in the wake of colonization, the center is choosing to provide services that perhaps families may have taken care of in the past. Initially, Judy Pamp expressed concern that the teachings associated with the use of cradleboards had always been taught by family members within the home. However, she believed that the community must adapt to changing circumstances and family dynamics— that Ziibiwing is and must be a "living cultural center." Flexibility and willingness to embrace change, while retaining core Anishinabe values, form the cornerstone of the center's philosophy, and this approach is certainly expressed in the development of the Cradleboard/Dikinaagan Project:

So it was just, alright, this is part of the twenty-first century reality, this is who we are today, so then, again, how do we accommodate and make them feel welcome, and that it's okay that your family's that way. And then still find a way to do those cultural teachings. So, through Seventh Generation they were able to work in their woodshop, and work with the men, and accomplish the boards; through the Nimkee Clinic, they developed the relationships with the young moms, and encouraged them to get here, and provided the food. And through Ziibiwing, we provided the center and the sewing machines, and the cultural teachings. So, everybody came together to make sure that this was accomplished, and then, when we were done, we celebrated. . . . "Look what's back in our community! Let's celebrate!" So we had a Dikinaagan Day . . . full of games and food and then [we] set up a photo opportunity for these families to have pictures with their new cradleboards. And even if they didn't have their baby yet, they had their stomach and were able to hold the cradleboard. Just a big day of celebration. . . . And then also letting them know, you now are the keeper of this knowledge. It's not something you have to wait for a class. When somebody in your family is ready to be a new parent, you now can offer this service 'cause you are the keeper of this knowledge. So you can say, "Do you plan on using a cradleboard? And if so, I can help."[47]

The idea that these individuals are now "keeper[s] of this knowledge" and in a position to assist others in the future is an important means by which the Ziibiwing Center is achieving its decolonizing mission. Teachings that would have been imparted within the home are now being transmitted through cultural programs that have evolved to address the current, twenty-first-century situation. Because the people had been separated from their traditional knowledge, which the fifth and sixth prophecies foretold and which did, in fact, occur during the period of these prophecies, the instruction in cultural ways must now be introduced in new ways. Even the cradleboard itself has evolved with changing circumstances. It is now made with backpack straps instead of a burden strap worn on the forehead, so that it is easier for today's mother to carry her baby with her. The evolution of the board reflects both the changing circumstances of Anishinabe life and the Ziibiwing Center's commitment to adapting to changing times.

Repatriation has also been a major area of work and programming, and it exemplifies Ziibiwing's decolonizing mission. Given the central role that repatriation played in the development of the museum itself, it is not surprising that the Ziibiwing Center's permanent exhibit includes a section on repatriation. But its commitment to this work, so critical to its overall mission, does not stop with the gallery. Throughout the Ziibiwing Center's history, the staff have worked tirelessly to repatriate their ancestors and cultural objects from museums and federal agencies. Staff members were instrumental in forming the statewide Native American tribal consortium in Michigan to address NAGPRA-related issues: the Michigan Anishinaabek Cultural Preservation and Repatriation Alliance. As I mention earlier in this chapter, the Nibokaan Ancestral Cemetery was established on the reservation for the ancestral remains that were reclaimed. Over 500 ancestors and 65,000 associated funerary objects have been reburied since 1996. In 2009–10, the center's staff successfully negotiated with Central Michigan University for the return of 160 ancestors and 374 associated funerary objects in the university's possession. These ancestors, along with another 9 individuals from another museum in Michigan, were reburied in the fall of 2010 at Nibokaan.[48]

The Ziibiwing staff's successful negotiation for the return of their ancestors in Central Michigan University's possession represents more than sixteen years of tireless work on this issue—an issue of vital importance to tribal communities across the country. No one can deny the impact of NAGPRA both on scientific communities and on the Indigenous nations that have reclaimed their ancestors and cultural items from museums and federal agencies. The repatriations have brought comfort and healing to Native people, while also giving the scientific community an opportunity to put things right in the present. That said, a great deal of work remains to be done to address the shortcomings and limitations of the law.

The central contentious issue standing in the way of NAGPRA compliance today concerns the fate of over 125,000 ancestors who are deemed "culturally unidentifiable" and who continue to be held in museums and federal agencies. Human remains are determined to be "culturally unidentifiable human remains" (CUHRs) if they have not been deemed to be affiliated with contemporary Native American tribes or Native Hawaiian organizations by museums or federal agencies. In an article I coauthored with Jon Daehnke, we identify three broad categories that explain why remains would be deemed CUHRs: "1) Insufficient evidence or provenience to identify the affiliation of remains; 2) Identification of remains to an earlier group for which there is no present day tribal organization; and 3) Affiliation of human remains to a modern day tribal organization that is *not* federally recognized as an Indian tribe."[49]

In his article "Decolonizing NAGPRA," James Riding In, a leading Pawnee repatriation scholar and activist, discusses the current state of NAGPRA compliance and this "unfinished business" regarding NAGPRA implementation. After providing a critical analysis of the current state of the CUHRs situation, Riding In advocates for tribes to assert ownership and control over all human remains in museums and federal agencies, including those designated CUHRs. He argues that Indigenous communities must engage in the following efforts to decolonize NAGPRA. Native people must

- assume responsibility for the proper care of ancestral remains in museums or those that remain in Mother Earth;
- understand and acquire traditional knowledge about their own respective tribe's burial practices;
- understand the history of past collecting practices and how it relates to the colonization process;
- comprehend the intricacies of NAGPRA implementation to ensure that the spirit and intent of the law as human rights legislation are achieved;
- collaborate with other Native nations and organizations; and
- establish coalitions to work cooperatively to reclaim objects and ancestors.[50]

Establishing coalitions is, according to Riding In, perhaps the most effective way to ensure that so-called CUHRs are repatriated under NAGPRA. As it currently stands, tribes can make "shared group identity" claims for ancestral remains, which is particularly effective in cases where museums and federal agencies remain resistant to repatriation.[51]

The Saginaw Chippewa Tribe of Michigan is currently addressing head-on the fate of its ancestors who were deemed CUHRs. By working collectively with MACPRA, it is seeking the return of the twelve hundred ancestors still held by the state's leading research university, the University of Michigan in Ann Arbor.[52] At the beginning of this chapter, I mention the central role that NAGPRA legislation played in forming the Ziibiwing Cultural Society, which eventually led to the development of the Ziibiwing Center. Additionally, the center's founding director Bonnie Ekdahl played a key role in establishing MACPRA, which brought together the state and federally recognized tribes in Michigan to address repatriation issues.

Perhaps the greatest strength of MACPRA is that it is a collective alliance. This consortium of tribes can more effectively offset challenges made by museums, universities, or federal agencies One of the main arguments made by scientists is that the ancestors cannot be affiliated to any one of the tribes in Michigan, and they need to retain possession in order to avoid repatriating to the wrong tribe. The scientists' argument is in direct opposition to the position held by the Anishinabek who believe that all the Michigan Anishinabek tribes are related according to their oral tradition. Standing together as a collective body allows the tribes to challenge the scientists' position more effectively. In practice, those who are reluctant to repatriate at all are the ones who consistently advance this argument. Their argument obfuscates the fact that scientists have not consulted with tribes during the process of determining possible affiliation in the first place. Yet consulting with tribes would be a core practice if the scientists' commitment to NAGPRA compliance were authentic.

In November 2007, following extensive research on the University of Michigan Museum of Anthropology's collection of culturally unaffiliated human remains and cultural items—research supported by a National Park Service grant—the Saginaw Chippewa Indian Tribe, along with MACPRA, made a formal request to the University of Michigan for the return of 405 sets of human remains in the university's possession. These ancestral remains were excavated from three sites in the state. The Saginaw Chippewa and MACPRA decided to focus on the remains from these three sites first, with ongoing efforts to reclaim the rest.[53] In a letter dated 29 November 2007, Saginaw Chippewa tribal chief Fred Cantu Jr. on behalf of the tribe and MACPRA, credited the work of the Ziibiwing Center staff in reaching this point: "The Ziibiwing Center of Anishinabe Culture & Lifeways, the Saginaw Chippewa Indian Tribe of Michigan's repatriation entity, has been researching and working diligently for many months with key American Indian elders, spiritual leaders, academic consultants and tribal representatives from MACPRA in order to arrive at this juncture."[54]

Along with the letter, Cantu sent a position statement about the so-called unaffiliated ancestors and cultural items at the University of Michigan Museum of Anthropology. In it, he stated that the research conducted by the Ziibiwing Center in collaboration with MACPRA on the three sites in question fully supports the affiliation of the ancestors found there with the modern-day Anishinabek tribes of Michigan. The researchers based this claim on their careful review of the archaeological and historical evidence collected by Sonya Atalay (Anishinabe) of Indiana University and other tribal historians who examined the cultural materials in the possession of the university. These individuals "noted the similarity of cultural materials from the burial items with those used today by Anishinabek people."[55] In other words, both scientific and Indigenous knowledge support the ancestors' affiliation with the contemporary Anishinabek. On this basis, the Saginaw Chippewa, with the support of MACPRA, put forward their claim to repossess the ancestral remains and cultural artifacts.

Their request for the return of the 405 ancestors occurred at a particularly critical juncture in the repatriation battle nationally. In October 2007, the U.S. Department of the Interior issued regulations for the disposition of culturally unidentifiable human remains and requested comments from interested parties. These regulations would finally address the fate of the CUHRs, and responses to the proposed regulations were varied and heated. While some Native people raised concerns about the proposed regulations, the National Congress of American Indians (the oldest pantribal political organization in the country), the Native American Rights Fund, and tribal nations from across the country expressed their support for the proposed regulations and sent letters to this effect to National NAGPRA by the January 2008 deadline.

In striking contrast, the two leading scientific organizations with vested interests in opposing NAGPRA compliance—the Society for American Archaeology (SAA) and the American Association of Physical Anthropologists —sent position statements critical of the regulations. Both organizations expressed great concern over the proposed regulations and openly opposed their promulgation.[56]

In January 2008, Stephen R. Forrest, vice president for research at the University of Michigan, responded to Chief Fred Cantu's letter, denying the request for tribal disposition. In his letter, Forrest cited a section of the proposed regulations dated 16 October 2007 that stated, "Current regulations implementing the Act require museums to retain possession of culturally unidentifiable human remains until final regulations are promulgated or the Secretary recommends otherwise."[57] His interpretation of this particular section in the proposed regulations gave the University of Michigan the excuse needed to retain possession. However, in a letter written in response to the denial, Saginaw Chippewa tribal attorney Rebecca Adams criticized Forrest's interpretation of the statement as "reading one provision of the Act out of context with the whole." She cited current regulations that refute the position that museums must retain possession of CUHRS. Adams wrote, "Current federal regulations specifically provide that they not 'be construed to . . . limit the authority of any museum or Federal Agency to return or repatriate human remains, funerary objects, sacred objects, or objects of cultural patrimony to Indian tribes, Native Hawaiian organizations, or individuals.'"[58]

The University of Michigan did not change its position on the disposition, and the Saginaw Chippewa, Ziibiwing Center staff, and MACPRA did not retreat. On 20 March 2008, the tribal public relations director, Joseph Sowmick, addressed the University of Michigan Board of Regents, protesting the museum's steadfast refusal to return the remains. In a powerful and eloquent statement written in collaboration with Ziibiwing director Shannon Martin, he summarized the ongoing struggles they were having with the university's museum. Sowmick cited the lack of consultation between the museum staff and Michigan tribes in determining affiliation and the steadfast refusal of the university to repatriate on the basis of its scientists' one-sided findings. He also made clear that the community will continue to engage this battle until the ancestors and cultural objects are returned. Most significantly, Sowmick emphasized that these are their relatives and that they are Anishinabek ancestors. I quote from his statement at length:

> My ancestors have also been mis-categorized through the years by your university's archaeologists and anthropologists as being "culturally unidentifiable."
>
> Over two years ago, the Saginaw Chippewa Indian Tribe, with support from MACPRA, began to research this issue and take matters into our own hands. Through a National Park Service consultative grant, a team of Elders, scholars, and historians was assembled.
>
> On November 29, 2006, our team traveled to this university to conduct research for our claim. Our team was allowed to view associated funerary objects. But, when it came time for our most important step of

visiting our ancestors' remains and conducting important protocols, we were told by Dr. John O'Shea [archaeologist at the University of Michigan and former NAGPRA representative], "Absolutely not, these burials are not affiliated with you."

This is shocking behavior on many levels. When was the decision of identity made for us? There was no consultation with Native communities in Michigan to determine cultural identity, as required by law under NAGPRA. And, why were our religious rights denied by Dr. John O'Shea?

Have we not evolved from 100 years ago when non-Native people decided for my people as to where we should live, how we should raise our children, and how we should pray?

The treatment our team received from Dr. John O'Shea was appalling and brought us back to those oppressive times.

"Culturally unidentifiable?" We undeniably say no to this miscategorization and are extremely offended by it. These individuals are related to us, the present day Anishinabek—the Original People of Michigan. At no time, throughout your university's history, has any Michigan tribe been consulted by your institution as to the "affiliation" of our ancestral relatives.

And, because of your university's mis-categorization of my ancestors as being "culturally unidentifiable," they have been de-humanized. Our ancestors' bodies and funerary objects have been written on with markers and pens, handled, and studied by professors, researchers, and students for far too long. Their bodies, laid out in cardboard boxes, on metal shelves, is your university's shameful reminder of the disrespect for human dignity.

Hear me now; your university is in direct violation of our basic human rights.

We ask, would you want your grandmothers and grandfathers to be treated in this way?

Is this the legacy you want to perpetuate for future generations?

Honorable Regents, I respectfully remind you today that the founding of your great institution is due to the generosity of our ancestors. For it was they who provided the first trust—land that was given through the Treaty of Detroit. I ask you now, is desecrating their grandmothers and grandfathers how you repay the first donors to the University of Michigan?

We have done all the research and provided your university with a strong and compelling case. We have the support of MACPRA. Tribal attorneys are diligently working on the legality of this issue. And, the Saginaw Chippewa Indian Tribe of Michigan has the resources to see this through to our satisfactory end.

Today, I am here to inform you that we will not stand idly by and condone this treatment, nor will we allow our research and perspective to be dismissed. Please rest assured that our perseverance and determination will carry us through once again—as this issue is of the utmost importance to us all.

Outside these doors are my relatives from other Michigan tribes who are standing witness. We are the direct descendants of the ancestors who lived on this land before your arrival and we are united on this issue. In the spirit of NAGPRA, we urge you to do the right thing—restore dignity to our ancestors and to your institution.[59]

On the day that Joseph Sowmick read his remarks as he stood in front of a group of Anishinaabek Ogitchedaw (warriors), close to fifty Michigan Native people and their allies held a rally in solidarity before the meeting. While the regents did not engage directly with Sowmick after he spoke, they did request additional information from the university regarding the case. Local newspapers, such as the university's *Michigan Daily* and the *Ann Arbor News*, covered the event, and later the *Detroit News* also picked up the story.[60] While the earlier press coverage provided mostly a summary of the day's activities, the *Detroit News* article, written close to a month after the University of Michigan Board of Regents meeting, included comments by John O'Shea on the case. In the article, O'Shea articulated his concern that, if the remains and objects were returned to the tribes, broader scientific knowledge would suffer a great loss. The journalist represented O'Shea's viewpoint as follows: "'What we lose if we give away this pot,' O'Shea said, his hand running along the edges of the quart-sized bowl dated to 700 A.D. . . . 'is all the layers of evidence that are in the porous matrix of the ceramic, which is why it is in a museum. . . . They have to realize that they are extremely valuable as evidence of the past and that they should be maintained.'"[61]

His position is shared by some archaeologists, who, from the earliest debates over NAGPRA, have argued that repatriating Native American human remains and cultural items would result in a great loss to science and, allegedly, to the greater public good. Indigenous communities have critiqued this position as ill informed and paternalistic. It also fails to recognize the disparity—indeed, contradiction—in how graves of Native people versus graves of other American citizens have been treated throughout history. Many people generally accept that what is at stake here are ultimately questions of power, ownership, and who has the right to control the Native American past. O'Shea's comments reflect a mind-set that is all too familiar to tribes who work tirelessly on this issue, and stances such as these will continue to pose an obstacle to future negotiations over the fate of the CUHRS.

As of this writing, the Saginaw Chippewa and MACPRA request for the ancestors and cultural objects at the University of Michigan Museum of Anthropology has not been resolved, even in the wake of formal promulgation of the final rule on the disposition of CUHRS in May 2010. In June 2008, the Ziibiwing Center hosted a strategy session called the "1390 Summit," which brought together Anishinaabek leaders from throughout the state and other repatriation experts to develop a plan to address the University of Michigan situation. Participants engaged in critical discussions about how to reclaim their relatives and cultural items, and those in attendance benefited immensely from the presentation of Paul Williams, the First Nations attorney who assisted the Whitefish Bay Anishinabe community of Ontario, Canada, in another high-profile repatriation battle with the University of Michigan.

I had the privilege of attending this event, and I listened attentively as the Michigan Native leaders developed a plan to address this pressing issue of NAGPRA compliance and the fate of their ancestors deemed CUHRS. I further saw the willingness of the Ziibiwing Center's staff to address this issue of great importance not only to the Michigan Anishinaabek but to all tribal nations in the United States as well. Indigenous people across the country are engaged in ongoing battles with museums and federal agencies over the fate of their ancestors who have been designated CUHRS, and university museums are some of the institutions most reluctant to repatriate.

The University of Michigan case has the potential to set a precedent, and a victory here would be a great step forward not only for the descendants of the Anishinabek ancestors, but for all tribal nations engaged in these struggles. As Joseph Sowmick stated in his speech before the University of Michigan Board of Regents, "Please rest assured that our perseverance and determination will carry us through once again—as this issue is of the utmost importance to us all." Repatriation efforts will certainly continue under the leadership of Ziibiwing's current director, Shannon Martin. The Ziibiwing staff's persistent work to decolonize NAGPRA and to bring their relatives home situates them as national leaders in this field of critical importance to all Indigenous communities.

CONCLUSION

Museums, as we know, are as much about the present and future as they are about the past. As we look to the future, I believe it is critical that museums support Indigenous communities in our efforts toward decolonization. This includes a commitment on the part of museums to privilege Indigenous voices and perspectives, to challenge stereotypical representations of Native people that were produced in the past, and to serve as educational forums for our own communities and the public. Furthermore, the hard truths of our history need to be stated to a nation that has willfully sought to silence our versions of the past. This is essential for the good of both our communities and the wider public. We need to tell the hard truths of colonization— explicitly and specifically—in our twenty-first-century museums.

My research on the Ziibiwing Center of Anishinabe Culture & Lifeways builds upon my previous work on the National Museum of the American Indian (NMAI) and my concern over labeling the NMAI as a "decolonizing museum." While I fully support the NMAI's collaborative methodology of working with tribal communities from throughout the hemisphere, my concern is about the absence in its exhibitions of a clear, coherent, and hard-hitting analysis of colonialism and its ongoing effects. Without this context, the museum falls short of moving us forward in our efforts toward decolonization.

As one of the newest tribally owned and operated museums, the Ziibiwing Center exemplifies a decolonizing museum practice in multiple ways. Its exhibits both privilege oral tradition and speak the hard truths of colonization, which together promote healing and understanding in the Saginaw Chippewa community, and its programming is designed to complement the decolonizing vision of the galleries. The complex story of this tribal nation is presented powerfully and beautifully in the galleries, which embody the best new representational strategies. Ziibiwing's work is heavily informed by important scholarship on historical unresolved grief and broader theoretical literature in Native American studies.

Conversations with staff members indicate that visitors respond very favorably to the museum's exhibitions, and tribal and nontribal members have even described their engagement with the *Diba Jimooyung: Telling Our Story* permanent exhibit as "a spiritual experience because of the way the ancient teachings are woven into the story."[62] This museum provides an important forum for Saginaw Chippewa members to understand their unique history and culture and thereby to empower current and future generations. Founding Director Bonnie Ekdahl has suggested that "healing our own community" is the primary goal for this museum. By honoring the Anishinabe oral tradition, engaging in truth telling, and serving as a "living cultural center," it is taking powerful steps in this healing direction.[63]

CONCLUSION

Transforming Museums into "Places that Matter"
for Indigenous Peoples

I would like to return for a moment to the lessons I learned while working at the Minnesota Historical Society (MHS) on community-collaborative
exhibitions. In chapter 2, I discuss the process of building the new Mille
Lacs Indian Museum that opened in 1996. From the start, the MHS curatorial team made the commitment to respond to the wishes of the Mille Lacs
Band and to give them final authority in content decisions. The following
exchange demonstrates the process of privileging their perspective during
the planning process.

I was in my late twenties at the time, and my academic training was fresh
in my mind. I was excited to have this job at MHS where I could work as an
exhibit researcher, especially on Indigenous themes and with Native communities. In the fall of 1994, I was assigned the task of developing the historic time line for the exhibit, beginning with the origin story of the Mille
Lacs Band. I immersed myself in the research and studied the Anishinabe
origin story as published in William Whipple Warren's *History of the Ojib-
way People* and as told by other Anishinabe writers. I also had conversations
with community members on this subject.

During the research process and in discussions with other MHS staff, the
idea emerged to include various other theories about the origins of the Mille
Lacs Band as well as about Native American origins in general. In line with
the then current academic approach of presenting multiple perspectives—
what Ruth Phillips has since referred to as the "multivocal exhibit model"—
we considered presenting a diversity of viewpoints on Native peoples' origins. With this in mind, I immersed myself in studying the Bering Strait

theory and other stories of Native origins—Native and non-Native. In retrospect, I realize the drawbacks of the multivocal approach when it comes to giving primacy to Native perspectives. Instead of privileging Native voices otherwise not heard, it potentially buries them in a hodgepodge of conflicting views, marginalizing and minimizing the wisdom embodied in Native origin stories. At the time, though, my academic training got the better of me. I thought we could offer all of these origin stories in one place and still privilege the perspective of the Mille Lacs Band.

What happened next was a painful but important lesson for me. During this period in the exhibit's development, the Minnesota Historical Society exhibit team met monthly with the Mille Lacs Band advisory board members to go over content ideas for the exhibit. The team members from MHS —Kate Roberts (curator), Shana Crosson (exhibit researcher), Rick Polenek (designer), Kendra Dillard (collections specialist), Dan Miller (production lead), Sarah Libertus (project manager), Jack Rumpel (designer), and myself (exhibit researcher)—would pile into a Minnesota State van for the ninety-minute drive to the Mille Lacs reservation for a daylong meeting with the Band's advisory board. At these meetings, we typically worked through various proposals for exhibit sections, which Kate Roberts and Joycelyn Shingobe Wedll outlined. In some instances, the team brought mock-ups of exhibit sections for the community to review. We also discussed areas to consider for next time and then enjoyed a lunch together at the casino buffet.

One of these meetings in 1994 was devoted to going over the historic timeline section. On that day, I took the floor and presented the research I had conducted on the various stories of tribal origins and mentioned the possibility of having a multivocal exhibit. I will never forget the Mille Lacs community members' reactions. They said firmly: "We do not care what other people say about our origins. We want to feature only our story." I immediately sunk in my chair, worried that I might have offended them. Thankfully, Kate Roberts took over the discussion. She assured them that this idea was just an idea and could certainly be abandoned if they saw fit. The multivocal approach I had proposed was abandoned, and I learned a valuable lesson that day.

For generations and in countless museums even today, tribal origin stories have not been privileged, and if they are mentioned, museums present them as quaint myths of primitive peoples. They are not taken seriously or treated as having profound and real meaning. A multivocal approach represented the effort by the more progressive museums of the 1990s to deal more fairly with such material. When museum professionals were faced with presenting sensitive topics, especially those of a more controversial nature, they would present a range of perspectives and leave it to visitors to weigh the value of each.

But the Mille Lacs Indian Museum was not about maintaining or following the status quo. It was not about presenting all views. Instead, it would be about privileging the voices, stories, history, and memory of the Mille Lacs Band of Ojibwe—on their reservation, in their museum. Presenting the origin story of the people in a powerful first-person voice was critical to maintaining the community-based curatorial practice in this "hybrid tribal museum."

I share this story not only to emphasize the role of the Mille Lacs advisory board in deciding exhibit content but also to show my own learning process—my development as a Native scholar devoted to decolonizing museums. At the time, I was deeply embarrassed that I did not realize how sensitive this issue would be—and that I even suggested such an approach to the community members. Moving to the place of respecting and privileging Native voices in museum work inevitably involves painful experiences, such as the one I just described. These experiences need not be a cause for negative judgments or taking things personally. Rather, they show that participants are engaged in an authentic, transformative process. As with any relationship, the challenge lies in how we respond to these experiences when they arise.

Developing community-collaborative exhibitions demands more than just being well versed in the scholarly literature on respective topics or on the latest in exhibition practices. It is about building trust, developing relationships, communicating, sharing authority, and being humble. As Linda Tuhiwai Smith states when she describes the process of working with Indigenous communities on collaborative research projects, "If I have one consistent message for the students I teach and the researchers I train it is that indigenous research is a humble and humbling activity."[1] I learned that lesson firsthand and will always be grateful for it. In the process, I realized that the voice and perspective of the Mille Lacs Band advisory board had to take the lead in making the overall content decisions in their new museum and that pursuing this type of methodology in community-collaborative exhibitions is a central part of a decolonizing museum practice.

Privileging Indigenous voices and perspectives, challenging stereotypes that have dominated museum representations of the past, and serving as sites of "knowledge making and remembering" for our own communities and the general public are only the beginning of a decolonizing museum practice. As the museum world explores further what a decolonizing museum practice involves, I believe it is critical for museums to speak the hard truths of colonization and to honor Indigenous ways of understanding history.

When museums shy away from telling these truths, they sadly limit their capacities to address the historical unresolved grief that is ever present in Native American communities. It does, however, take considerable vision to do this work. Shying away from speaking the hard truths leads to tragically missed opportunities. The good that museums could do for addressing and healing historical grief and trauma and for putting Native peoples on a positive, self-empowering path can be squandered all too easily.

The three museum case studies I have included in this book illuminate the various facets and stages of a decolonizing museum practice. I have analyzed the practices of the three museums not only within this decolonizing framework but also during a period of considerable change in the relationship between the museum world and Indigenous communities. Each of the museums tells a different piece of this story. When I think back to where the best of the museum world was in the mid-1990s (much less the worst) and then think about what the Ziibiwing museum is doing today, I realize that I have been a firsthand witness to this transformation toward clear Indigenous voices and empowerment through museums. While there is a great deal of work that remains, I believe museums have the potential—through both their exhibits and their programming—to promote healing, revitalization, and nation building for Indigenous peoples.

What happens when museums do the decolonizing work? Museums become places for building momentum for healing, for community, and for restoring dignity and respect. By using the focus of Indigenous peoples to guide their work, those involved in developing museums change what museums are all about. Museums cease to function as places of oppression or for perpetrating colonizer-serving images and models. The decolonizing direction enables museums to become places for decolonizing the representations of Native peoples and for promoting community healing and empowerment. In other words, museums become a means for repairing colonization's harm.

But this does not happen overnight. The story I have told in this book spans nearly two decades. Decolonizing museums by transforming what museums are all about has been—and continues to be—a process. What is happening in the museum world for Native peoples has not been a dramatic takeover but is the result of a long history of activism and a persistent push to honor and privilege Native voices, perspectives, and understandings.

DECOLONIZING ENGAGES A COLLABORATIVE METHODOLOGY

The three museums I have discussed have played different roles in shifting the consciousness and practice around decolonizing and indigenizing museums. As my analysis of the Mille Lacs Indian Museum highlights, this museum emerged at a critical moment in the larger shift in the museum world. It clearly embodied new museum theory put into practice. This happened because of a commitment on the part of the Minnesota Historical Society to change the site from an MHS-controlled site to a "hybrid tribal museum." Those involved on both sides stepped up to the challenges posed by museum theorists to remake museums "from a site of worship and awe to one of discourse and critical reflection that is committed to examining unsettling histories with sensitivity to all parties."[2]

Furthermore, these theorists advocated for museums to be "transparent in [their] decision making and willing to share power. New museum theory is about decolonizing, giving those represented control over their own cultural heritage."[3] During the seventeen-year process of transforming the museum at Mille Lacs, my colleagues and I clearly witnessed the "power sharing" on the part of MHS. Only by sharing power could a museum emerge—MHS funded as it is—that ultimately features the voice and tribal memory of the Mille Lacs Band of Ojibwe.

By pursuing a rigorous, community-based, collaborative methodology, the two groups—the Mille Lacs Band and MHS—helped set a precedent for what would follow in the larger museum world, most notably, the Smithsonian's National Museum of the American Indian. The limited programming efforts of the Mille Lacs Indian Museum reflect the hybrid nature of the museum and the challenges inherent in such a relationship. However, I must emphasize that the approach pursued there not only helped set the stage for the NMAI, but also provided the foundation from which the Ziibiwing Center of Anishinabe Culture & Lifeways in Michigan could later emerge.

DECOLONIZING: FROM SITES OF OPPRESSION
TO PLACES THAT MATTER

Some Native American scholars and activists have questioned my decision to study museums and their potential to serve as sites of decolonization. "Aren't museums just colonial sites that should basically just release our stuff?" My two decades of experience leads me to see more. Yes, museums have a terrible history as places intimately tied to the colonization process. Of course, ancestral remains, associated funerary objects, sacred objects, and objects of cultural patrimony should be returned to those to whom they belong, and I remain deeply committed to repatriation efforts. However, righting wrongs is only the beginning of decolonizing. The possibility of decolonizing and indigenizing museums lies in transforming these sites of colonial harm into sites of healing, and restoring community well-being. Decolonizing is powerful not only because it ends and mends harms, but also because it opens opportunities. What was impossible for generations is slowly becoming possible. Sites of oppression have the potential to transform into sites of revitalization and autonomy.

In these endeavors, I have found that the emerging work of tribal museums can make a difference in places like the Saginaw Chippewa community. Since my first engagement with the Ziibiwing Center in 2006, I have witnessed its growth far beyond being a place that stands frozen as a site of static representation. The Ziibiwing Center has become a focal point for important community work on many levels. It champions ongoing efforts to repatriate ancestors, including the recent reburial of 160 ancestors and 374 associated funerary objects from Central Michigan University at the tribe's Nibokaan Ancestral Cemetery, which took place in 2010. It has stepped up and protected ancestors who were dug up from graves in Flint, Michigan, as a result of an inadvertent discovery of a tribal burial ground during a real estate development project in 2009. And it is developing school curriculum to assist public schools in understanding the difficult history of boarding schools. This place matters. Tremendously. And not just to a few history buffs in the community who may take a guest there once in a while. The community actively uses this place to help its tribal citizens understand who they are as Anishinabek people.

DECOLONIZING GOES BEYOND SURVIVANCE

The Mille Lacs Indian Museum and the National Museum of the American Indian matter tremendously as well, as they too carry forward important educational objectives. I offer my critiques of them not to diminish their potential but to support them in becoming even more effective as forces for decolonizing and for supporting Native peoples. As I argue throughout, decolonizing must include narratives that allow for truth telling and for a critical analysis of colonialism and its ongoing effects. The time for exhibits that merely state "we are still here" through an emphasis on our contemporary survival is past.

Without question, survivance is a powerful and affirmative message to communicate in the face of the American master narrative that depends on our erasure and silence. There is no denying our continuance. But if museums are to serve as sites of decolonization and are to follow Indigenous community-based practices, I believe we need to speak the hard truths of our history as well. We need the hard truths spoken both for our own communities and for the general public. And we need the hard truths told so we can confront fully where we are now. Only from this honest and balanced assessment can we move forward.

DECOLONIZING IS SHARING INDIGENOUS KNOWLEDGE

By comparing these three museums—how they developed and what they have become—I have been examining the changing relationship between Indigenous communities and museums. My desire is to give voice to those sites that are doing the challenging, transformative work, as I understand it. How are they changing the cultural institutions that have been so deeply tied to colonization? I have sought to understand the unique subjectivity of each institution and to trace the genealogy of each museum's current exhibitions and programming. Through this comparative process, I believe we can gain many insights into the best practices—those that our Native communities need in order to develop museums into "places that matter." Linda Tuhiwai Smith reminds us:

> What is more important than what alternatives indigenous peoples offer the world is what alternatives indigenous people offer each other. . . . The spiritual, creative and political resources that indigenous peoples can draw on from each other provide alternatives for each other. Sharing is a good thing to do, it is a very human quality. To be able to share,

to have something worth sharing gives dignity to the giver. To accept a gift and to reciprocate gives dignity to the receiver. To create something new through that process of sharing is to recreate the old, to reconnect relationships and to recreate our humanness.[4]

My hope is that what I have written based on my research and experiences can help us all understand how to make museums more Indigenous based and transformative for our communities. To advance our museum work in these directions, we must embrace the role of museums in helping Native peoples confront the hard truths of our history and continue our efforts to move toward decolonization and community empowerment.

notes

PREFACE

1. For additional historical coverage of the war, see Gary Clayton Anderson and Woolworth, *Through Dakota Eyes*; Meyer, *History of the Santee Sioux*; Carly, *Sioux Uprising of 1862*; Gary Clayton Anderson, *Little Crow*; Schultz, *Over the Earth I Come*; and for more recent coverage of the war as part of a larger text on Minnesota history, see Wingerd, *North Country*. On the legacy of the war and its aftermath, see Waziyatawin Angela Wilson, *In the Footsteps of Our Ancestors*, and Waziyatawin, *What Does Justice Look Like?*

2. Quoted in Waziyatawin Angela Wilson, "Decolonizing the 1862 Death Marches," 190.

3. In 2004 and 2006, I participated in a commemorative event to honor the thousands of Dakota people who were forced out of the state of Minnesota following the U.S.-Dakota War of 1862. During the commemorative march, participants retraced the original 150-mile route that the sixteen hundred mostly Dakota women and children were forced to walk in 1862. The Dakota Commemorative March, held every two years in Minnesota, is viewed by many as an important act of decolonization and Indigenous commemoration and as a powerful act of healing, remembrance, truth telling, and reclamation. The event has profoundly influenced my personal and professional life, and in an essay based on my participation, "Transforming Lives by Reclaiming Memory," I examine the commemorative march not only as an act of healing but also as an expression of Indigenous memory and a Dakota challenge to the master narrative of the U.S.-Dakota War. The essay also has personal importance because thousands of Ho-Chunk people were exiled from Minnesota at the same time and the forced removal of my people has largely been erased from the memory of this event. Through my participation, I challenged the erasure of Ho-Chunk forced removal from Minnesota and therefore added another layer of memory to this decolonizing project.

4. For a summary of their lives, see Ramona Kitto Stately's touching essay on her participation in the Dakota Commemorative March, "Pazahiyayewin and the Importance of Remembering Dakota Women."

CHAPTER 1

1. Gail Anderson, "Introduction," 1.
2. McLean, "Museum Exhibitions and the Dynamics of Dialogue," 193.
3. Penney, "Poetics of Museum Representations," 47.
4. Erikson, *Voices of a Thousand People*, 189.
5. Erikson, *Voices of a Thousand People*.
6. Ibid., 27–28.

7. Bodinger de Uriarte, *Casino and Museum*, and Isaac, *Mediating Knowledges*.

8. The literature on collaboration has been growing over the last decade. Important titles include Parezo, "Indian Fashion Show"; Peers and Brown, *Museums and Source Communities*; Clifford, *Routes*; Clifford, "Looking Several Ways"; Erikson, *Voices of a Thousand People*; Bowechop and Erikson, "Forging Indigenous Methodologies on Cape Flattery"; Archambault, "American Indians and American Museums"; Krmpotich and Anderson, "Collaborative Exhibitions and Visitor Reactions"; Shannon, "Construction of Native Voice at the National Museum of the American Indian"; and Simpson, *Making Representations*.

9. Phillips, "Re-placing Objects."

10. On the new museum theory and practice, see Ames, *Cannibal Tours and Glass Boxes*; Gail Anderson, *Reinventing the Museum*; Clavir, *Preserving What Is Valued*; Erikson, *Voices of a Thousand People*; Greenberg, Ferguson, and Nairne, *Thinking about Exhibitions*; Hooper-Greenhill, *Museums and the Shaping of Knowledge*; Karp et al., *Museum Frictions*; Karp and Lavine, *Exhibiting Cultures*; Kreps, *Liberating Culture*; Lonetree and Cobb, *National Museum of the American Indian*; Marstine, *New Museum Theory and Practice*; Message, *New Museums and the Making of Culture*; Peers and Brown, *Museums and Source Communities*; and Simpson, *Making Representations*.

11. I borrow this phrase from Patricia Pierce Erikson. See Erikson, *Voices of a Thousand People*, 30, and Erikson, "A-Whaling We Will Go."

12. Brave Heart, "Historical Trauma Response among Natives and Its Relationship with Substance Abuse," 7.

13. Brave Heart, "Gender Differences in the Historical Trauma Response among the Lakota," 3.

14. Brave Heart and DeBruyn, "American Indian Holocaust," 72.

15. Poupart, "Familiar Face of Genocide," 96.

16. Paul Chaat Smith, in his recent publication *Everything You Know about Indians Is Wrong*, expresses his reluctance to discuss the specifics of the history of colonialism within the introductory sections of his book. This reluctance to recount the specifics of this history, I would argue, is also present in the "Evidence" section of the *Our Peoples* gallery at the NMAI, which Smith co-curated.

17. Waziyatawin, "Colonialism on the Ground."

18. Miller, "Native America Writes Back."

19. Susan Miller emphasizes the influence of a 1960s, U.S.-based Native American intellectual tradition that includes Vine Deloria Jr., Clyde Warrior, Robert K. Thomas, Rupert Costo, and Jeannette Henry Costo.

20. Miller, "Native America Writes Back," 14.

21. Ibid.

22. Ibid., 17–18.

23. Stevenson, "Decolonizing Tribal Histories," 212, quoted in Waziyatawin Angela Wilson, *Remember This!*, 13–14.

24. Miller, "Native America Writes Back," 15–16.

25. Shepherd, *We Are an Indian Nation*, 8.

26. Hoxie, Mancall, and Merrell, "Cultural and Political Transformations," 263. The phrase "the Dark Ages of Native history" is used by the authors to describe the period

roughly from 1900 to 1950. I have always found this to be an apt phrase, because it captures how poorly represented this period in Native history has been in the historical record. I am referring in this section to the earlier part of "the Dark Ages of Native history" when most of the collecting took place.

27. Berlo, *Early Years of Native American Art History*, 3.

28. Hoxie, "Exploring a Cultural Borderland," 267.

29. Ibid.

30. See Thornton, *American Indian Holocaust and Survival*; Stannard, *American Holocaust*; and Stannard, "Disease and Infertility."

31. McDonnell, *The Dispossession of the American Indian*, 121.

32. Iverson, *"We Are Still Here,"* 26.

33. Cole, *Captured Heritage*, 286.

34. Tweedie, *Drawing Back Culture*, 52.

35. Ibid., 60.

36. Thornton, "Who Owns Our Past?," 387.

37. Ibid., 388.

38. Riding In, "Our Dead Are Never Forgotten," 298.

39. Ibid.

40. Harjo, introduction to Meister, *Mending the Circle*. See also Riding In, "Six Pawnee Crania."

41. As cited in Riding In, "Our Dead Are Never Forgotten," 306.

42. Ibid.

43. Watkins, "Antiquities Act at One Hundred Years."

44. Dumont, "Politics of Scientific Objections to Repatriation," 117.

45. Echo-Hawk and Echo-Hawk, "Repatriation, Reburial and Religious Rights," 179–80.

46. Maurer, "Presenting the American Indian," 19–20.

47. Ames, *Cannibal Tours and Glass Boxes*, 50.

48. Ibid., 51.

49. Ibid.

50. Ibid.

51. Nason, "'Our' Indians," 37.

52. Ames, *Cannibal Tours and Glass Boxes*, 53.

53. Ibid., 56.

54. Boast, "Neocolonial Collaboration," 56.

55. Phillips, introduction to "Community Collaboration in Exhibitions," 158.

56. Ibid.

57. Erikson, *Voices of a Thousand People*, 33.

58. Ames, "Are Changing Representations of First Peoples in Canadian Museums and Galleries Challenging the Curatorial Prerogative?," 74.

59. Trope and Echo-Hawk, "Native American Graves Protection and Repatriation Act," 141.

60. Bower and Putnam, "Walter Echo-Hawk Fights for His People's Right to Rest in Peace—Not in Museums."

61. Simpson, *Making Representations*, 137.

62. Abrams, *Tribal Museums in America*, 4.

63. Ibid.

64. Cooper and Sandoval, *Living Homes for Cultural Expression*, 8.

65. Abrams, *Tribal Museums in America*, 3.

66. Archambault, "American Indians and American Museums," 21–22.

67. Hernandez, "Past Is Perfect in the Present Tense," 157.

68. Phillips, introduction to "Community Collaboration in Exhibitions," 158.

69. Ibid., 163.

70. Nicks, introduction to "Museums and Contact Work," 21.

71. Tisdale, "Cocopah Identity and Cultural Survival," 286–350.

72. Boast, "Neocolonial Collaboration," 67.

73. For an excellent analysis of the current state of NAGPRA compliance and the efforts of members of the scientific community to rewrite the legislative history of the act to serve their needs in the present, see Dumont, "Contesting Scientists' Narrations of NAGPRA's Legislative History."

CHAPTER 2

1. W. Richard West to the American Association for State and Local History, 14 March 1997, "American Association for State and Local History Awards Nomination Materials," Exhibit Curator Files, Minnesota Historical Society/Mille Lacs Indian Museum, Saint Paul.

2. Tooker interview. Jennifer Stampe, in her dissertation, refers to the museum as "The Tribal Museum that Wasn't" ("'You *Will* Learn about Our Past," 67).

3. Archabal interview.

4. Quoted in Coleman, "Spirit Unbroken," 6a.

5. Treuer, *Ojibwe in Minnesota*, 10–11.

6. Ibid., 11.

7. "National Endowment for the Humanities Implementation Grant," 1993, 6, Exhibit Curator Files, Minnesota Historical Society/Mille Lacs Indian Museum, Saint Paul.

8. Wedll, "Learn about Our Past to Understand Our Future," 90.

9. "Top 10 Things to Know about the Mille Lacs Band of Ojibwe," Mille Lacs Band of Ojibwe, http://www.millelacsband.com/Page_FactSheet_Top10.aspx (accessed 6 September 2010).

10. Vizenor, introduction to Vizenor, *Native American Literature*, 6. Curator Kate Roberts, when asked which scholarship influenced her content decisions for the new museum, mentioned Ojibwe authors Gerald Vizenor and Kimberly Blaeser, whom she believed convey through their poetry and short stories the spirit of the Ojibwe people. Roberts interview.

11. Treuer, *Living Our Language*, 50.

12. Ibid.

13. Ibid.

14. "National Endowment for the Humanities Implementation Grant," 1993, 9, Exhibit Curator Files.

15. Wedll, "Learn about Our Past to Understand Our Future," 90.

16. Buffalohead and Buffalohead, *Against the Tide of American History*, 74.

17. Libertus, "Preview: The New Mille Lacs Indian Museum," 33–34.

18. Roberts interview.

19. Mille Lacs Indian Museum: Interpretation Files, n.d., Minnesota Historical Society, State Archives, Saint Paul, Box 799.

20. "National Endowment for the Humanities Implementation Grant," 1993, 37, Exhibit Curator Files.

21. Quoted in Meier, "Continuing Story," E4.

22. "National Endowment for the Humanities Implementation Grant," 1993, 81, Exhibit Curator Files.

23. Thomas Vennum, report submitted as part of the 1979 self-study of the Mille Lacs Indian Museum, Exhibit Curator Files, Minnesota Historical Society/Mille Lacs Indian Museum, Saint Paul.

24. Ibid.

25. The consultants working with MHS in 1984 included Carey T. Caldwell, director of the Suquamish Tribal Cultural Center and Museum; George P. Horse Capture, curator at the Plains Indian Museum; Freda McDonald, supervisor of the Native Encampment at Old Fort William; John D. Nichols, a professor in the Department of Native Studies at the University of Manitoba; and Dave Warren, director of Cultural Studies, Resource and Research Center at the Institute of American Indian Arts.

26. During the 1984 review process, George Horse Capture advocated that the site focus on the Mille Lacs Band: "For now we should only focus on a good Mille Lacs Chippewa Indian Museum. The museum can stress anything they desire, in general terms, but must do the best job on their own band's history and culture, because no one else will ever do it as well as themselves." George Horse Capture, report submitted as part of the 1984 self-study of the Mille Lacs Indian Museum, Exhibit Curator Files, Minnesota Historical Society/Mille Lacs Indian Museum, Saint Paul.

27. Vennum, report submitted as part of the 1979 self-study, Exhibit Curator Files.

28. Archabal interview.

29. Ibid.

30. These individuals are listed in "A Concept Plan for the New Indian Museum and Cultural Center," 1985, 16, Historic Sites Department Records, Minnesota Historical Society/Mille Lacs Indian Museum. The following individuals are listed in an undated document in the Historic Sites Department records as also contributing to the project: Arthur Gahbow (tribal chair), Doug Sam, Lanette Bellacourt, and Raining Boyd. Internal Historic Sites Department memo, undated, ibid.

31. Archabal interview.

32. Krmpotich and Anderson, "Collaborative Exhibitions and Visitor Reactions," 380.

33. "A Building Program for the Mille Lacs Indian Museum and Historic Site," May 1992, 17, Historic Sites Department Records, Minnesota Historical Society/Mille Lacs Indian Museum, Saint Paul.

34. Simpson, *Making Representations*, 137.

35. "Concept Plan for the New Indian Museum and Cultural Center," 1984–85, 5, Historic Sites Department Records.

36. Other funding sources for the project included $100,000 from the Mille Lacs Band, $250,000 from the McKnight Foundation, $257,334 from the Intermodal Surface Transportation Efficiency Act Highway Enhancement Funds, and $150,000 from the Laura Jane Musser Foundation. Public Relations Materials, 1996, Historic Sites Department Records, Minnesota Historical Society/Mille Lacs Indian Museum, Saint Paul.

37. Archabal interview.

38. Tooker interview.

39. Horse Capture, report submitted as part of the 1984 self-study, Exhibit Curator Files.

40. Mille Lacs Band of Chippewa Indians, Legislative Branch of Tribal Government, "A Resolution Approving the Grant of an Easement to the Minnesota Historical Society and Authorizing a Land Exchange between the Minnesota Historical Society and the Mille Lacs Band of Ojibwe," 30 March 1993, Historic Sites Department Records, Minnesota Historical Society/Mille Lacs Indian Museum, Saint Paul. Negotiations to resolve the land issue spanned several years. The project manager at the time, Rachel Tooker, made note of it in a progress report on the project to Marge Anderson (chief executive officer of the Mille Lacs Band) and Dave Matrious on 15 April 1992. Historic Sites Department Records, Minnesota Historical Society/Mille Lacs Indian Museum, Saint Paul.

41. Wedll, "Learn about Our Past to Understand Our Future," 92.

42. Ibid.

43. Clifford, "Looking Several Ways," 9.

44. Roberts interview.

45. Ibid.

46. Ibid.

47. "American Association for State and Local History Awards Nomination Materials," 1997, 9, Exhibit Curator Files, Minnesota Historical Society/Mille Lacs Indian Museum, Saint Paul.

48. Ibid.

49. Ames, "Are Changing Representations of First Peoples in Canadian Museums and Galleries Challenging the Curatorial Prerogative?," 82–83.

50. "American Association for State and Local History Award Nomination Materials," 1997, 3.

51. Opening text panel, introductory section, Mille Lacs Indian Museum.

52. Roberts interview.

53. During a site visit to the Mille Lacs Indian Museum in June 2010, I learned from Travis Zimmerman, the site manager, that the plaque with the headline "Onamia Indians Starving, Nun Says" was taken down by request. He explained that a tribal member asked for its removal because she felt "it makes it look like our grandparents were not taking care of the children."

54. Introductory text panel: "Our Living Culture," Mille Lacs Indian Museum.

55. Members of the Minnesota Historical Society exhibition team visited several museums that they believed would provide ideas for them as they developed the Mille Lacs Indian Museum. Team members visited several tribal museums in the Pacific Northwest, including the Museum at Warm Springs in Oregon and the Makah Cultural and Research Museum in Washington. Curator Kate Roberts believes that the spirit of the

Mille Lacs Indian Museum is very similar to that of the Museum at Warm Springs. Roberts interview.

56. Crosson interview.

57. Archabal interview.

58. Cobb, "Understanding Tribal Sovereignty," 124.

59. Introductory text panel: "Nation within a Nation," Mille Lacs Indian Museum.

60. For more information on the lawsuit, see McClurken, *Fish in the Lakes, Wild Rice, and Game in Abundance.*

61. Table flip-books: "Nation within a Nation," Mille Lacs Indian Museum.

62. "American Association for State and Local History Awards Nomination Materials," 1997, 3, Exhibit Curator Files.

63. Text panel: "Making a Living," Mille Lacs Indian Museum.

64. Ibid.

65. Roberts interview.

66. Bauer, *We Were All like Migrant Workers Here*, 2.

67. Interactive media: "Making a Living," Mille Lacs Indian Museum.

68. Ibid.

69. Ibid.

70. "American Association for State and Local History Awards Nomination Materials," 1997, 4, Exhibit Curator Files.

71. Wedll, "Learn about Our Past to Understand Our Future," 92.

72. Quoted in Meier, "Continuing Story."

73. Following completion of the survey, some on the Mille Lacs Indian Museum team were concerned that this section might reinforce commonly held stereotypes of a vanishing culture. Steps would later be taken to address this concern by making stronger connections to other sections of the gallery that focus on twentieth-century themes.

74. Margaret Dubin, *Native America Collected*, 86.

75. Text panel, "Trading Post" exhibit, Mille Lacs Indian Museum.

76. Horse Capture, report submitted as part of the 1984 self-study, Exhibit Curator Files.

77. Coleman, "Spirit Unbroken."

78. Adam Bickford, "Summative Evaluation of the Mille Lacs Indian Museum," October 1996, Exhibit Curator Files, Minnesota Historical Society/Mille Lacs Indian Museum, Saint Paul.

79. "Final Report to the National Endowment for the Humanities Museum Programs Division," 11 June 1997, ibid.

80. Bickford, "Summative Evaluation of the Mille Lacs Indian Museum," October 1996, Exhibit Curator Files.

81. Quoted in Meier, "Continuing Story."

82. West to the American Association for State and Local History, 14 March 1997, Exhibit Curator Files.

83. Ibid.

84. Stampe, "Views from Here," 134.

85. Ibid., 135.

86. Tooker interview.

87. Archabal interview.

88. Vennum, report submitted as part of the 1979 self-study, Exhibit Curator Files.

89. Tweedie, *Drawing Back Culture*, 60.

90. Archabal interview.

91. The museum is also open during the months of April, May, September, and October on Wednesday through Saturday from 11 A.M. to 4 P.M. School groups can also make appointments during the year.

92. Zimmerman interview.

CHAPTER 3

1. During my internship, the Smithsonian's National Museum of American History had two wonderful exhibitions: *A More Perfect Union* and *From Field to Factory*. Both left an indelible impression on me, given their critical interpretation of American history. Most notably, *A More Perfect Union* focused on the experiences of Japanese Americans during World War II. This was my first introduction to the history of the internment camps (as the Smithsonian called them) or concentration camps (the terminology used by many Asian American activists and scholars). Although these exhibitions were widely well received, they also spurred a major shift at the Smithsonian toward developing exhibits less critical of U.S. policies. It is safe to say that under its current leadership, and given exhibition controversies in the 1990s, the Smithsonian's choices today—both of exhibits and of how to present them—demonstrate a desire to acquiesce to the interests of Congress. For a discussion on the "culture wars" at the Smithsonian, see Linenthal and Engelhardt, *History Wars*, and Dorf, "Culture Wars in the Nation's Attic."

2. Quoted in Force, *Politics and the Museum of the American Indian*, 402.

3. The number of organizations, tribes, and communities featured in the exhibitions has been scaled back to eight.

4. Linenthal, *Preserving Memory*.

5. NMAI curatorial staff person, personal communication, 2001.

6. Lonetree, "Continuing Dialogues," "Missed Opportunities," and "'Acknowledging the Truth of History'" (a revised and expanded version of "Missed Opportunities").

7. Lonetree, "Critical Engagements with the National Museum of the American Indian," and Lonetree and Cobb, *National Museum of the American Indian*.

8. Ostrowitz, "Concourse and Periphery," 85.

9. McMullen, "Reinventing George Heye," 71. McMullen states that when Heye died in 1957, "the collections numbered over 225,000 catalog numbers representing perhaps more than 700,000 individual items"; according to McMullen, the NMAI's current collection totals "825,000 items" (ibid., 90)."

10. Kidwell, "Every Last Dishcloth," 250.

11. Jacknis, "A New Thing?," 10.

12. McMullen, "Reinventing George Heye," 86.

13. Thompson, "Mission Statement and Its Relationship to Museum Interpretative Practices," 91.

14. Force, *Politics and the Museum of the American Indian*, 8–12.

15. In his essay "A New Thing?," Jacknis claims that Vine Deloria became a trustee in 1977. But at a congressional hearing, Deloria himself stated that he served on the board for "about 20 years," which means his tenure began in roughly 1969. See *Establishment of the National Museum of the American Indian*, 18.

16. Thompson, "Mission Statement and Its Relationship to Museum Interpretative Practices," 102.

17. Ibid., 95–97.

18. *Establishment of the National Museum of the American Indian*, 23.

19. Jacknis, "A New Thing?," 20.

20. Ibid., 21.

21. *Establishment of the National Museum of the American Indian*, 23.

22. Ibid., 100.

23. McMullen, "Reinventing George Heye," 79.

24. Force, *Politics and the Museum of the American Indian*, xviii.

25. *Establishment of the National Museum of the American Indian*, 22.

26. Ibid, 20.

27. The influence of the Iroquois Confederacy on the Founding Fathers has been a cause of great scholarly controversy over the years. Historians such as Donald Grinde have argued that the Great Law of Peace that governed the Six Nations of the Iroquois Confederacy greatly influenced the Founding Fathers at the time of the signing of the U.S. Constitution. See Grinde and Johansen, *Exemplar of Liberty*.

28. *Establishment of the National Museum of the American Indian*, 102.

29. Erikson, "Decolonizing the 'Nation's Attic,'" 49–50.

30. McMaster interview.

31. West, "National Museum of the American Indian."

32. Volkert interview. Beginning in 1990, the museum held regional and urban meetings with tribal people to discuss their vision of the museum and how it should develop its facilities. For more information on the planning of the sites, see Venturi, Scott Brown and Associates, *Way of the People*.

33. Volkert interview.

34. Ibid.

35. Tom Hill and Hill, *Creation's Journey*.

36. Volkert interview.

37. West, "National Museum of the American Indian."

38. Cotter, "New Museum Celebrating American Indian Voices."

39. Volkert interview.

40. Arieff, "Different Sort of (P)Reservation," 81.

41. Ibid.

42. White, "Representing Indians," 29.

43. Ibid., 30.

44. National Museum of the American Indian, *All Roads Are Good*, 15.

45. West, "Who Gets the Talking Stick."

46. Margaret Dubin, *Native America Collected*, 90–92.

47. Cotter, "New Museum Celebrating American Indian Voices."

48. Margaret Dubin, *Native America Collected*, 94.

49. Hilden and Huhndorf, "Performing 'Indian' in the National Museum of the American Indian," 167.

50. Ibid., 176.

51. Ibid., 178.

52. Arieff, "Different Sort of (P)Reservation," 88.

53. Bernstein interview.

54. Venturi, Scott Brown and Associates, *Way of the People*.

55. Shannon, "Ethnography of 'Our Lives,'" 61.

56. "Mall Exhibition Guiding Principles," 1999, Curatorial Department Records, Cultural Resources Center, National Museum of the American Indian, Smithsonian Institution, Suitland, Md.

57. "Mall Exhibition Statement," dated 25 September 1999, ibid.

58. "Our Universes Exhibition Narrative," n.d., 1, ibid.

59. Ibid.

60. Her Many Horses interview.

61. Ibid.

62. Ibid.

63. See Cooper, *Spirited Encounters*, 15–49.

64. "Our Universes Exhibition Narrative," n.d., 5, Curatorial Department Records.

65. Quoted in Shannon, "Ethnography of 'Our Lives,'" 176.

66. Bernstein interview.

67. This decision was of particular interest to me in light of my previous research on the Mille Lacs Ojibwe community in Minnesota. They decided not to include any information related to their ceremonial life in the exhibitions developed for the new Mille Lacs Indian Museum.

68. Her Many Horses interview.

69. McMaster interview.

70. NMAI staff person, interview by author, December 2001.

71. "'Our Peoples' Information Prepared for the Senior Management Group," 13 September 2000, Curatorial Department Records, Cultural Resources Center, National Museum of the American Indian, Smithsonian Institution, Suitland, Md. The number of communities featured in the galleries would eventually be scaled back, and the museum would open with eight communities featured.

72. NMAI curatorial staff person, interview by author, 2001.

73. "'Our Peoples' Information Prepared for the Senior Management Group," 13 September 2000, Curatorial Department Records.

74. NMAI curatorial staff person, interview by author, 2001.

75. Ibid.

76. National Campaign Office, *Great American Spirit* [fund-raising document] (Washington, D.C.: National Museum of the American Indian, Smithsonian Institution, 2001), 13.

77. Tristine Smart to Bruce Bernstein, *Our Lives* progress report memo, 9 June 2000, Curatorial Department Records, Cultural Resources Center, National Museum of the American Indian, Smithsonian Institution, Suitland, Md.

78. NMAI staff member, personal communication.

79. Bruce Bernstein, quoted in Shannon, "Ethnography of 'Our Lives,'" 166.

80. Volkert interview.

81. During the 2002 annual meeting of the American Association of Museums, the following sessions dealt with audience and visitor experiences: "Standards of Excellence: Designing Accessible Exhibitions and Activities"; "Enhancing Visitor Observation Skills: Museum Collaborations with Untraditional Partners"; "Connecting with Our Visitors: A Community of Interpretation Professionals"; and "Can We Talk? Building a Language for Judging the Visitor Experience." These are only a few samples of the many sessions offered on the topic.

82. Shannon, "Ethnography of 'Our Lives,'" 178–79.

83. Ibid., 179.

84. Smith, "Ten Years of Accidental Victories, Brilliant Mistakes, and Useless Lessons."

85. Jacknis, Storage Box of Tradition, 105–6.

86. Gerald McMaster used this term when describing NMAI's evolving exhibition strategy. McMaster interview.

87. For scholars' critiques, see DeLugan, "'South of the Border' at the National Museum of the American Indian"; Carpio, "(Un)disturbing Exhibitions: Indigenous Historical Memory at the National Museum of the American Indian"; and Atalay, "No Sense of the Struggle: Creating a Context for Survivance at the National Museum of the American Indian." For reviews by journalists and cultural critics, see Fisher, "Indian Museum's Appeal, Sadly, Only Skin Deep"; Richard, "Shards of Many Untold Stories"; Rothstein, "Who Should Tell History"; Jenkins, "Museum of Political Correctness"; Achenbach, "Within These Walls"; and Noah, "National Museum of Ben Nighthorse Campbell."

88. Shannon, "Ethnography of 'Our Lives,'" 282.

89. Ibid., 283.

90. Claire Smith, "Decolonising the Museum"; Doyle, "National Museum of the American Indian Opens in Washington, D.C."; Cobb, "National Museum of the American Indian as Cultural Sovereignty"; Cobb, "National Museum of the American Indian"; and Archuleta, "Gym Shoes, Maps, and Passports, Oh My!"

91. Carpio, "(Un)disturbing Exhibitions: Indigenous Historical Memory at the NMAI," 297.

92. For an excellent study of the United States Holocaust Memorial Museum, see Linenthal, Preserving Memory.

93. Signed statement by American Indian Movement leaders Floyd Red Crow Westerman, Dennis Banks, and Clyde and Vernon Bellecourt, quoted in Rave, "Indian Museum Looks at Life, Death."

94. Quoted in Achenbach, "Within These Walls."

95. Claire Smith, "Decolonising the Museum," and Doyle, "National Museum of the American Indian."

96. Smithsonian TV, "Curator's Talk."

97. Ibid.

98. Ibid.

99. Isaac, "What Are Our Expectations Telling Us?," American Indian Quarterly, 585.

100. Ibid., 586.

101. Isaac, "What Are Our Expectations Telling Us?," in Lonetree and Cobb, *National Museum of the American Indian*, 255.

102. Barker and Dumont, "Contested Conversations," 124.

103. Peers, "Native Americans in Museums," 11.

104. Claire Smith, "Decolonising the Museum," 433.

105. Philip Porter, "Interpreters' Manual, Indian Encampment, Colonial Michilimackinac" (internal document for site use, 1992), quoted in Peers, *Playing Ourselves*, 100.

106. Peers, *Playing Ourselves*, 100.

107. Ibid., 104.

108. Paul Chaat Smith, *Making History*, narrated by Floyd Favel, "Evidence" video, National Museum of the American Indian.

109. Lonetree, "Continuing Dialogues," 60.

110. Mithlo, "History Is Dangerous," 57.

111. Claire Smith, "Decolonising the Museum," 437.

112. Waziyatawin and Yellow Bird, "Beginning Decolonization," 2.

113. Wakeham, "Performing Reconciliation at the National Museum of the American Indian," 354.

114. Ibid., 355.

115. West, "Remarks on the Occasion of the Grand Opening Ceremony."

116. Tsosie, "BIA's Apology to Native Americans," 201.

CHAPTER 4

1. Brave Heart, "Historical Trauma Response among Natives and Its Relationship with Substance Abuse," 7.

2. Brave Heart, "Gender Differences in the Historical Trauma Response among the Lakota," 3.

3. Brave Heart, "Historical Trauma Response among Natives and Its Relationship with Substance Abuse," 7.

4. Ibid., 11.

5. "Honoring Nations 2008 Online Application," 5, Ziibiwing Center of Anishinabe Culture & Lifeways, Mount Pleasant, Mich. Director Shannon Martin wrote the application and shared a copy with me.

6. Ekdahl interview.

7. Paul Johnson interview.

8. Ekdahl interview.

9. Ibid.

10. Paul Johnson interview.

11. Ekdahl interview.

12. Ibid.

13. McLean, "Museum Exhibitions and the Dynamics of Dialogue," 193.

14. I do not want to diminish in any way the importance of objects in exhibitions. What I am referring to here is the recent move to allow themes rather than objects to drive exhibit content. In newer types of exhibitions, objects are still very important but are used to illustrate certain themes.

15. Waziyatawin Angela Wilson, *Remember This!*, 50.

16. Denetdale, *Reclaiming Diné History*, 7.

17. The fall 2006 issue of *Museum Design* magazine features an interview with Bianca Message—president of André and Associates, the center's exhibit design firm—describing the uniqueness of the center's approach to presenting Anishinabe tribal philosophies. "Conversation with Bianca Message."

18. "Narrative: History of the Diba Jimooyung Permanent Exhibit/Two Voices," 3.

19. Erikson, *Voices of a Thousand People*, 30.

20. "Honoring Nations 2008: Semifinalist Application," 1, Ziibiwing Center of Anishinabe Culture & Lifeways, Mount Pleasant, Mich.

21. Text panel, area 1: "Petroglyphs," Ziibiwing Center of Anishinabe Culture & Lifeways.

22. Text panel, area 3: "Teaching Lodge," Ziibiwing Center of Anishinabe Culture & Lifeways.

23. Ekdahl interview.

24. "Narrative: History of the Diba Jimooyung Permanent Exhibit/Two Voices," 5.

25. Text panel, area 7: "Effects of Colonization," Ziibiwing Center of Anishinabe Culture & Lifeways.

26. Text panel, ibid.

27. Text panel, ibid.

28. "Narrative: History of the Diba Jimooyung Permanent Exhibit/Two Voices," 7.

29. Ibid.

30. Text panel, area 9: "Blood Memory," Ziibiwing Center of Anishinabe Culture & Lifeways.

31. Phillips, "Re-placing Objects," 108.

32. Ekdahl interview.

33. Ibid.

34. Rand, "Why I Can't Visit the National Museum of the American Indian."

35. William Johnson interview.

36. "Narrative: History of the Diba Jimooyung Permanent Exhibit/Two Voices," 7.

37. Text panel, area 14: "Spirit of Sovereignty," Ziibiwing Center of Anishinabe Culture & Lifeways.

38. The Three Fires Confederacy is comprised of the following three tribal nations: Ishkodaywatomi (also known as the Pottawatomi), Odawa, and Ojibwe or Anishinabe.

39. Erikson, *Voices of a Thousand People*, 189.

40. "Honoring Nations 2008: Semifinalist Application," 1, Ziibiwing Center of Anishinabe Culture & Lifeways.

41. Ziibiwing Center of Anishinabe Culture & Lifeways, *4-Year Annual Report, 2004–2008*, 15.

42. Pamp interview.

43. See Waziyatawin, "Defying Colonization through Language Survival," and McCarty, Romero, and Zepeda, "Reclaiming the Gift."

44. Pamp interview.

45. Ibid.

46. Ibid.

47. Ibid.

48. Shannon Martin, e-mail communication with author, 22 July 2009.

49. Daehnke and Lonetree, "Repatriation in the United States," 219.

50. Riding In, "Decolonizing NAGPRA," 61.

51. Ibid.

52. The Saginaw Chippewa have made their first request for 405 ancestral remains from the following sites: Younge (59), Bussinger (114), and Riviere aux Vase (232). Eventually they will seek repatriation of all 1,200.

53. "Position Statement regarding 'Unaffiliated' Human Remains and Cultural Materials Currently Held at the University of Michigan's Museum of Anthropology," June 2007, Ziibiwing Center of Anishinabe Culture & Lifeways, Mount Pleasant, Mich.

54. Chief Fred Cantu Jr. to Mary Sue Coleman, president of the University of Michigan, 29 November 2007, Ziibiwing Center of Anishinabe Culture & Lifeways, Mount Pleasant, Mich.

55. "Position Statement regarding 'Unaffiliated' Human Remains and Cultural Materials Currently Held at the University of Michigan's Museum of Anthropology," June 2007, Ziibiwing Center of Anishinabe Culture & Lifeways.

56. Lonetree, "Repatriation Matters."

57. Stephen R. Forrest, vice president for research at the University of Michigan, to Chief Fred Cantu Jr., 11 January 2008, Ziibiwing Center of Anishinabe Culture & Lifeways, Mount Pleasant, Mich.

58. Rebecca L. Adams, associate general council, Saginaw Chippewa Indian Tribe of Michigan, to the University of Michigan Board of Regents, 20 March 2008, Ziibiwing Center of Anishinabe Culture & Lifeways, Mount Pleasant, Mich.

59. Joseph Sowmick and Shannon Martin, "Remarks from Saginaw Chippewa to the University of Michigan Board of Regents," 20 March 2008, Ziibiwing Center of Anishinabe Culture & Lifeways, Mount Pleasant, Mich.

60. "From the Daily," and Gershman, "Groups Want Bones Reburied but Cultural Affiliations Unknown."

61. Wilkinson, "Tribe Demands U-M Hand Over Remains."

62. "Narrative: History of the Diba Jimooyung Permanent Exhibit/Two Voices," 3.

63. Bonnie Ekdahl, quoted in "Conversation with Bianca Message," 16. Ekdahl also shared this view during a panel presentation at the Embracing a Community: A 21st Century Tribal Museum Model Symposium at the Ziibiwing Center of Anishinabe Culture & Lifeways in May 2006.

CHAPTER 5

1. Linda Tuhiwai Smith, *Decolonizing Methodologies*, 5.

2. Marstine, introduction to Marstine, *New Museum Theory and Practice*, 5.

3. Ibid.

4. Linda Tuhiwai Smith, *Decolonizing Methodologies*, 105.

bibliography

PRIMARY SOURCES

Unpublished

Curatorial Department Records. Cultural Resources Center. National Museum of the American Indian, Smithsonian Institution, Suitland, Md.

Exhibit Curator Files. Minnesota Historical Society/Mille Lacs Indian Museum, Saint Paul, Minn.

Historic Sites Department Records. Minnesota Historical Society/Mille Lacs Indian Museum, Saint Paul, Minn.

Mille Lacs Indian Museum Exhibit Archive Files. State Archives. Minnesota Historical Society, Saint Paul, Minn.

Records related to the Diba Jimooyung Permanent Exhibition. Ziibiwing Center of Anishinabe Cultue & Lifeways, Mount Pleasant, Mich.

Published

Establishment of the National Museum of the American Indian: Joint Hearings before the Committee on Interior and Insular Affairs, House of Representatives, and the Subcommittee on Libraries and Memorials of the Committee on House Administration, and the Subcommittee on Public Buildings and Grounds of the Committee on Public Works and Transportation, One Hundred First Congress, First Session, Oversight . . . Hearing Held in Washington, D.C., March 9, 1989, H.R. 2668 . . . Hearing Held in Washington, D.C., July 20, 1989. Washington, D.C.: Government Printing Office, 1992.

Ziibiwing Center of Anishinabe Culture & Lifeways. *4-Year Annual Report, 2004–2008.* Mount Pleasant: Ziibiwing Center of Anishinabe Culture & Lifeways, Saginaw Chippewa Indian Tribe of Michigan, 2008.

Interviews by the Author

Agosto, Amanda (former visitor services coordinator, Ziibiwing Center). Tape recording. Mount Pleasant, Mich., 20 December 2007.

Archabal, Nina (director, Minnesota Historical Society). Tape recording. Saint Paul, Minn., 18 May 2001.

Bernstein, Bruce (assistant director for cultural resources, National Museum of the American Indian). Tape recording. Suitland, Md., 20 December 2001.

Crosson, Shana (former exhibit researcher, Minnesota Historical Society). Tape recording. Saint Paul, Minn., 15 May 2001.

Ekdahl, Bonnie (founding director, Ziibiwing Center). Tape recording. Mount Pleasant, Mich., 19 December 2007.

Her Many Horses, Emil (associate curator, National Museum of the American Indian). Tape recording. Suitland, Md., 19 December 2001.

Horse Capture, George (senior counselor to the director and special assistant for cultural resources, National Museum of the American Indian). Tape recording. Suitland, Md., 18 September 2000.

Johnson, Paul (planner, Ziibiwing Center). Tape recording. Mount Pleasant, Mich., 19 December 2007.

Johnson, William (curator, Ziibiwing Center). Tape recording. Mount Pleasant, Mich., 19 December 2007.

Lowe, Truman (curator, National Museum of the American Indian). Tape recording. Suitland, Md., 11 December 2001.

Markowitz, Harvey (field-worker, National Museum of the American Indian). Tape recording. Suitland, Md., 19 December 2001.

McMaster, Gerald (deputy assistant director for cultural resources, National Museum of the American Indian). Tape recording. Suitland, Md., 11 December 2001.

Pamp, Judy (assistant director, Ziibiwing Center). Tape recording. Mount Pleasant, Mich., 20 December 2007.

Roberts, Katherine (curator, Minnesota Historical Society). Tape recording. Saint Paul, Minn., 18 May 2001.

Secakuku, Susan (training program specialist, National Museum of the American Indian). Tape recording. Suitland, Md., 13 December 2001.

Tooker, Rachel (director, Historic Sites Department, Minnesota Historical Society). Tape recording. Saint Paul, Minn., 15 May 2001.

Volkert, James (associate director, National Museum of the American Indian). Tape recording. Suitland, Md., 14 December 2001.

Zimmerman, Travis (site manager, Mille Lacs Indian Museum). Onamia, Minn., 18 June 2010.

SECONDARY SOURCES

Books, Articles, Catalogues, Etc.

Abrams, George H. J. *Tribal Museums in America*. Nashville, Tenn.: American Association for State and Local History, 2004.

Achenbach, Joel. "Within These Walls, Science Yields to Stories." *Washington Post*, 19 September 2004.

Adams, David Wallace. *Education for Extinction: American Indians and the Boarding School Experience, 1875–1928*. Lawrence: University Press of Kansas, 1995.

Aguilar, Liz. "The Opening of the National Museum of the American Indian." *News from Native California* 18, no. 2 (Winter 2004–5): 4–12.

Alexander, Edward P., and Mary Alexander. *Museums in Motion: An Introduction to the History and Functions of Museums*. 2nd ed. Lanham, Md.: AltaMira Press, 2008.

Alfred, Taiaiake. *Wasáse: Indigenous Pathways of Action and Freedom*. Peterborough, Ontario: Broadview Press, 2005.

Ames, Michael M. "Are Changing Representations of First Peoples in Canadian Museums and Galleries Challenging the Curatorial Prerogative?" In National Museum of the American Indian, *Changing Presentation of the American Indian*, 73–88.

———. *Cannibal Tours and Glass Boxes: The Anthropology of Museums*. Vancouver: University of British Columbia Press, 1992.

———. "How to Decorate a House: The Renegotiation of Cultural Representations at the University of British Columbia Museum of Anthropology." In Peers and Brown, *Museums and Source Communities*, 171–80.

———. "How to Decorate a House: The Re-negotiation of Cultural Representations at the University of British Columbia Museum of Anthropology." *Museum Anthropology* 22, no. 3 (1999): 41–51.

———. *Museums, the Public and Anthropology: A Study in the Anthropology of Anthropology*. Vancouver: University of British Columbia Press, 1986.

Anderson, Gail. "Introduction: Reinventing the Museum." In Anderson, *Reinventing the Museum*, 1–7.

———, ed. *Reinventing the Museum: Historical and Contemporary Perspectives on the Paradigm Shift*. Walnut Creek, Calif.: AltaMira Press, 2004.

Anderson, Gary Clayton. *Little Crow: Spokesman for the Sioux*. Saint Paul: Minnesota Historical Society Press, 1986.

Anderson, Gary Clayton, and Alan R. Woolworth. *Through Dakota Eyes: Narrative Accounts of the Minnesota Indian War of 1862*. Saint Paul: Minnesota Historical Society Press, 1988.

Archambault, JoAllyn. "American Indians and American Museums." *Zeitschrift für Ethnologie* 118 (1994): 7–22.

Archuleta, Elizabeth. "Gym Shoes, Maps, and Passports, Oh My! Creating Community or Creating Chaos at the NMAI?" *American Indian Quarterly* 29, nos. 3–4 (2005): 426–49.

Arieff, Allison. "A Different Sort of (P)Reservation: Some Thoughts on the National Museum of the American Indian." *Museum Anthropology* 19, no. 2 (1995): 78–90.

Assembly of First Nations and the Canadian Museums Association. "Task Force Report on Museums and First Peoples." *Museum Anthropology* 16, no. 2 (1992): 12–20.

Atalay, Sonya. "No Sense of the Struggle: Creating a Context for Survivance at the National Museum of the American Indian." In Lonetree and Cobb, *National Museum of the American Indian*, 267–89.

———. "No Sense of the Struggle: Creating a Context for Survivance at the NMAI." *American Indian Quarterly* 30, nos. 3–4 (2006): 597–618.

Baiesi, Nadia, Marzia Gigli, Elena Monicelli, and Roberta Pellizzoli. "Places of Memory as a Tool for Education: The 'Peace in Four Voices Summer Camps' at Monte Sole." *Public Historian* 30, no. 1 (2008): 27–37.

Barker, Joanne, and Clayton Dumont. "Contested Conversations: Presentations, Expectations, and Responsibility at the National Museum of the American Indian." *American Indian Culture and Research Journal* 30, no. 2 (2006): 111–40.

Barnes, John. "The Struggle to Control the Past: Commemoration, Memory, and the Bear River Massacre of 1863." *Public Historian* 30, no. 1 (2008): 81–104.

Bataille, Gretchen M., ed. *Native American Representations: First Encounters, Distorted Images, and Literary Appropriations.* Lincoln: University of Nebraska Press, 2001.

Bauer, William J., Jr. *We Were All Like Migrant Workers Here: Work, Community, and Memory on California's Round Valley Reservation, 1850–1941.* Chapel Hill: University of North Carolina Press, 2009.

Bennett, Tony. *The Birth of the Museum: History, Theory, Politics.* London: Routledge, 1995.

Benz, Charmaine M., Ronald Todd Williamson, and Saginaw Chippewa Indian Tribe of Michigan, Ziibiwing Cultural Society. *Diba Jimooyung, Telling Our Story: A History of the Saginaw Ojibwe Anishinabek.* Mount Pleasant, Mich.: Saginaw Chippewa Indian Tribe of Michigan, Ziibiwing Cultural Society, 2005.

Berkhofer, Robert. *The White Man's Indian.* New York: Alfred A. Knopf, 1978.

Berlo, Janet Catherine. "Introduction: The Formative Years of Native American Art History." In Berlo, *Early Years of Native American Art History,* 1–21.

———, ed. *The Early Years of Native American Art History: The Politics of Scholarship and Collecting.* Seattle: University of Washington Press, 1992.

Berlo, Janet Catherine, and Aldona Jonaitis. "'Indian Country' on Washington's Mall—The National Museum of the American Indian: A Review Essay." *Museum Anthropology* 28, no. 2 (2005): 17–30.

Berlo, Janet Catherine, and Ruth B. Phillips. *Native North American Art.* Oxford: Oxford University Press, 1998.

———. "Our (Museum) World Turned Upside-Down: Re-presenting Native American Arts." *Art Bulletin* 77 (1995): 6–10.

———. "'Visualizing the Things of the Past': Museum Representations of Native North American Art in the 1990s." *Museum Anthropology* 16, no. 1 (1992): 29–43.

Berry, Susan. "Voices and Objects at the National Museum of the American Indian." *Public Historian* 28, no. 2 (2006): 63–67.

Blatti, Jo. "Public History as Contested Terrain: A Museum Perspective." *Public Historian* 19, no. 2 (1997): 57–60.

———, ed. *Past Meets Present: Essays about Historic Interpretation and Public Audiences.* Washington, D.C.: Smithsonian Institution Press, 1987.

Blue Spruce, Duane, ed. *Spirit of a Native Place: Building the National Museum of the American Indian.* Washington, D.C.: National Museum of the American Indian, Smithsonian Institution, in association with National Geographic, 2004.

Boast, Robin. "Neocolonial Collaboration: Museum as Contact Zone Revisited." *Museum Anthropology* 34, no. 1 (2011): 56–70.

Bodinger de Uriarte, John J. *Casino and Museum: Representing Mashantucket Pequot Identity.* Tucson: University of Arizona Press, 2007.

———. "Imagining the Nation with House Odds: Representing American Indian Identity at Mashantucket." *Ethnohistory* 50, no. 3 (2003): 549–65.

Bodnar, John. *Remaking America: Public Memory, Commemoration, and Patriotism in the Twentieth Century.* Princeton: Princeton University Press, 1992.

Bowechop, Janine, and Patricia Pierce Erikson. "Forging Indigenous Methodologies on Cape Flattery." *American Indian Quarterly* 29, nos. 1–2 (2005): 263–73.

Bowen, Blair. "American Indians vs. American Museums: A Matter of Religious Freedom." Pts. 1 and 2. *American Indian Journal* (May 1979): 13–21; (June 1979): 2–6.

Bower, Montgomery, and Conan Putnam. "Walter Echo-Hawk Fights for His
People's Rights to Rest in Peace—Not in Museums." *People Magazine*,
4 September 1989.

Brave Heart, Maria Yellow Horse. "Gender Differences in the Historical Trauma
Response among the Lakota." *Journal of Health and Social Policy* 10, no. 4 (1999):
1–21.

———. "The Historical Trauma Response among Natives and Its Relationship with
Substance Abuse: A Lakota Illustration." *Journal of Psychoactive Drugs* 35, no. 1
(2003): 7–13.

———. "Oyate Ptayela: Rebuilding the Lakota Nation through Addressing Historical
Trauma among Lakota Parents." *Journal of Human Behavior in the Social Environment* 2, nos. 1–2 (1999): 109–26.

Brave Heart, Maria Yellow Horse, and Lemyra M. DeBruyn. "The American Indian
Holocaust: Healing Historical Unresolved Grief." *American Indian and Alaska
Native Mental Health Research* 8, no. 2 (1998): 56–78.

Brave Heart–Jordan, Maria Yellow Horse. "The Return to the Sacred Path: Healing
from Historical Trauma and Historical Unresolved Grief among the Lakota; A
Dissertation Based upon an Independent Investigation." Ph.D. diss., Smith
College, 1995.

Bray, Tamara L., and Thomas W. Killion, eds. *Reckoning with the Dead: The Larsen Bay
Repatriation and the Smithsonian Institution.* Washington, D.C.: Smithsonian
Institution Press, 1994.

Brown, Alison K., and Laura Peers. *"Pictures Bring Us Messages" = Sinaakssiiksi
Aohtsimaahpihkookiyaawa: Photographs and Histories from the Kainai Nation.*
Toronto: University of Toronto Press, 2006.

Buffalohead, W. Roger, and Priscilla Buffalohead. *Against the Tide of American History:
The Story of the Mille Lacs Anishinabe.* Cass Lake: Minnesota Chippewa Tribe,
1985.

Carly, Kenneth. *The Sioux Uprising of 1862.* 2nd ed. Saint Paul: Minnesota Historical
Society Press, 2001.

Carpio, Myla Vicenti. "(Un)disturbing Exhibitions: Indigenous Historical Memory at
the National Museum of the American Indian." In Lonetree and Cobb, *National
Museum of the American Indian*, 290–304.

———. "(Un)disturbing Exhibitions: Indigenous Historical Memory at the NMAI."
American Indian Quarterly 30, nos. 3–4 (2006): 619–31.

Castle, Elizabeth A., Madonna Thunder Hawk, Marcella Gilbert, and Lakota Harden.
"'Keeping One Foot in the Community': Intergenerational Indigenous Women's
Activism from the Local to the Global (and Back Again)." *American Indian
Quarterly* 27, nos. 3–4 (2003): 840–61.

Cattelino, Jessica. "Tribal Gaming and Indigenous Sovereignty, with Notes from
Seminole Country." In "Indigeneity at the Crossroads of American Studies,"
special issue, *American Studies* 46, nos. 3–4 (Fall–Winter 2005): 187–204.

Clavir, Miriam. *Preserving What Is Valued: Museums, Conservation, and First Nations.* Vancouver: University of British Columbia Press, 2002.

Clifford, James. "Four Northwest Coast Museums: Travel Reflections." In Karp and Lavine, *Exhibiting Cultures,* 212–54.

———. "Looking Several Ways: Anthropology and Native Heritage in Alaska." *Current Anthropology* 45, no. 1 (2004): 5–30.

———. *The Predicament of Culture: Twentieth-Century Ethnography, Literature, and Art.* Cambridge, Mass.: Harvard University Press, 1988.

———. *Routes: Travel and Translation in the Late Twentieth Century.* Cambridge, Mass.: Harvard University Press, 1997.

Clifford, James, and George E. Marcus, eds. *Writing Culture: The Poetics and Politics of Ethnography.* Berkeley: University of California Press, 1986.

Cobb, Amanda J. "Interview with W. Richard West, Director, National Museum of the American Indian." *American Indian Quarterly* 29, nos. 3–4 (2005): 517–37.

———. "The National Museum of the American Indian as Cultural Sovereignty." *American Quarterly* 57, no. 2 (2005): 485–506.

———. "The National Museum of the American Indian: Sharing the Gift." *American Indian Quarterly* 29, nos. 3–4 (2005): 361–83.

———. "Understanding Tribal Sovereignty: Definitions, Conceptualizations, and Interpretations." In "Indigeneity at the Crossroads of American Studies," special issue, *American Studies* 46, nos. 3–4 (Fall–Winter 2005): 115–32.

Cole, Douglas. *Captured Heritage: The Scramble for Northwest Coast Artifacts.* Seattle: University of Washington Press, 1985.

Cole, Douglas, and Ira Chaikin. *An Iron Hand upon the People: The Law against the Potlatch on the Northwest Coast.* Seattle: University of Washington Press, 1990.

Coleman, Nick. "A Spirit Unbroken." *Saint Paul Pioneer Press,* 19 May 1996.

Conaty, Gerald. "Glenbow's Blackfoot Gallery: Working towards Co-Existence." In Peers and Brown, *Museums and Source Communities,* 227–41.

Conn, Steven. "Heritage vs. History at the National Museum of the American Indian." *Public Historian* 28, no. 2 (2006): 69–74.

———. *History's Shadow: Native Americans and Historical Consciousness in the Nineteenth Century.* Chicago: University of Chicago Press, 2004.

———. *Museums and American Intellectual Life, 1876–1926.* Chicago: University of Chicago Press, 1998.

"A Conversation with Bianca Message." *Museum Design,* Fall 2006, 1–16.

Cooper, Karen Coody. *Spirited Encounters: American Indians Protest Museum Policies and Practices.* Lanham, Md.: AltaMira Press, 2008.

Cooper, Karen Coody, and Nicolasa I. Sandoval, eds. *Living Homes for Cultural Expression: North American Native Perspectives on Creating Community Museums.* Washington, D.C.: National Museum of the American Indian, Smithsonian Institution, 2006.

Cotter, Holland. "New Museum Celebrating American Indian Voices." *New York Times,* 28 October 1994.

Crane, Susan A., ed. *Museums and Memory.* Stanford, Calif.: Stanford University Press, 2000.

Cummings, Mary-Ellen, and Caroline Gebhard. "Treaties and Memorials: Interpreting Horseshoe Bend National Military Park." *Public Historian* 18, no. 4 (1996): 19–36.

Daehnke, Jon, and Amy Lonetree. "Repatriation in the United States: The Current State of NAGPRA." In *Handbook of Postcolonial Archaeology*, edited by Uzma Rizvi and Jane Lydon, 245–55. Walnut Creek, Calif.: Left Coast Press, 2010.

Deloria, Philip J. *Playing Indian*. New Haven: Yale University Press, 1998.

Deloria, Philip J., and Neal Salisbury, eds. *A Companion to American Indian History*. Oxford: Blackwell, 2002.

DeLugan, Robin Maria. "'South of the Border' at the National Museum of the American Indian." In Lonetree and Cobb, *National Museum of the American Indian*, 384–404.

Denetdale, Jennifer. *Reclaiming Diné History: The Legacies of Navajo Chief Manuelito and Juanita*. Tucson: University of Arizona Press, 2007.

Dixon, Susan R. "Reclaiming Interpretation: An Interview with W. Richard West, Jr." *Akwe:kon Journal* 9, no. 4 (1992): 4–10.

Dorf, Michael C. "Culture Wars in the Nation's Attic." *Social Identities* 13, no. 2 (March 2007): 201–15.

Doyle, Debbie Ann. "National Museum of the American Indian Opens in Washington, D.C." *Perspectives*, November 2004, http://www.historians.org/perspectives/issues/2004/0411/0411new2.cfm (accessed May 2005).

Dubin, Margaret. *Native America Collected: The Culture of an Art World*. Albuquerque: University of New Mexico Press, 2001.

Dubin, Steven C. *Displays of Power: Memory and Amnesia in the American Museum*. New York: New York University Press, 1999.

Dumont, Clayton, Jr. "Contesting Scientists' Narrations of NAGPRA's Legislative History: Rule 10.11 and the Recovery of 'Culturally Unidentifiable' Ancestors." *Wicazo Sa Review* 26, no. 1 (2011): 5–41.

———. "The Politics of Scientific Objections to Repatriation." *Wicazo Sa Review* 18, no. 1 (2003): 109–28.

———. Review of *Opening Archaeology: Repatriation's Impact on Contemporary Research and Practice*, edited by Thomas Killion. *Wicazo Sa Review* 24, no. 1 (2009): 113–18.

Echo-Hawk, Walter R., and Roger C. Echo-Hawk. "Repatriation, Reburial and Religious Rights." In *American Indians in American History, 1870–2001: A Companion Reader*, edited by Sterling Evans, 177–93. Westport, Conn.: Greenwood Publishing Group, 2002.

Edwards, Elizabeth, Chris Gosden, and Ruth B. Phillips. *Sensible Objects: Colonialism, Museums and Material Culture*. Oxford: Berg, 2006.

Erikson, Patricia Pierce. "A-Whaling We Will Go: Encounters of Knowledge and Memory at the Makah Cultural and Research Center." *Cultural Anthropology* 14, no. 4 (1999): 556–83.

———. "Decolonizing the 'Nation's Attic': The National Museum of the American Indian and the Politics of Knowledge-Making in a National Space." In Lonetree and Cobb, *National Museum of the American Indian*, 43–83.

———. "'Defining Ourselves through Baskets': Museum Autoethnography and the

Makah Cultural and Research Center." In Mauzé, Harkin, and Kan, *Coming to Shore*, 339–61.

———. "Encounters in the Nation's Attic: Native American Community Museums/ Cultural Centers, the Smithsonian Institution, and the Politics of Knowledge-Making." Ph.D. diss., University of California, Davis, 1996.

———. "Exhibition Review: The Mashantucket Pequot Museum and Research Center." *Museum Anthropology* 23, no. 2 (1999): 46–53.

———. *Voices of a Thousand People: The Makah Cultural and Research Center*. With Helma Ward and Kirk Wachendorf. Lincoln: University of Nebraska Press, 2002.

———. "Welcome to This House: A Century of Makah People Honoring Identity and Negotiating Cultural Tourism." *Ethnohistory* 50, no. 3 (2003): 523–47.

Evelyn, Douglas. "The Smithsonian's National Museum of the American Indian: An International Institution of Living Cultures." *Public Historian* 28, no. 2 (2006): 51–56.

Evelyn, Douglas, and Mark G. Hirsch. "At the Threshold: A Response to Comments on the National Museum of the American Indian's Inaugural Exhibitions." *Public Historian* 28, no. 2 (2006): 85–90.

Ewers, John C. "A Century of American Indian Exhibits in the Smithsonian Institution." In *Annual Report of the Board of Regents of the Smithsonian Institution . . . 1958*, 513–25. Washington, D.C.: Government Printing Office, 1959.

Faragher, John Mack. "'A Nation Thrown Back upon Itself': Frederick Jackson Turner and the Frontier." In *Rereading Frederick Jackson Turner: "The Significance of the Frontier in American History" and Other Essays*, with commentary by John Mack Faragher, 1–10. New York: Henry Holt, 1994.

Fienup-Riordan, Ann. "Collaboration on Display: A Yup'ik Eskimo Exhibit at Three National Museums." *American Anthropologist* 101, no. 2 (1999): 339–58.

Fine-Dare, Kathleen S. *Grave Injustice: The American Indian Repatriation Movement and NAGPRA*. Lincoln: University of Nebraska Press, 2002.

Fisher, Marc. "Indian Museum's Appeal, Sadly, Only Skin Deep." *Washington Post*, 21 September 2004.

Fixico, Donald L., ed. *Rethinking American Indian History*. Albuquerque: University of New Mexico Press, 1998.

Force, Roland. *Politics and the Museum of the American Indian: The Heye and the Mighty*. Honolulu: Mechas Press, 1999.

Franco, Barbara. "Public History and Memory: A Museum Perspective." *Public Historian* 19, no. 2 (1997): 65–67.

"From the Daily: A Grave Mistake." *Michigan Daily*, 26 March 2008.

Gershman, Dave. "Groups Want Bones Reburied but Cultural Affiliations Unknown." *Ann Arbor News*, 21 March 2008.

Graburn, Nelson. "Weirs in the River of Time: The Development of Historical Consciousness among Canadian Inuit." *Museum Anthropology* 22, no. 1 (1998): 18–32.

Greenberg, Reesa, Bruce W. Ferguson, and Sandy Nairne, eds. *Thinking about Exhibitions*. London: Routledge, 1996.

Grinde, Donald A., Jr., and Bruce E. Johansen. *Exemplar of Liberty: Native America and the Evolution of Democracy*. Native American Politics Series 3. Los Angeles: American Indian Studies Center, University of California, Los Angeles, 1991.

Guembe, Maria Laura. "Challenges on the Road to Memory." *Public Historian* 30, no. 1 (2008): 63–71.

Gulliford, Andrew. "Bones of Contention: The Repatriation of Native American Human Remains." *Public Historian* 18, no. 4 (1996): 119–43.

———. "Curation and Repatriation of Sacred and Tribal Objects." *Public Historian* 14, no. 3 (1992): 23–38.

———. "Reply to 'Another View on Repatriation.'" *Public Historian* 14, no. 3 (1992): 47–50.

———. *Sacred Objects and Sacred Places: Preserving Tribal Traditions.* Boulder: University of Colorado Press, 2000.

Hall, Stuart, ed. *Representation: Cultural Representations and Signifying Practices.* London: Sage Publications, 1997.

Handler, Richard, and Eric Gable. *The New History in an Old Museum: Creating the Past at Colonial Williamsburg.* Durham, N.C.: Duke University Press, 1997.

Harjo, Suzan Shown. Introduction to Meister, *Mending the Circle,* 3–7.

Henderson, Amy, and Adrienne L. Kaeppler, eds. *Exhibiting Dilemmas: Issues of Representation at the Smithsonian.* Washington, D.C.: Smithsonian Institution Press, 1996.

Henry, James Pepper. "Challenges in Maintaining Culturally Sensitive Collections at the National Museum of the American Indian." In *Stewards of the Sacred,* edited by Lawrence E. Sullivan and Alison Edwards, 105–12. Washington, D.C.: American Association of Museums, 2004.

Henshall, John. "Visions of Another America." *New Statesman,* 26 July 1999, 30.

Hensher, Philip. "Treasure Trove of Thunderbirds and Tomahawks." *Mail on Sunday —London,* 11 July 1999, A10.

Hernandez, Rebecca. "Identified Indian Objects: An Examination of Category." *American Indian Culture and Research Journal* 31, no. 3 (2007): 121–40.

———. "Past Is Perfect in the Present Tense: Exhibiting Native America in Museums and Cultural Centers." Ph.D. diss., University of New Mexico, 2004.

Hilden, Patricia Penn, and Shari M. Huhndorf. "Performing 'Indian' in the National Museum of the American Indian." *Social Identities* 5, no. 2 (1999): 161–83.

Hill, Richard. "Indians and Museums: A Plea for Cooperation." *Museum Anthropology* 4, no. 2 (1980): 22–25.

———. "The Museum Indian: Still Frozen in Time and Mind." *Museum News,* May–June 2000, 40–44, 58–63, 66–67, 74.

———. "Reclaiming Cultural Artifacts." *Museum News* 55 (1977): 43–46.

Hill, Tom, and Richard W. Hill Sr., eds. *Creation's Journey: Native American Identity and Belief.* Washington, D.C.: Smithsonian Institution Press in association with the National Museum of the American Indian, Smithsonian Institution, 1994.

Hill, Tom, and Trudy Nicks. *Turning the Page: Forging New Partnerships between Museums and First Peoples.* Ottawa: Assembly of First Nations and the Canadian Museums Association, 1992.

Hinsley, Curtis M. *Savages and Scientists: The Smithsonian Institution and the Development of American Anthropology, 1846–1910.* Washington, D.C.: Smithsonian Institution Press, 1981.

———. *The Smithsonian and the American Indian: Making a Moral Anthropology in Victorian America*. Washington, D.C.: Smithsonian Institution Press, 1994.

———. "The World as Marketplace: Commodification of the Exotic at the World's Columbian Exposition, Chicago, 1893." In Karp and Lavine, *Exhibiting Cultures*, 344–65.

Hobsbawn, Eric, and Terance Ranger, eds. *The Invention of Tradition*. Cambridge: Cambridge University Press, 1983.

Hoffman, Jill. "Issues of Education Surrounding Native American Art as Reflected within the Iroquois Indian Museum." Ph.D. diss., Pennsylvania State University, 1998.

Hooper-Greenhill, Eilean. *Museums and Education: Purpose, Pedagogy, Performance*. London: Routledge, 2007.

———. *Museums and the Interpretation of Visual Culture*. London: Routledge, 2000.

———. *Museums and Their Visitors*. London: Routledge, 1994.

———. *Museums and the Shaping of Knowledge*. London: Routledge, 1992.

———, ed. *The Educational Role of the Museum*. 2nd ed. Leicester Readers in Museum Studies. London: Routledge, 2000.

———, ed. *Museum, Media, Message*. London: Routledge, 1999.

Horse Capture, George P. "From the Reservation to the Smithsonian via Alcatraz." *American Indian Culture and Research Journal* 18, no. 4 (1994): 135–49.

———. "The Way of the People." In Blue Spruce, *Spirit of a Native Place*, 30–45.

Howe, Craig. "The Morality of Exhibiting Indians." In *Embedding Ethics: Shifting Boundaries of the Anthropological Profession*, edited by Lynn Meskell and Peter Pels, 219–37. Oxford: Berg, 2005.

Hoxie, Frederick E. "Exploring a Cultural Borderland: Native American Journeys of Discovery in the Early Twentieth Century." In Hoxie, Mancall, and Merrell, *American Nations*, 265–87.

———. *A Final Promise: The Campaign to Assimilate the Indians, 1880–1920*. Lincoln: University of Nebraska Press, 1984.

Hoxie, Frederick E., Peter C. Mancall, and James H. Merrell. "Cultural and Political Transformations, 1900–1950." In Hoxie, Mancall, and Merrell, *American Nations*, 263–64.

———, eds. *American Nations: Encounters in Indian Country, 1850 to the Present*. New York: Routledge, 2001.

Huhndorf, Shari M. *Going Native: Indians in the Cultural Imagination*. Ithaca: Cornell University Press, 2001.

Isaac, Gwyneira. *Mediating Knowledges: Origins of a Zuni Tribal Museum*. Tucson: University of Arizona Press, 2007.

———. "What Are Our Expectations Telling Us? Encounters with the National Museum of the American Indian." *American Indian Quarterly* 30, nos. 3–4 (2006): 574–96.

———. "What Are Our Expectations Telling Us? Encounters with the National Museum of the American Indian." In Lonetree and Cobb, *National Museum of the American Indian*, 24–66.

Iverson, Peter. *"We Are Still Here": American Indians in the Twentieth Century.* Wheeling, Ill.: Harlan Davidson, 1998.

Jacknis, Ira. "Franz Boas and Exhibits: On the Limitations of the Museum Method of Anthropology." In Stocking, *Objects and Others*, 75–111. Madison: University of Wisconsin Press, 1985.

———. "'A Magic Place': The Northwest Coast Indian Hall at the American Museum of Natural History." In Mauzé, Harkin, and Kan, *Coming to Shore*, 221–50.

———. "A New Thing? The National Museum of the American Indian in Historical and Institutional Context." In Lonetree and Cobb, *National Museum of the American Indian*, 3–42.

———. "Repatriation as Social Drama: The Kwakiutl Indians of British Columbia, 1922–1980." In Mihesuah, *Repatriation Reader*, 266–81.

———. *The Storage Box of Tradition: Kwakiutl Art, Anthropologists, and Museums, 1881–1981.* Washington, D.C.: Smithsonian Institution Press, 2002.

Jackson, Robert H., and Edward Castillo. *Indians, Franciscans, and Spanish Colonization: The Impact of the Mission System on California Indians.* Albuquerque: University of New Mexico Press, 1995.

Jacobson, Lisa. "Editor's Introduction." *Public Historian* 28, no. 2 (2006): 45–50.

Jenkins, Tiffany. "The Museum of Political Correctness." *Independent Review*, 25 January 2005.

Jessup, Lynda, ed. *On Aboriginal Representation in the Gallery.* With Shannon Bagg. Mercury Series. Hull, Quebec: Canadian Museum of Civilization, 2002.

Johnson, Tim, ed. *Spirit Capture: Photographs from the National Museum of the American Indian.* Washington, D.C.: Smithsonian Institution Press in association with the National Museum of the American Indian, Smithsonian Institution, 1998.

Johnson, Troy, Joane Nagel, and Duane Champagne, eds. *American Indian Activism: Alcatraz to the Longest Walk.* Urbana: University of Illinois Press, 1997.

Kammen, Michael. *Mystic Cords of Memory: The Transformation of Tradition in American Culture.* New York: Vintage Press, 1993.

Karp, Ivan, Corinne A. Kratz, Lynn Szwaja, and Tomás Ybarra-Frausto, eds. *Museum Frictions: Public Cultures/Global Transformations.* Durham, N.C.: Duke University Press, 2006.

Karp, Ivan, Christine Mullen Kreamer, and Steven D. Lavine, eds. *Museums and Communities: The Politics of Public Culture.* Washington, D.C.: Smithsonian Institution Press, 1992.

Karp, Ivan, and Steven D. Lavine. *Exhibiting Cultures: The Poetics and Politics of Museum Display.* Washington, D.C.: Smithsonian Institution Press, 1991.

Kidwell, Clara Sue. "Every Last Dishcloth: The Prodigious Collecting of George Gustav Heye." In Krech and Hail, *Collecting Native America, 1870–1960*, 232–58.

Kidwell, Clara Sue, and Ann Marie Plane. "Representing Native American History: Introduction." *Public Historian* 18, no. 4 (1996): 9–18.

King, C. Richard. "Surrounded by Indians: The Exhibition of Comanche and the Predicament of Representing Native American History." *Public Historian* 18, no. 4 (1996): 37–52.

Kline, Andrew. "Who Are the Culturally Unidentifiable?" In *National NAGPRA Report*, 2007. www.nps.gov/history/nagpra/review/Who%20are%20the%20 Culturally%20Unidentifiable.pdf

Krech, Shepard, III, and Barbara A. Hail, eds. *Collecting Native America, 1870–1960*. Washington, D.C.: Smithsonian Institution Press, 1999.

Kreps, Christina F. *Liberating Culture: Cross-Cultural Perspectives on Museums, Curation, and Heritage Preservation*. London: Routledge, 2003.

Krmpotich, Cara, and David Anderson. "Collaborative Exhibitions and Visitor Reactions: The Case of 'Nitsitapiisinni: Our Way of Life.'" *Curator: The Museum Journal* 48, no. 4 (2005): 377–405.

Kurin, Richard. *Reflections of a Culture Broker: A View from the Smithsonian*. Washington, D.C.: Smithsonian Institution Press, 1997.

Lacayo, Richard. "A Place to Bring the Tribe." *Time*, 20 September 2004.

Lavine, Steven D., and Ivan Karp. "Introduction: Museums and Multiculturalism." In Karp and Lavine, *Exhibiting Cultures*, 1–9.

Lawlor, Mary. *Public Native America: Tribal Self-Representations in Casinos, Museums, and Powwows*. New Brunswick, N.J.: Rutgers University Press, 2006.

Layne, Valmont. "The District Six Museum: An Ordinary People's Place." *Public Historian* 30, no. 1 (2008): 53–62.

Legget, Jane. *Restitution and Repatriation: Guidelines for Good Practice*. London: Museums and Galleries Commission, 2000.

Leon, Warren, and Roy Rosenzweig, eds. *History Museums in the United States: A Critical Assessment*. Urbana: University of Illinois Press, 1989.

Lewis, Catherine M. *The Changing Face of Public History: The Chicago Historical Society and the Transformation of an American Museum*. DeKalb: Northern Illinois University Press, 2005.

Libertus, Sarah. "Preview: The New Mille Lacs Indian Museum." *Minnesota History*, Spring 1996, 32–39.

Linenthal, Edward T. *Preserving Memory: The Struggle to Create America's Holocaust Museum*. New York: Columbia University Press, 2001.

———. "Problems and Promise in Public History." *Public Historian* 19, no. 2 (1997): 45–48.

———. *Sacred Ground: Americans and Their Battlefields*. Urbana: University of Illinois Press, 1991.

Linenthal, Edward T., and Tom Engelhardt, eds. *History Wars: The Enola Gay and Other Battles for the American Past*. New York: Metropolitan Press, 1996.

Lonetree, Amy. "'Acknowledging the Truth of History': Missed Opportunities at the National Museum of the American Indian." In Lonetree and Cobb, *National Museum of the American Indian*, 305–27.

———. "Continuing Dialogues: Evolving Views of the National Museum of the American Indian." *Public Historian* 28, no. 2 (2006): 57–62.

———. "Guest Editor's Remarks." *American Indian Quarterly* 30, nos. 3–4 (2006): 507–10.

———. "Missed Opportunities: Reflections on the NMAI." *American Indian Quarterly* 30, nos. 3–4 (2006): 632–45.

———. "Museums as Sites of Decolonization: Truth Telling in National and Tribal Museums." In Sleeper-Smith, *Contesting Knowledge*, 322–37.

———. Review of the *Diba Jimooyung: Telling Our Story* permanent exhibit. *Journal of American History* 95, no. 1 (June 2008): 158–63.

———. "Transforming Lives by Reclaiming Memory: The Dakota Commemorative March of 2004." In Wilson, *In the Footsteps of Our Ancestors*, 246–56.

———, ed. "Critical Engagements with the National Museum of the American Indian." Special issue, *American Indian Quarterly* 30, nos. 3–4 (2006).

Lonetree, Amy, and Amanda J. Cobb, eds. *The National Museum of the American Indian: Critical Conversations*. Lincoln: University of Nebraska Press, 2008.

Lurie, Nancy O. "American Indians and Museums: A Love-Hate Relationship." *Old Northwest* 2, no. 3 (1976): 235–51.

Macdonald, Sharon, and Gordon Fyfe. *Theorizing Museums: Representing Identity and Diversity in a Changing World*. Cambridge, Mass.: Blackwell, 1996.

Madikida, Churchill, Lauren Segal, and Clive van den Berg. "The Reconstruction of Memory at Constitution Hill." *Public Historian* 30, no. 1 (2008): 17–25.

Marstine, Janet. Introduction to Marstine, *New Museum Theory and Practice*, 1–36.

———, ed. *New Museum Theory and Practice: An Introduction*. Malden, Mass.: Blackwell, 2006.

Maurer, Evan M. "Presenting the American Indian: From Europe to America." In National Museum of the American Indian, *Changing Presentation of the American Indian*, 15–28.

Mauzé, Marie. "Two Kwakwaka'wakw Museums: Heritage and Politics." *Ethnohistory* 50, no. 3 (2003): 503–22.

Mauzé, Marie, Michael E. Harkin, and Sergei Kan, eds. *Coming to Shore: Northwest Coast Ethnology, Traditions, and Visions*. Lincoln: University of Nebraska Press, 2004.

Maxwell, Anne. *Colonial Photography and Exhibitions: Representations of the "Native" and the Making of European Identities*. London: Leicester University Press, 1999.

McCarty, Teresa L., Mary Eunice Romero, and Ofelia Zepeda. "Reclaiming the Gift: Indigenous Youth Counter-Narratives on Native Language Loss and Revitalization." *American Indian Quarterly* 30, nos. 1–2 (2006): 28–48.

McClurken, James M., comp. *Fish in the Lakes, Wild Rice, and Game in Abundance: Testimony on Behalf of Mille Lacs Ojibwe Hunting and Fishing Rights*. East Lansing: Michigan State University Press, 2000.

McDonnell, Janet A. *The Dispossession of the American Indian, 1887–1934*. Bloomington: Indiana University Press, 1991.

McKeown, C. Timothy. "Considering Repatriation Legislation as an Option: The National Museum of the American Indian Act (NMAIA) and the Native American Graves Protection and Repatriation Act (NAGPRA)." In *Utimut: Past Heritage—Future Partnerships*, edited by Mille Gabriel and Jens Dahl, 134–47. Copenhagen: IWGIA, 2008.

McKeown, C. Timothy, and Sherry Hutt. "In the Smaller Scope of Conscience: The Native American Graves Protection and Repatriation Act Twelve Years After." *UCLA Journal of Environmental Law and Policy* 21, no. 2 (2002): 153–212.

McLaughlin, Castle. *Arts of Diplomacy: Lewis and Clark's Indian Collection.* Cambridge, Mass.: Peabody Museum of Archaeology and Ethnology; Seattle: University of Washington Press, 2003.

McLean, Kathleen. "Museum Exhibitions and the Dynamics of Dialogue." In Anderson, *Reinventing the Museum,* 193–211.

McMaster, Gerald, ed. *Reservation X: The Power of Place in Aboriginal Contemporary Art.* Seattle: University of Washington Press; Hull, Quebec: Canadian Museum of Civilization, 1998.

McMullen, Ann. "Reinventing George Heye: Nationalizing the Museum of the American Indian and Its Collections." In Sleeper-Smith, *Contesting Knowledge,* 65–105.

Meier, Peg. "A Continuing Story." *Minneapolis Star Tribune,* 16 May 1996.

Meister, Barbara, ed. *Mending the Circle: A Native American Repatriation Guide.* New York: American Indian Ritual Object Repatriation Foundation, 1996.

Message, Kylie. *New Museums and the Making of Culture.* Oxford: Berg, 2006.

Meyer, Roy. *History of the Santee Sioux: United States Indian Policy on Trial.* Lincoln: University of Nebraska Press, 1967.

Mihesuah, Devon A., ed. *Repatriation Reader: Who Owns American Indian Remains?* Lincoln: University of Nebraska Press, 2000.

Miller, Susan A. "Native America Writes Back: The Origin of the Indigenous Paradigm in Historiography." *Wicazo Sa Review* 23, no. 2 (2008): 9–28.

Mitchell, Jean. "The National Museum of the American Indian, Smithsonian Institution: The Establishment of a National Museum." Master's thesis, American University, 1992.

Mithlo, Nancy Marie. "Blood Memory and the Arts: Indigenous Genealogies and Imagined Truths." *American Indian Culture and Research Journal* 35, no. 4 (2011): 103–18.

———. "History Is Dangerous." *Museum Anthropology* 19, no. 2 (1995): 50–57.

———. "'Red Man's Burden': The Politics of Inclusion in Museum Settings." *American Indian Quarterly* 28, nos. 3–4 (2004): 743–63.

Munk, Jan. "Activities of Terezín Memorial." *Public Historian* 30, no. 1 (2008): 73–79.

Nason, James D. "'Our' Indians: The Unidimensional Indian in the Disembodied Local Past." In National Museum of the American Indian, *Changing Presentation of the American Indian,* 29–46.

National Museum of the American Indian. *All Roads Are Good: Native Voices on Life and Culture.* Washington, D.C.: Smithsonian Institution Press in association with the National Museum of the American Indian, Smithsonian Institution, 1994.

———. *The Changing Presentation of the American Indian: Museums and Native Cultures.* Washington, D.C.: National Museum of the American Indian, Smithsonian Institution; Seattle: University of Washington Press, 2000.

Nelson, Melissa K. "Ravens, Storms, and the Ecological Indian at the National Museum of the American Indian." *Wicazo Sa Review* 21, no. 2 (2006): 41–60.

Nesper, Larry. "Commentary: Of 'Historical Ambivalence in a Tribal Museum.'" *Museum Anthropology* 32, no. 1 (2009): 47–50.

———. "Historical Ambivalence in a Tribal Museum." *Museum Anthropology* 28, no. 2 (2005): 1–16.

———. "Simulating Culture: Being Indian for Tourists in Lac du Flambeau's Wa-Swa-Gon Indian Bowl." *Ethnohistory* 50, no. 3 (2003): 447–72.

Nicks, Trudy. "Dr. Oronhyatekha's History Lessons: Reading Museum Collections as Texts." In *Reading beyond Words: Contexts for Native History*, edited by Jennifer S. H. Brown and Elizabeth Vibert, 483–508. Petersborough, Ontario: Broadview Press, 1996.

———. Introduction to "Museums and Contact Work." Pt. 1 in Peers and Brown, *Museums and Source Communities*, 19–27.

Niezen, Ronald. *Spirit Wars: Native North American Religions in the Age of Nation Building.* Berkeley: University of California Press, 2000.

Noah, Timothy. "The National Museum of Ben Nighthorse Campbell: The Smithsonian's New Travesty." *Slate*, 29 September 2004, http://slate.msn.com/id/2107140/ (accessed 13 October 2004).

Ostrowitz, Judith. "Concourse and Periphery: Planning the National Museum of the American Indian." In Lonetree and Cobb, *National Museum of the American Indian*, 84–127.

Oxendine, Linda. "Tribally Operated Museums: A Reinterpretation of Indigenous Collections." Ph.D. diss., University of Minnesota, 1992.

Parezo, Nancy. "The Indian Fashion Show: Manipulating Representations of Native Attire in Museum Exhibits to Fight Stereotypes in 1942 and 1998." *American Indian Culture and Research Journal* 31, no. 3 (2007): 5–48.

Pearce, Susan M. *Museums, Objects, and Collections: A Cultural Study.* Washington, D.C.: Smithsonian Institution Press, 1993.

Peers, Laura. "Curating Native American Art: The North American Perspective." *British Museum Magazine*, Summer 1999, 24–27.

———. "Native Americans in Museums: A Review of the Chase Manhattan Gallery of North America." *Anthropology Today* 16, no. 6 (December 2000): 8–13.

———. "'Playing Ourselves': First Nations and Native American Interpreters at Living History Sites." *Public Historian* 21, no. 4 (1999): 39–59.

———. *Playing Ourselves: Interpreting Native Histories at Historic Reconstructions.* Lanham, Md.: AltaMira Press, 2007.

Peers, Laura L., and Alison K. Brown, eds. *Museums and Source Communities: A Routledge Reader.* New York: Routledge, 2003.

Penney, David W. "The Poetics of Museum Representations: Tropes of Recent American Indian Art Exhibitions." In National Museum of the American Indian, *Changing Presentation of the American Indian*, 47–65.

Phillips, Ruth B. "Disrupting Past Paradigms: The National Museum of the American Indian and the First Peoples Hall at the Canadian Museum of Civilization." *Public Historian* 28, no. 2 (2006): 75–80.

———. Introduction to "Community Collaboration in Exhibitions: Toward a Dialogic Paradigm." Pt. 3 in Peers and Brown, *Museums and Source Communities*, 155–70.

———. "Re-placing Objects: Historical Practices for the Second Museum Age." *Canadian Historical Review* 86, no. 1 (2005): 83–110.

———. "Reply to James Clifford's 'Looking Several Ways: Anthropology and Native Heritage in Alaska.'" *Current Anthropology* 45, no. 1 (2004): 25–26.

————. *Trading Identities: The Souvenir in Native North American Art from the Northeast, 1700–1900.* Seattle: University of Washington Press; Montreal: McGill-Queen's University Press, 1998.

Phillips, Ruth B., and Christopher B. Steiner, eds. *Unpacking Culture: Art and Commodity in Colonial and Postcolonial Worlds.* Berkeley: University of California Press, 1999.

Poupart, Lisa. "The Familiar Face of Genocide: Internalized Oppression among American Indians." *Hypatia* 18, no. 2 (2003): 86–100.

Price, Sally. *Primitive Art in Civilized Places.* Chicago: University of Chicago Press, 1989.

Raibmon, Paige. *Authentic Indians: Episodes of Encounter from the Late-Nineteenth-Century Northwest Coast.* Durham, N.C.: Duke University Press, 2005.

Rand, Jacki Thompson. "Why I Can't Visit the National Museum of the American Indian: Reflections of an Accidental Privileged Insider, 1989–1994." *Common-Place* 7, no. 4 (July 2007), http://www.common-place.org/vol-07/no-04/rand/ (accessed 15 July 2009).

Rave, Jody. "Indian Museum Looks at Life, Death." *Bismarck Tribune*, 24 September 2004.

Reinhardt, Akim. "Defining the Native: Local Print Media Coverage of the NMAI." *American Indian Quarterly* 29, nos. 3–4 (2005): 450–65.

Richard, Paul. "Shards of Many Untold Stories: In Place of Unity, a Melange of Unconnected Objects." *Washington Post*, 21 September 2004.

Riding In, James. "Decolonizing NAGPRA." In Wilson and Yellow Bird, *For Indigenous Eyes Only*, 53–66.

————. "Graves Protection and Repatriation: An Unresolved Universal Human Rights Problem Affected by Institutional Racism." In *Human Rights in Global Light: Selected Papers, Poems, and Prayers, SFSU Annual Human Rights Summit, 2004–2007*, edited by Mariana Leal Ferreira, 37–42. Treganza Museum Anthropology Papers, nos. 24–25. San Francisco: San Francisco State University, 2008.

————. "Our Dead Are Never Forgotten: American Indian Struggles for Burial Rights and Protections." In *"They Made Us Many Promises": The American Indian Experience, 1524 to the Present*, edited by Philip Weeks, 291–323. Wheeling, Ill.: Harlan Davidson, 2002.

————. "Six Pawnee Crania: Historical and Contemporary Issues Associated with the Massacre and Decapitation of Pawnee Indians in 1869." *American Indian Culture and Research Journal* 16, no. 2 (1992): 101–19.

Ringle, Ken. "Where's Tonto? You Won't Find Out at the New Indian Museum." *Weekly Standard*, 4 April 2005.

Rosoff, Nancy B. "Integrating Native Views into Museum Procedures: Hope and Practice at the National Museum of the American Indian." *Museum Anthropology* 22, no. 1 (1998): 33–42.

Rothstein, Edward. "Who Should Tell History: The Tribes or the Museums?" *New York Times*, 21 December 2004.

Ruffins, Fath Davis. "Culture Wars Won and Lost: Ethnic Museums on the Mall." Pt. 1, "The National Holocaust Museum and the National Museum of the American Indian." *Radical History Review* 68 (Spring 1997): 79–100.

——. "Culture Wars Won and Lost." Pt. 2, "The National African-American Museum Project." *Radical History Review* 70 (Winter 1998): 78–101.

Russell-Ciardi, Maggie. "The Museum as a Democracy-Building Institution: Reflections on the Shared Journeys Program at the Lower East Side Tenement Museum." *Public Historian* 30, no. 1 (2008): 39–52.

Sadongei, Alyce; Arizona State Museum; Arizona State Library, Archives and Public Records; and Institute of Museum and Library Services (U.S.). *Tribal Archive, Library and Museum Directory.* Tucson: American Indian Program, Arizona State Museum, University of Arizona, 2005.

Schultz, Duane. *Over the Earth I Come: The Great Sioux Uprising of 1862.* New York: St. Martin's Press, 1992.

Ševčenko, Liz, and Maggie Russell-Ciardi. Foreword to "Sites of Conscience: Opening Historic Sites for Civic Dialogue." *Public Historian* 30, no. 1 (2008): 9–15.

Shannon, Jennifer Ann. "The Construction of Native Voice at the National Museum of the American Indian." In Sleeper-Smith, *Contesting Knowledge,* 218–47.

——. "An Ethnography of 'Our Lives': Collaborative Exhibit Making at the National Museum of the American Indian." Ph.D. diss., Cornell University, 2008.

Shepherd, Jeffrey. *We Are an Indian Nation: A History of the Hualapai People.* Tucson: University of Arizona Press, 2010.

Simpson, Moira G. *Making Representations: Museums in the Post-Colonial Era.* Rev. ed. London: Routledge, 2001.

Sleeper-Smith, Susan, ed. *Contesting Knowledge: Museums and Indigenous Perspectives.* Lincoln: University of Nebraska Press, 2009.

Smith, Claire. "Decolonising the Museum: The National Museum of the American Indian in Washington, D.C." *Antiquity* 79, no. 304 (2005): 424–39.

Smith, Linda Tuhiwai. *Decolonizing Methodologies: Research and Indigenous Peoples.* London: Zed Books, 1999.

Smith, Paul Chaat. "Critical Reflections on the Our Peoples Exhibit: A Curator's Perspective." In Lonetree and Cobb, *National Museum of the American Indian,* 131–43.

——. *Everything You Know about Indians Is Wrong.* Minneapolis: University of Minnesota Press, 2009.

Smith, Paul Chaat, and Robert Allen Warrior. *Like a Hurricane: The Indian Movement from Alcatraz to Wounded Knee.* New York: New Press, 1996.

Smithsonian Institution. Center for Museum Studies. *Tribal Museum Directory.* Washington, D.C.: Center for Museum Studies, Smithsonian Institution, 1998.

Stampe, Jennifer. "Views from Here: Working the Field, Looking at Tourists, Mapping Touristic Terrain." *Tourist Studies* 8, no. 1 (April 2008): 123–40.

——. "'You *Will* Learn about Our Past': Cultural Representation, Self-Determination, and Problems of Presence." Ph.D. diss., University of Minnesota, 2007.

Stannard, David E. *American Holocaust: The Conquest of the New World.* New York: Oxford University Press, 1992.

——. "Disease and Infertility: A New Look at the Demographic Collapse of Native Populations in the Wake of Western Contact." *Journal of American Studies* 24, no. 3 (1990): 325–50.

Starn, Orin. *Ishi's Brain: In Search of America's Last "Wild" Indian.* New York: Norton, 2004.

Stately, Ramona Kitto. "Pazahiyayewin and the Importance of Remembering Dakota Women." In Wilson, *In the Footsteps of Our Ancestors,* 192–95.

Stevenson, Winona Lu-Ann. "Decolonizing Tribal Histories." Ph.D. diss., University of California, Berkeley, 2000.

Stocking, George W., Jr., ed. *Objects and Others: Essays on Museums and Material Culture.* Madison: University of Wisconsin Press, 1985.

Stoffman, Judy. "Natives Tell Their Own Story at Smithsonian: Controversy in Calgary Led to Collaboration; Native Groups Consulted on Every Aspect of Museum." *Vancouver Sun,* 21 August 2004.

Task Force on Museums and First Peoples, Assembly of First Nations, and Canadian Museums Association. *Turning the Page: Forging New Partnerships between Museums and First Peoples = Tourner la page: Forger de nouveaux partenariats entre les musées et les Premières Nations.* 3rd ed. Ottawa: Task Force on Museums and First Peoples, 1994.

Thomas, David Hurst. *Skull Wars: Kennewick Man, Archaeology, and the Battle for Native American Identity.* New York: Basic Books, 2000.

Thompson, Laura Dickstein. "The Mission Statement and Its Relationship to Museum Interpretative Practices: A Case Study of the National Museum of the American Indian." Ph.D. diss., Columbia University, 2001.

Thornton, Russell. *American Indian Holocaust and Survival: A Population History since 1492.* Norman: University of Oklahoma Press, 1987.

———. "Health, Disease, and Demography." In Deloria and Salisbury, *Companion to American Indian History,* 68–84.

———. "Who Owns Our Past? The Repatriation of Native American Human Remains and Cultural Objects." In Thornton, *Studying Native America,* 385–415.

———, ed. *Studying Native America: Problems and Prospects.* Madison: University of Wisconsin Press, 1998.

Tisdale, Shelby. "Cocopah Identity and Cultural Survival: Indian Gaming and the Political Ecology of the Lower Colorado River Delta, 1850–1996." Ph.D. diss., University of Arizona, 1997.

Treuer, Anton. *Ojibwe in Minnesota.* Saint Paul: Minnesota Historical Society Press, 2010.

———, ed. *Living Our Language: Ojibwe Tales and Oral Histories.* Saint Paul: Minnesota Historical Society Press, 2001.

Trope, Jack F. "The Native American Graves Protection and Repatriation Act." In Meister, *Mending the Circle,* 8–18.

Trope, Jack F., and Walter R. Echo-Hawk. "The Native American Graves Protection and Repatriation Act: Background and Legislative History." In Mihesuah, *Repatriation Reader,* 123–68.

Tsosie, Rebecca. "The BIA's Apology to Native Americans: An Essay on Collective Memory and Collective Conscience." In *Taking Wrongs Seriously: Apologies and Reconciliation,* edited by Elazar Barkan and Alexander Karn, 185–212. Stanford, Calif.: Stanford University Press, 2006.

Tweedie, Ann M. *Drawing Back Culture: The Makah Struggle for Repatriation*. Seattle: University of Washington Press, 2002.

Venturi, Scott Brown and Associates. *The Way of the People: National Museum of the American Indian Master Facilities Programming, Phase 1, Revised Draft Report*. Washington, D.C.: Smithsonian Institution Office of Design and Construction, 1991.

Vergo, Peter, ed. *The New Museology*. London: Reaktion Books, 1989.

Vizenor, Gerald. "Bone Courts: The Rights and Representation of Tribal Bones." *American Indian Quarterly* 10, no. 4 (1986): 319–31.

——. *Fugitive Poses: Native American Indian Scenes of Absence and Presence*. Lincoln: University of Nebraska Press, 1998.

——. Introduction to Vizenor, *Native American Literature*, 1–15.

——. *Manifest Manners: Narratives on Postindian Survivance*. Lincoln: University of Nebraska Press, 1999.

——, ed. *Native American Literature: A Brief Introduction and Anthology*. New York: HarperCollins College Publishers, 1995.

Wakeham, Pauline. "Performing Reconciliation at the National Museum of the American Indian: Postcolonial Rapprochement and the Politics of Historical Closure." In Lonetree and Cobb, *National Museum of the American Indian*, 353–83.

Watkins, Joe E. "The Antiquities Act at One Hundred Years: A Native American Perspective." In *The Antiquities Act: A Century of American Archaeology, Historic Preservation, and Nature Conservation*, edited by David Harmon, Francis P. McManamon, and Dwight T. Pitcaithley, 187–98. Tucson: University of Arizona Press, 2006.

Waziyatawin. "Defying Colonization through Language Survival." In Wilson and Yellow Bird, *For Indigenous Eyes Only*, 109–26.

——. "Relieving Our Suffering: Indigenous Decolonization and a United States Truth Commission." In Wilson and Yellow Bird, *For Indigenous Eyes Only*, 189–205.

——. *What Does Justice Look Like? The Struggle for Liberation in Dakota Homeland*. Saint Paul, Minn.: Living Justice Press, 2008.

Waziyatawin and Michael Yellow Bird. "Beginning Decolonization." In Wilson and Yellow Bird, *For Indigenous Eyes Only*, 1–7.

Weaver, Hilary N., ed. *Voices of First Nations People: Human Services Considerations*. New York: Haworth Press, 1999.

Wedll, Joycelyn. "Learn about Our Past to Understand Our Future: The Story of the Mille Lacs Band of Ojibwe." In National Museum of the American Indian, *Changing Presentation of the American Indian*, 89–98.

West, W. Richard. "Cultural Rethink." In National Museum of the American Indian, *Changing Presentation of the American Indian*, 99–102.

——. "A New Idea of Ourselves: The Changing Presentation of the American Indian." In National Museum of the American Indian, *Changing Presentation of the American Indian*, 7–13.

West, W. Richard, Barbara Isaac, Hartman Lomawaima, Timothy McKeown, and Suzan Shown Harjo. "NAGPRA at 10: Examining a Decade of the Native American Graves Protection and Repatriation Act." *Museum News* 79 (2000): 42–49, 67–75.

White, Richard. "Representing Indians: Art, History, and the New Museums." *New Republic*, 21 April 1997, 28–34.

Wilkins, David E., and K. Tsianina Lomawaima. *Uneven Ground: American Indian Sovereignty and Federal Law*. Norman: University of Oklahoma Press, 2001.

Wilkinson, Mike. "Tribe Demands U-M Hand Over Remains." *Detroit News*, 17 April 2008.

Wilson, Thomas H., Georges Erasmus, and David W. Penney. "Museums and First Peoples in Canada." *Museum Anthropology* 16, no. 2 (1992): 6–11.

Wilson, Waziyatawin Angela. "Decolonizing the 1862 Death Marches." *American Indian Quarterly* 28, nos. 1–2 (2004): 185–215.

———. *Remember This! Dakota Decolonization and the Eli Taylor Narratives*. Lincoln: University of Nebraska Press, 2005.

———, ed. *In the Footsteps of Our Ancestors: The Dakota Commemorative Marches of the 21st Century*. Saint Paul, Minn.: Living Justice Press, 2006.

Wilson, Waziyatawin Angela, and Michael Yellow Bird, eds. *For Indigenous Eyes Only: A Decolonization Handbook*. School of American Research Native America Series. Santa Fe: School of American Research Press, 2005.

Wingerd, Mary Lethert. *North Country: The Making of Minnesota*. Minneapolis: University of Minnesota Press, 2010.

Witcomb, Andrea. *Re-Imagining the Museum: Beyond the Mausoleum*. London: Routledge, 2003.

Yellow Bird, Michael. "Cowboys and Indians: Toys of Genocide, Icons of American Colonialism." *Wicazo Sa Review* 19, no. 2 (2004): 33–48.

Zurier, Sarah E. "Collections Same, Museum Different: Object Lessons at the George Gustav Heye Center of the National Museum of the American Indian." *Public Historian* 18, no. 4 (1996): 185–92.

Lectures and Conference Presentations

Lonetree, Amy. "Repatriation Matters: University Museums and the Struggle over NAGPRA Compliance." Paper presented at the annual meeting of the American Anthropological Association, San Francisco, 19–23 November 2008.

Smith, Paul Chaat. "Ten Years of Accidental Victories, Brilliant Mistakes, and Useless Lessons." Paper presented at "The Task of the Curator: Translation, Intervention and Innovation in Exhibitionary Practice," conference hosted by Museum and Curatorial Studies at the University of California, Santa Cruz, 14–15 May 2010.

Smithsonian TV. "Curator's Talk: Paul Chaat Smith." 4 March 2005. National Museum of the American Indian. http://smithsonian.tv/videos/nmai/ Curator_Talks/2005-03-04_ChaatSmith.htm (accessed 14 May 2005).

Vizenor, Gerald. "Bone Courts and Native American Sovereignty." Paper presented at "Who Owns the Body," conference held at the University of California, Berkeley, International House, 22 September 2000. Video recording held at the Media Resources Center, University of California, Berkeley.

Waziyatawin. "Colonialism on the Ground." Paper presented at "Keywords in Native American Studies," conference hosted by the Native American Studies Program at the University of Michigan, Ann Arbor, January 2008. Also available online at http://waziyatawin.net/commentary/?page_id=20 (accessed 23 August 2011).

West, W. Richard. "Museums and Controversy in Exhibitions." Paper presented at the annual meeting of the American Association of Museums, Philadelphia, Pa., 21–25 May 1995. Audiotape recording held at the Smithsonian Center for Education and Museum Studies, Washington, D.C.

———. "The National Museum of the American Indian: Perspectives on Museums in the 21st Century." Paper presented at a meeting of the New England Museum Association, Newport, Rhode Island, 10 November 1993.

———. "Remarks on the Occasion of the Grand Opening Ceremony." 21 September 2005. National Museum of the American Indian, Washington, D.C. http://newsdesk.si.edu/kits/nmai (accessed 23 August 2006; page no longer available).

———. "Who Gets the Talking Stick: Voice and Authority in Exhibitions." Paper presented as part of a session organized by James Volkert at the annual meeting of the American Association of Museums, Atlanta, Ga., 1997. Audiotape recording held at the Smithsonian Center for Education and Museum Studies, Washington, D.C.

index

Italic page numbers refer to illustrations.

and, 25, 29–32, 36, 38–42, 43, 48–69, 71–72,
132–33, 168–70, 172, 181 (n. 30); Mille Lacs
Indian Museum development, 2000–2010
and, 32–33, 66–72; opening exhibitions of
new Mille Lacs Indian Museum and, 38,
49–67, 103; State Indian Museum and, 36;
visitor surveys to museum and, 63, 64–66
Minnesota Historical Society American Indian
Advisory Board, 45
Minnesota Scenic Highway 169, 35, 57
Mitchell, Jennie, 62
Mitewiwin. *See* Midewiwin Society
Mithlo, Nancy, 119–20
Moccasins display (*All Roads are Good*
exhibition), 88, *89*
Monadnock Media, 129
Moose, Darren, 37, 54
Morton, Samuel G., 12–13
Mount Pleasant Indian Industrial Boarding
School, 140, 154
Musée de l'Homme, 15
Museum Anthropology, 24
Museum at Warm Springs, 20, 48, 136, 182–83
(n. 55)
Museum exhibitions: addressing unresolved
grief, 5, 9, 70; community-based
collaboration and, 2–3, 21–22; indigenous
activism against, 17–18; indigenous
collaboration and, xi, xii–xv, 1–4, 16–17,
21–25, 42–43, 66, 71–72, 101; specialists
required for, 103; spirituality and, 95–99,
136–38; thematic vs. object-oriented, 22,
47, 108, 131, 188 (n. 14). *See also* Mille Lacs
Indian Museum; Museums; National
Museum of the American Indian; Ziibiwing
Center of Anishinabe Culture & Lifeways
Museum of Indian Arts and Culture/
Laboratory of Anthropology (Santa Fe), 23
Museum of the American Indian (MAI),
78–79, 80–82; indigenous involvement and,
79, 81, 185 (n. 15); transfer to Smithsonian,
79, 80, 81–82, 84
Museums: collaborative approaches and, xi,
1, 4, 29, 169–70, 172; decolonizing process,
5–6, 9, 25, 171–72, 173; early collecting of

Native American materials, 9–14, 35, 36,
63, 78–80, 178–79 (n. 26), 184 (n. 9); early
displays of Native American materials,
9–10, 14–16, 36–37, 79, 97–98; human
remains and, 12–14, 17, 18, 80, 82, 126–27,
158–66, 173; human rights and, 4, 17; Indian
spirituality and, 79, 95–99, 186 (n. 67);
natural history museums, 13–14, 15–16, 23,
79, 80, 97–98; truth-telling function of,
5–6, 16, 109, 119, 138–39, 174, 175. *See also*
Colonialism; Mille Lacs Indian Museum;
Museum exhibitions; Museum of the
American Indian; National Museum of
the American Indian; Ziibiwing Center of
Anishinabe Culture & Lifeways
Museums and Source Communities (Peers and
Brown, eds.), 21

Nahua peoples, 99
National Congress of American Indians, 161
National Endowment for the Humanities
(NEH), xi, 20, 38, 44, 45
National Museum of American History, 73, 74,
184 (n. 1)
National Museum of Natural History
(NMNH), 15, 81, 82, 97–98
National Museum of the American Indian
(NMAI), 29, 53, 66, 71, 184 (n. 9); author's
involvement with, 73–78; colonialism and,
107, 108–13, 119–22, 145; community-based
collaboration and, 23, 92–93, 94–99,
100; contemporary survival portrayed
and, 75, 93, 98, 108, 110, 119; Cultural
Resources Center (Suitland, Md.) and,
74, 75; decolonization process and, 109,
111, 119–22, 166; early development, 76,
77, 78, 83–86, 185 (n. 32); establishment
of, 73–74, 81–82; exhibition philosophy
of, 82, 87, 90–91, 92–93, 107, 187 (n. 86);
exhibition planning for, 2, 75–76, 92–107;
indigenous collaboration and, 22, 25, 26,
75–76, 77, 101–4, 105–7, 119, 121, 166, 172,
185 (n. 32); opening exhibitions of, 75, 76,
93–101, 107–17, 118–19, 184 (n. 3), 186 (n. 71);
opening of, 72, 77; *Our Lives* exhibition, 75,

123–25, 144–46, 166; opening of, 129–30; oral traditions and, 25–26, 131, 132, 133, 136, 152; origins of, 126–30; programs created around exhibition, 152–66, 173; repatriation of human remains and, 18, 149–51, 158–66, 173; Seven Prophecies/Seven Fires of Anishinabe Indians and, 131–32, 133–34, 136, 137, 147, 152, 158; sovereignty display, 148–49, *150*; spirituality and, 136–37, 151–52, 189 (n. 17); as tribal museum, 2, 19, 25–26, 122, 123, 126, 146–47, 166–67, 172; truth-telling and, 138–39, 146–47

Ziibiwing Cultural Society (ZCS), 126; cultural center beginnings and, 128–30; gaming and, 127–28; human remains and, 127, 160

Zimmerman, Travis, 32–33, 70, 71, 182 (n. 53)

Zuni Museum, 3